The Individual and the Social Self

Edited with an Introduction by
David L. Miller

The Individual and the Social Self

Unpublished Work of George Herbert Mead

The University of Chicago Press
Chicago and London

DAVID L. MILLER is professor of philos-
ophy emeritus at the University of Texas.
He is the author of *The Philosophy of
Alfred North Whitehead; Modern Science
and Human Freedom; Individualism,
Personal Achievement, and the Open
Society;* and *George Herbert Mead: Self,
Language, and the World*, which is pub-
lished by the University of Chicago Press.

The University of Chicago Press, Chicago 60637
The University of Chicago Press, Ltd., London

Library of Congress Cataloging in Publication Data

Mead, George Herbert, 1863–1931.
    The individual and the social self.

    Includes index.
    1. Social psychology. 2. Self. 3. Consciousness.
4. Socialization. I. Miller, David L., 1903–
II. Title.
HM251.M4192   1982   302   82–4885
ISBN 0–226–51673–3   AACR2
ISBN 0–226–51674–1 (paper)

To Mary, Valentine and Reese

Contents

Introduction

The class notes of 1914 and 1927 were given to me in 1968 by Dr. Irene Tufts Mead, Mr. Mead's daughter-in-law. I had decided to do the book *George Herbert Mead: Self, Language, and the World* as early as 1965. I visited Dr. Mead at Chicago in 1968 and talked to her extensively about my project. Later, in 1970, we both attended the conference on Mead at Winterthur, Switzerland (directed by Walter Corti), where we met and again had long discussions about Mead. Thereafter from time to time Dr. Mead sent me many of Mr. Mead's unpublished manuscripts (now in the archives at Regenstein Library of the University of Chicago).

The persons who transcribed the notes published here are unknown. On the first page of the 1914 notes is "Philosophy 321, Social Psychology." These notes were typewritten and were not in good shape. The final draft is my third, starting from the original. I have done extensive editing in punctuation; I have also inserted words to make grammatically correct and clear sentences. In no case have I changed what I strongly believe was the actual intention and original meaning of what Mead said.

All references in these notes to the works of persons other than Mead were cryptic and for the most part incomplete; much time was spent in the library in clarifying and completing them. For example, on page 37 of the original notes one reads, "'this has been the function of mating and care of the young. Cf. Craif's study of pigeons." Instead of "Craif," the author is Wallace Craig, as stated in the final draft. There were more than a few such problems. Many of the original notes were underlined. I have deleted all underlining. Also, I have furnished all subtitles, made many corrections in spelling, and I have changed the word order in several places.

The 1927 notes consist of forty lectures given in Gates Hall during the spring quarter. They are typed, single-spaced, and cover 60 pages. Here again I have deleted all underlining and furnished the subtitles.

1

The original copy is in much better shape than that for the 1914 class notes.

The essay by Mead on "Consciousness, Mind, the Self, and Scientific Objects," was written by him probably around 1917, prior to the influence of Whitehead's writings. It is a profound article involving problems in epistemology and metaphysics. His chief aim is to offer a philosophical justification for his theory of mind, self, and reflective intelligence. This requires a careful distinction between scientific (physical) objects and mind and selves that emerged from them—a distinction between them that does not lead to metaphysical dualism or a complete separation of mind from bodily behavior. There is a discussion of the nature of the physical thing, how we come to have a concept of it, and our experience of it in connection with the nature of physical objects treated by physical scientists.

The essays "Functional Identity of Response" and "Functional Identity of Stimulus," with several other items, were given to me in 1963 by the late Dr. John M. Brewster, to use as I deemed appropriate. I have thought much about who might have written them, but I have not reached a conviction about it. I can only suggest that it might have been W. I. Thomas or Ellsworth Faris or A. W. Moore. Of course many others come to mind, but none fit into my speculation. I judge the essays were written about 1925. They are concerned with a very important problem and I think they are among the very finest of any written about Mead. They required some, but very little, editing.

Ellsworth Faris's review of *Mind, Self, and Society* (*American Journal of Sociology*, 41 [1936]:909-13) suggested that the organization of topics in the book should have been reversed. "Not mind and then society; but society first and then minds arising within that society—such would probably have been the preference of him who spoke these words" (p. 810). All will agree with Faris that Mead propounded the thesis that selves and minds emerge in individuals from society, out of social interactions, that there can be societies without minds and selves but not the reverse. Consequently the topic-order by the editor, Charles Morris, may be somewhat misleading. However I believe that *Mind, Self, and Society*, as published, presents Mead's thinking in the order he presented it to his classes. Mead always approached his problems from the historical standpoint. For example, in his course on Hume in the fall of 1930, Mead began by saying "The Aristotelian object was an object of experience; the individual added nothing to the object in contrast to that of Galileo and Descartes" (from my own class notes). In his social psychology course in fall of 1929 Mead began by saying: "Human behavior, that is, conduct like the behavior of lower animals, springs from impulses" (from my class notes).

On page 1 of *Mind, Self, and Society* Mead says: "The point of approach I wish to suggest is that of dealing with experience from the standpoint of society." In the 1914 notes Mead begins by discussing the nature of the act, the primitive unit of existence, and later discusses social acts and how selves and minds emerge from them. In the 1927 notes there is a close similarity in approach to that in *Mind, Self, and Society*. Mead begins by discussing Watsonian behaviorism, and later comes to a discussion of the origin of minds and selves. We can safely conclude that Mead's method of leading up to his basic claims and his defense of them is the historical approach. Always in the back of his mind were the writings of, especially, Darwin, Wilhelm Dilthey, Wilhelm Wundt, and the work of William James, Charles Cooley, and John Dewey.

Mead's Chief Problems

Having taken seven courses given by Mead and having studied his works and the writings about him, including many dissertations and theses, I make bold to offer a statement of what I believe were Mead's chief problems or, as he would say, what lay in the back of his mind as he began his work in philosophy. Also, a brief statement should be made about how these class notes fit into his overall purpose.

While at Oberlin College from 1879-1883, Mead, with his close friend, Henry Castle, rebelled against the theological claim that the mind (or the soul) is a supernatural substance, that it can exist apart from the body, and against the implications of this claim for morality and for ethical systems. Nor was he satisfied with the contention that man is born into a moral order.

At Harvard University, in 1887-88, Mead took courses with Josiah Royce and lived in William James's home. There he learned about Hegel and absolute idealism. During his schooling at Leipzig and Berlin, 1888-91, Mead became acquainted with Wilhelm Wundt's laboratory in physiological psychology and he studied with Wilhelm Dilthey. (Mead intended to complete his dissertation at Berlin under Dilthey's direction, but this did not happen.) Clearly, Darwin's writings about the emotions of animals and Wundt's theory of gestures, as well as Dilthey's thesis that we can understand the thinking of individuals only by knowing their historical, social, and cultural backgrounds, must have influenced Mead's social theory of the self. Still there were other factors of a more philosophic, metaphysical, and epistemological nature influencing him.

First, his revolt against the belief in a spiritual self as a substance distinct from matter was a revolt against Cartesian dualism. Hegel's absolute idealism, claiming that the essence of the real is mental or spiritual and that all relations are internal, was also distasteful, inasmuch as it assimilated the self to, and smothered the individual in, the timeless, seamless unchanging whole, the Absolute; it left no room for the creativity of the individual. Nor did it allow for an open universe nor even for an open society of open selves where evolution and advance are possible. Not only was this monistic Hegelian system unsatisfactory to Mead as an answer to Cartesian dualism, but so was the Lockean, Berkeleyan, and Humean claim that the real is built up from experienceable atomic units, each having existence apart from all others. Mead was no doubt influenced by the laboratory method of research and by James's and Dewey's claim that one must begin with experience as the basis for developing a system. To start with Hegel's abstractions and then to try to arrive at the nature of the real is to put the cart before the horse. Similarly, Humean atomic impressions are abstractions from concrete experience. "The unit of existence is the act." Selves, minds, and our knowledge about matters of fact all emerge from acts that are experienced. Mind cannot be separated from action. There can be no self apart from action, more specifically, from social action.

Here we can see some very important implications of Mead's basic commitment. (1) He has evaded the sensuous atomism of Locke, Berkeley, and Hume, as well as the later logical atomism of Bertrand Russell and Ludwig Wittgenstein and that of the early logical positivists. (2) He has rejected Cartesian dualism by making a functional, not a substantive, distinction between mental (symbolic) processes and overt bodily behavior. (3) He has rejected both Hegelian idealism and phenomenalism.

On the positive side, Mead committed himself (1) to being a pragmatist, emphasizing that mind without action is impossible, that belief, knowledge, and truth are all related to conduct.

2. He became a "process philosopher" long before the term was used extensively by philosophers. This meant for him that the temporal dimension cannot be excluded from the real; the real is not timeless but consists of acts, happenings, or events. There can be no world at an "instant," as that term is defined by mathematicians.

3. History and time do not consist simply of the instantiation of eternal Platonic forms, but gives rise to novel, emergent, unpredictable events. Thus Mead embraces Darwinism and its implications, emergent evolution and creative evolution.

4. The individual and society are continually in the process of adjustment.

5. Neither habits nor customs are adequate for meeting the demands of many (new) kinds of situations, and reflective intelligence, made possible because of the social component of minds, comes to our aid upon the breakdown of custom. The "I" component of the self is creative in proposing new hypotheses, new ideas, many of which are true because they enable us successfully to meet problems at hand; they thereby result in a satisfactory continuation of the social process.

6. Mead, with his basic commitment, is able to show how reflective intelligence, involving the manipulation of physical objects by the hand, fits perfectly the scientific method, which requires the creativity of individual thinkers. Neither the ancient Greeks nor Cartesian dualists could show how the manipulation of objects by the hand is functionally related to reason, the mental, or to reflective intelligence.

7. Inadequate attention by sociologists and psychologists, as well as therapists, has been paid to one of Mead's central doctrines, which might well be called *objective relativism*. Mead opposes the long-standing belief that if x is objective and therefore ultimately real, it must "stand on its own feet," that its existence cannot depend on any other thing. For example, Descartes, Locke, and Berkeley held that colors, sounds, and so-called secondary qualities depend upon a perceiver for their existence and therefore they are not real in themselves. They were said to be "subjective," not objective, and for the scientists they had the ontological status of being less real than such qualities as mass, figure, and resistance.

Introspective psychology treated ideas, concepts, and all mental phenomena as belonging to each individual subject, and it could not get rid of solipsism; it could not make knowledge shareable, nor could it understand the meaning of shared perspectives. Mead, in his doctrine of objective relativism, is able to relieve ideas and knowledge of their subjectivity. The individual mind can exist only in relation to other minds with shared meanings. If one can evoke in himself, by his gesture, the same (functionally identical) response that he evokes in the other, then the gesture's meaning is relieved of its privacy, it is objective and also real, even as an irrevocable past is real but only in relation to a present perspective. Similarly, colors, odors, sounds, tastes may exist only in relation to perceivers, but they are there, objectively; they belong to the objective world. Thus, as Mead says, "we have returned these stolen goods to the world." If it is the function of analysts to relieve the patient of the troublesome hidden subjective elements of experience, the *ex-*

pression of those ideas is necessary, and, according to Mead, expressing an idea is essential for both its clarity and its objectivity. A hypothesis, proposed by an individual, is relieved of its subjectivity when it is tested and when the proposal is accepted by others.

Probably one of the most important consequences of Mead's objective relativism is his claim that through language we literally construct many objects; they exist only in relation to a society which creates new meanings and makes many cuts of an otherwise disorganized, undifferentiated collocation of events. Such things as chairs, homes, knives, scholars, kings, and possibly everything that is classified depends on our doing the classifying. Much finer distinctions can be made than are made to date. This may be the basis for the sociology of knowledge. Still, items that fall under our concepts are objective and real, though relative. Our whole human environment is real and objective, but only in relation to us. So it is that lower animals and we confer many characters on the world, and these characters are by no means subjective. By this doctrine Mead is able to answer Hegel, Locke, Berkeley, the positivists, and the phenomenalists. As I see it, this doctrine was in the back of Mead's mind in all of his teaching and writing, as stated in his famous essay "The Objective Reality of Perspectives."

8. Finally, his system explains how democracy, as we have known it recently in the West, is indispensable to an open society of open selves in which there is continuous need for the reformation and enrichment of our social perspective and the generalized other. Every new idea, every innovation, according to Mead, comes from an individual.

The Class Notes and Mead's System

The 1914 notes indicate that Mead was faithful to his early commitment as stated above. He says: "We consider the act as the primitive unit." Herbert Spencer, Mead says, conceives of the act as arising, and he does not see the importance of making it primary. For Mead, the act does not itself emerge but is there as the basis for all other emergence. Both Mead's pragmatism and his commitment to process philosophy are exhibited throughout these notes. Compared to later notes they are more closely related to and conditioned by the psychologists and sociologists of that time, such as James, Hobhouse, Spencer, James R. Angell, William McDougall, and Cooley. Beginning with the impulse, which means the animal is seeking stimuli that will release an act (of pecking, say), Mead explains how, from sensing stimuli (which he calls perceptual consciousness), the human, because of conflicting stimuli and the inhibition of the act, arrived at reflective consciousness, which is social in character. Reflective consciousness, involving an awareness of the consequences of behavior, requires a consciousness of meanings, which occurs prior to one's being aware of himself. In some of Mead's later still unpublished essays he is concerned with the meaning of consciousness. I believe he is driving toward the conlusion that perceptual consciousness is simply a taking into account, by way of the senses, an immediately present object, whereas in reflective consciousness we take into account some absent possible object or situation, and this requires symbols and is social in nature.

In the 1927 notes Mead's main purpose is to account for the nature and genesis of the self. He explains his behavioristic approach and contrasts it with introspectionism and Watsonian behaviorism which is, for Mead, too mechanical in that Watson treats stimuli as if they are physical forces compelling the organism to act. Although many problems treated in the notes are identical with those in *Mind, Self, and Society*, they are approached from a different point of view. Also, two topics in that work, the generalized other and the "I" and the "me," are practically overlooked in these notes. But special attention is paid to some topics in the notes that are practically ignored in *Mind, Self, and Society*. First, though Mead states there (p. 237) that language and the hand provide the mechanism for reflective intelligence, he does not explain the function of the hand in arriving at a conception of the *physical thing*. This is done in Mead's essay "Consciousness, Mind, the Self, and Scientific Objects," as well as in the present notes, and I believe that Mead, in so doing, had more than one problem he wanted to solve: (*a*) he had the metaphysical problem of not succumbing to the Berkeleyan-Humean claim that no distinction can be made between (Cartesian and Lockean) primary and secondary qualities. (*b*) He wanted to show that our concept of the physical thing arises out of the pulls and pushes we experience in the manipulation of objects, which is done through role-taking, something that is not possible for lower animals. (*c*) He wanted to stress the function of the hand in what he calls the manipulatory phase of the act, that phase in which reflective intelligence is most involved. (*d*) He wanted to show how mind and body (the symbolic process and overt behavior), though they are different phases of the act, still are necessarily functionally related.

Second, in these notes Mead emphasizes that the child's world is first a completely social world. At first the child does not have a conception of the physical thing, the physical world. By words the child can move other people to act; why not so move all other things? To abstract the physical thing from the mental is a social accomplishment requiring language.

Third, Mead discusses how attitudes can be gestures and he states the conditions under which they are not gestures. For a lower animal without a language, an attitude of a given animal cannot also be a gesture to that animal, whereas man can be aware of the meaning of his attitude to another, and in that case it is also a gesture to him.

Fourth, in these notes Mead discusses more extensively the nature of morality and how it arises. Also, the meaning of human freedom is discussed in conjunction with rules, laws, and customs. In these notes, as in *Mind, Self, and Society,* it seems that Mead wants to furnish a theory of the self consistent with all of the latest developments in the physical sciences.

The 1914 Class Notes

These notes are from the course Social Psychology, Philosophy 321, given by Professor Mead at the University of Chicago in the winter quarter, 1914. In this course Mead was concerned mainly with the genesis of the mind and the self. Emanating from his chief concern were many other problems, such as the origin and function of language; the functions of emotion, inhibition, and gestures in the social process of adjustment; the nature of significant symbols and shared meanings of gestures; the nature of perception, conception, analysis and synthesis; conversation and communication; the relationship between attitudes and gestures; putting oneself in the "place of the other," the "I" and the "me"; the "looking glass" theory of how one becomes self-conscious, how an individual self is distinguished from the other; and the importance of frustration, emotion, and inhibition in the development of significant symbols.

These lectures are rich in suggestions about such things as the social nature of crime, the function of artists in the solution of social, economic, political, and educational problems. Behind Mead's thinking there is his strong belief in evolution, democracy, the scientific method of solving problems, and technology as a means of attaining and preserving shared values or social goals. In all of this Mead subscribes to the view that we live in an open universe, an open society in which we construct and reconstruct a moral and environmental order, and in which the individual serves as the source of new ideas, new hypotheses, leading continually to the reformation and reconstruction of social behavior. I am confident that readers will find in these notes many hints and fertile suggestions about how to clarify and attack various problems encompassed by philosophy and social theory. In the following remarks I shall consider only a few of the concepts used by Mead. About some of these concepts there have been vigorous discussions and sometimes differences of interpretation by those who have been interested in Mead's philosophy.

Frustration, Inhibition, and Emotion

Mead's claim that the act is the unit of existence means, for example, that stimulus and response are actually so correlated that one cannot occur without the other occurring also. They occur as a unit and, consequently, each by itself is an abstraction from concrete reality. Mead assumes that all animals, including humans, have impulses, pre-potent responses, and thus that an animal seeks stimuli that will release them. Learning consists in the rejecting of certain stimuli and the selecting of others that are more adequate for continuing the life process. Objects in the environment serve as stimuli, but often the same object tends to evoke conflicting, incompatible responses. For example, bait in a wolf-trap may attract the wolf, but human odor on the bait may elicit the response of running away. The same object has these two properties, one signifying food, the other danger. And although the act of taking the bait is cut short of completion, is frustrated and inhibited, the wolf, in contrast to a human, does not analyze the object into its different properties (stimuli) but, rather, acts toward the object at one time as food and then immediately frustrates that act by acting toward the object as danger. But these conflicting responses (meanings) are not comprehended, internalized, or conceived of by the wolf. It does not say, "What do we have here? How can I reconcile these conflicting responses?"

Mead has an ingenious way of explaining how analysis, the thought process, emerges from conflicting responses (attitudes) and how inhibition is essential to the emergence of gestures, which serve as stimuli to animals other than those that are making the gestures. He also explains how these nonsignificant gestures (gestures whose meanings are not shared, the meaning of a gesture being the response it evokes) become significant gestures, gestures evoking in those who make them the same (functionally identical) responses that they evoke in the other. Gestures arise in connection with inhibition or frustration, and such things as grimacing, baring the teeth, ruffing the fur, crying, doubling the fist, taking certain postures, etc., result from inhibitions of acts and may be thought of as tendencies to act in certain ways or as the beginnings of acts. If they are sensed by other animals, they may indicate to the other the oncoming phases of acts of which they are the initial phases. They are not, as Darwin supposed, attempts to express an emotion. Lower animals do not intend anything by their gestures, just as we do not when we jump from a loud noise. Still, gestures are associated with emotions and we say that a person jumped because he was afraid or that a dog bared its teeth because it was angry. Mead explains that several emotions that are very important and necessary for social control, e.g., guilt and sympathy, could not be had apart from role-taking.

Attitudes and Gestures

In these lectures Mead uses "attitude" and "gesture" almost synonymously. If looked at simply as the behavior of an animal (as bodily movement or activity, including the voice), the two things are identical, and any gesture can also be called an attitude. However, bodily posture or activity does not serve as a gesture unless it evokes a response in another. In this sense there can be attitudes that do not serve as gestures. Mead wants to define "attitude," in his early work, in purely behavioristic terms, not referring to awareness or consciousness of meaning. "Attitude" and "posture" are the same in behavioristic terms. If, however, the attitude or posture serves as a stimulus to another animal, then it is a sign indicating to the other the oncoming phase of the act of which the attitude or posture is the first phase. Used in this sense we often say "it was a good gesture on his part," "he has the right attitude," "he presents a good posture." All of these meanings involve awareness of the further implications of one's behavior. A posture or an attitude becomes a gesture when it evokes a response by the other. Also, Mead uses "attitude" to mean "a set of the organism," a readiness to carry out an act. He says "gestures are attitudes of people who are going to act" (p. 40–41). "We have the gesture representing the attitude of the individual" (p. 48).

Mead says: "A conversation of gestures consists simply in the continued readjustment of one individual to another" (p. 43). Here he is thinking of nonsignificant gestures which function apart from an awareness (a consciousness) of their meanings.

The significant symbol emerges when the one who makes it is aware of its meaning to the other, i.e. when one can anticipate the response it will evoke in the other. Mead's most profound insight consists in understanding that the significant symbol, the language symbol, consists of a gesture whose meaning is had by both the one who makes the gesture and the other to whom it is addressed. He spent most of his intellectual life unraveling the implications of this insight. I believe the profundity of this insight is still not fully grasped. Here I can only make a few suggestions of its import.

The Significant Symbol

By means of gestures whose meanings are shared (significant symbols) we break out of a present. Thus there is not, when we communicate by language, simply a conversation of gestures, but a conversation of the meanings of gestures. One's response is not to the immediately sensed gesture but to its meaning. There is an awareness, a consciousness of the meaning of the gesture. The meaning is the distant, future, possible oncoming phase of the social act. Meanings of which we are conscious refer to both what is possible, but which may never become actual, and to what actually occurs. Hence shareable meanings are expressed in abstract terms, and concepts are required for expressing them. By concepts we can indicate possible objects and situations in their absence, as well as the kinds of responses we will make to them (later). Breaking out of a present, which is impossible apart from symbols whose meanings are shared, is essential for the existence of both minds and selves; lower animals, Mead believes, have neither. Breaking out of a present requires taking the role of the other, putting oneself in the place of the other. Awareness and self-consciousness both imply a breaking out of a present, indicating to oneself some possible phenomenon in its absence.

Apparently Mead believes lower animals have no experience corresponding to man's conception of the possible. They live in an eternal present. If the wolf could think of the meat in the trap as having alternative meanings, if it could think of it as "bait," it would have analyzed the object and it would think of alternative possible objects and the corresponding reactions to them. It would be able to indicate to itself alternative possible consequences of its behavior. It seems to me that Mead is supporting the view that an analysis of the various meanings of objects and situations depends finally on role-taking and the use of significant symbols, that analysis requires a mind having a social component which is constitutive and necessary to every individual mind. Only by symbols whose meanings are shared or shareable, can we be conscious of a past (remember) and anticipate a future. The details of these suggestions have not yet been fully worked out.

Caste and Profession

Mead considers the nature and origin of castes and holds that they first arose in societies when one group captured outsiders and used them as slaves. The owners of slaves considered themselves as socially superior, as elite. This elitist attitude is nurtured further in civilized industrial societies in the distinction between classes of people who perform different kinds of roles, such as the laboring class, management, professional role-performers such as teachers, ministers, doctors, lawyers, politicians, military personnel, etc. When members of such classes or professional groups think they are superior to members of another class, we have the "caste" attitude (pp. 84ff.). Mead believes one of the chief functions of democracy is to give people of various "classes" and backgrounds the opportunity to choose professions and roles of their liking. One who understands that his own role depends upon the roles of others, and that his performance is an integral part of and supported by a larger whole, will forsake the notion of elitism. "If a doctor wants to be superior, he will use big words, be secretive, etc. But if he is seeking to help to the fullest degree, he seeks to get the fullest understanding on the part of the patient, and thus professionalism tends to disappear." Mead contrasts his theory of caste with that of Cooley's (pp. 82ff.).

The Physical Thing

Mead is continually concerned with refuting Cartesian dualism, which holds that there is a substantive difference between mind and body. But when George Berkeley dealt with the problem he could not make a distinction of any kind between primary and secondary qualities; both, he held, were in the mind (spiritual), and he assimilated Cartesian matter to mind. Mead, however, in making not a substantive but a functional distinction between mental phenomena and bodily activities, is able to explain the difference and the functional relationship between what traditionally have been called primary and secondary qualities of matter. Mead calls secondary qualities, such as odors, sounds, and colors, "distance experiences," whereas the primary qualities are found in "contact experiences." Mead is a haptic philosopher, holding that the test of the reality of objects is found in contact experiences. We press or pull on an object and it, at the same time, offers numerically equal resistance to our efforts. The physical thing is experienced here and now, whereas the color of the object is experienced at a distance and indicates the physical object experienced in contact. Mead also explains that we do not project ourselves into objects or into other selves (p. 62), and thus he evades the phenomenological fallacy. (For a further discussion of this subject, see Mead's The Philosophy of the Present, Supplementary Essay II, "The Physical Thing." See also the accompanying essay by Mead in this volume, "Consciousness, Mind, the Self, and Scientific Objects.")

The reader may have the feeling that there is unwarranted repetition in the lectures, but I find that in repeated statements Mead is always attacking the same problems from different standpoints. We do not find, in these lectures, a discussion of the meaning of "the generalized other," a phrase Mead used extensively in his later writings. He means by it "the organization of roles," whereby the individual is able to comprehend the various phases of the social act as these phases or roles are performed by the various participants. To have a conception of a baseball game, say, is to have a conception of the rules of the game as well as the spatiotemporal relationship between all of the roles of the members of the team. A baseball game is a social object. To share a conception of all of the phases of the acts in the game that answer to the social object is to take the role of the generalized other. Here I can only suggest that in this very important concept he was directing his thought against absolutism and finality, against especially absolute idealism (Hegelianism) which holds that there is an absolute, final, all-inclusive perspective transcending the perspective of any and all particular individual members of society. This view would not permit changes in the "true" perspective. We would not have an open society, nor could the individual's perspective be effective in widening the community perspective, the generalized other.

The 1927 Class Notes

These notes are from Mead's course on Social Psychology given in Gates Hall during the spring quarter of 1927. This is an entirely different set of notes from those published in *Mind, Self, and Society.* Many of the same topics in the present lectures are discussed in that work but often from a different point of view. These lectures offer new insights into Mead's overall philosophy; compared with those of 1914, they develop a theory of the self, perception, the generalized other, the physical thing, the manipulatory phase of the act, in a way that coordinates and unifies Mead's earlier social theory with the epistemology and metaphysics of pragmatism as well as with cosmology, in which he deals with space and time and relatively theory. Not enough attention has been given to Mead's general outlook stated succinctly in *The Philosophy of The Present* as "the principle of sociality" and the social nature of the present. A careful study of Mead's works will show that whatever particular problem he is discussing, in the back of his mind there is always a more general philosophical position *(Weltanschauung)* from which he approaches the problem at hand. Consequently, any student of Mead's will find it profitable to get hold of his more general outlook, in that a better, more significant understanding of Mead's discussion of particular subjects will be a welcome consequence. Here I will discuss briefly some of Mead's claims that have implications not easily detected.

Mead speaks of "the fallacy of the stimulus-response theory." He wants to make clear that a stimulus "does not hold the control mandate that psychology assumes" (p.142). If psychologists were correct in thinking that stimuli force animals to respond in a sort of mechanical way, then Watsonian behaviorism could be easily defended as well as the generally accepted belief that the environment determines the nature of the organism and all of its activities. Mead's view, rather, is that the organism is equipped with impulses, with tendencies to act, and by virtue of these impulses it *seeks and selects* stimuli that will release these impulses, these pre-potent responses. He assumes, further, that the selection of a stimulus by the organism is conducive to the continuation of the life process of the particular organism as well as to the continuation of the species of which the particular form is a member. For example, the chick has the impulse to peck. From this basic contention Mead concludes that the form helps determine its environment, that it actually confers new characters on the environment, and that a clear conception of "environment" involves a conception of the form and vice versa. By following this claim, Mead's philosophy serves as a basis for refuting the various kinds of determinisms: environmental, hereditary, cultural, and technological. It supports his later claim that by use of language gestures we can select, in their absence, the kinds of stimuli (objects) to which we are going to respond later. This is the basis for human freedom and for the place of the individual in helping determine the nature of the social process. New forms, as well as new ideas, are responsible for new environments and for an open universe.

Mead makes much of what has been neglected by most psychologists, namely, the manipulatory phase of the act, that phase involving the human hand. I think recent students of Mead have not worked out the fuller implications of Mead's insight. First, we notice that Mead speaks of "phases" of the act, not of "parts" (atomic parts) that happen one after the other. He means that the act is the unit (of existence) and only by abstraction do we divide it into its various phases. We may designate these as the impulsive, the perceptual, the conceptual, the manipulatory, and the consummatory phases of the act. A striking characteristic of humans is that they greatly excel in handling objects, in dissecting them and in recombining the parts in multifarious ways. A considerable portion of the brain is devoted to controlling the hand. Instruments further facilitate the manipulation of objects, but the significance of all this for Mead is that reflective intelligence is concerned basically with manipulation, with that phase of the act lying between the impulsive and the consummatory phases of the act. For lower animals the manipulatory and the consummatory phases of the act are often one and the same, as when the wolf both kills and devours its prey by the same means and without a temporal span between the two. Also, the act of storing honey by bees or nuts by squirrels takes place instinctively without reflection and without knowledge of what is being done. (To know what one is doing means understanding the relationship between doing, as a means, and the result of doing or the result of manipulating objects.) What we call civilization and differences in cultures are due mainly to what the hand has wrought under the control of intellect. All of our instruments and technological devices fit in, directly or indirectly, with the human hand. Reflective intelligence, Mead contends, would be impossible apart from manipulation, and language would be surplus baggage.

Closely allied with Mead's conception of manipulation is his definition of "the physical *thing*." We notice that Mead did not use the expression "the physical óbject." Generally speaking, *things* according to Mead are socially constructed, they are constructed from a series of events or happenings. For example, a fountain pen is a thing because our conception of it includes not just what is here and now in our seeing of it or in our writing with it but also includes a whole series of possible future transactions between it and ourselves and other things many of which may never transpire. All things are social constructions, and if things constitute what is real for us then we have a basis for the sociology of knowledge claim that the real is a social construction. But Mead is concerned with other problems also in offering a definition of the physical thing. There is something unique about our experience of physical things in contrast with our experience of colors, sounds, and odors, or the so-called secondary qualities. The latter Mead calls "distance experiences," but we experience the physical thing by direct contact, immediately, not in a future or at a distance. (For a fuller discussion of the physical thing, see the accompanying essay by Mead, "Consciousness, Mind, the Self, and Scientific Objects," as well as my introduction to it.)

Our conception of the physical thing is central in our ability to separate space from time, and it has a direct bearing on Mead's notion of perception and his theory of physical relativity, something not fully brought out by followers of Mead. Let us consider his theory of perception, which is noticeably different from all standard theories. First, human perception, according to Mead, includes a social element. We perceive *things*. We do not perceive simply colors and shapes. Rather, perception or perceiving includes one's tendencies to act in a certain way. The meaning of things perceived is the implicit reaction, the attitude of the perceiver. We perceive, not by simply gazing and allowing what is there to produce a "photographic picture" on the brain or on the mind. Rather, what one perceives depends upon one's interest, on what one is doing or what one may possibly do. In this sense perception is a process of filtering, whereby relevant stimuli are admitted and others excluded. Thus perception, for Mead, involves a taking into account, and by colors, shapes, sounds, and odors we take into account distant objects. This taking into account is stated in terms of conduct or behavior. Perception, thus, involves an attitude, an implicit and therefore temporarily inhibited response to the physical thing, say. The child of two does not first see an object and then decide to reach for it. Its seeing and the act of reaching constitute one and the same undivided act. But later when the child realizes it is reaching for a pencil, say when it knows the kind of thing it is reaching for (when it has a concept of the thing), then there is a social element in its perception. The meaning of "pencil" is shared by other members of society. Its meaning is a social construction, and the pencil as a mere physically present object is now a thing for the child. Insofar as objects from which distance-experiences emanate have conscious meanings for us, they are things; i.e., our conception of them includes what is both actual about them and what we believe is really (in accordance with the laws of nature) possible, though many possible happenings may never become actual. When we perceive, say, a delicate Dresden figurine, we perceive it as fragile, breakable, which means, among other things, handle with care, don't drop. Basically the function of perception is to control behavior. It both filters out and admits stimuli conditioned by interest and the ongoing act. It has both its inhibitory and its releasing aspects. To be aware of the kind of object perceived requires also a social component.

Mead's theory of space and time, and of how space is separated from time, depends upon his theory of perception. Lower animals, he says, live in a present, but by use of significant symbols and role-taking we break out of a present and have conceptions of past and future. To conceive of a distant object as a thing requires breaking out of a present. Still, when an object becomes a thing for us we interpret the space in which both we as organisms and the distant object exist as static; i.e., it does not pass, whereas the action required to reach and handle it transpires or is temporal. Without a conception of things, this separation of space and time would be impossible. When we react to the distant object as if it were present, we have separated space from time; we have wrenched the distant object from its futurity. Also, to see a thing as distant requires being in a perspective which includes both the organism and the distant object. The perspective is objective (some would say "true") when, by acting with reference to the distant object, our act terminates in the anticipated results or, in pragmatic terms, when the act is successful.

The term "perspective" was not used to any extent by Mead until after about 1920. I am confident that A. N. Whitehead's use of the term influenced Mead. In his later years Mead often used "being in the perspective of the other" instead of "taking the role of the other." This shows the influence of the general theory of physical relativity on both Whitehead and Mead. Some writers have used the expression "having a perspective on" something, but Mead, as far as I know, does not do so inasmuch as he, like Whitehead, believed the individual belongs to or is in perspectives, thus evading both subjectivism and dualism. The community perspective, or the attitudes common to members of the group, precedes, for the child, an awareness of self. That is, the child is first in the perspective of the community, or the generalized other comes first in its conscious life. Since private perspectives emerge from a community perspective, the child first takes the role of the other before it is conscious of itself. It becomes conscious of itself by looking at its behavior from the standpoint of the other. This happens when the child has inclinations and desires of which it is aware but which are contrary to the community attitude. Self-consciousness is most prominent in any of us when we do something of which both we and others are aware and which is contrary to socially approved ways of behaving.

Mead's conception of the generalized other is central to his theory of universals and his notion of the community perspective. Always in the back of Mead's mind is a revolt against Hegel's and F. H. Bradley's Absolute. Mead is opposed to the idealist's claim that there is an absolute perspective, known to God, a perspective which transcends all human perspectives and is final, or fixed and unchanging. Corresponding to the Hegelian absolute is the Newtonian conception of absolute space and time which purportedly are conceivable but not manifested in sense experience. Newton said space and time are the sensoria of God, by which he meant, I presume, that God alone is witness to absolute motion or the motion of bodies with reference to an absolute, transcendent perspective of which human perspectives are mere aspects, in which case they would be infected with subjectivity and would not, of course, be objective, even as Newton claimed that sensed motion is not objective but relative. For Mead, perspectives are both social, conditioned by human beings, *and* objective. Again, Mead's view is contrary to that of Durkheim's, which is that there is a "social mind" or a group mind that controls the minds of individuals, a mind that transcends the minds of individuals. Mead's generalized other is neither a collection of individual perspectives nor a transcendent perspective. Rather it is *an organization of perspectives,* an awareness of how the behavior of individual role-performers are to be coordinated so that each is an effective phase of the more inclusive social act. The implications of Mead's "generalized other" have never been made fully explicit.

Mead speaks of the universal, or of universals, in two different senses. First, concepts indicated by common nouns are universal in that they connote, or indicate the meanings particular items (of a class) have for us; they also denote, in that they apply to an indefinite number of particulars. Universality also applies to generalized others, which vary in degree and comprehensiveness. A generalized other may be confined to a particular limited community or culture. The highest, most abstract, or most universal generalized other would be an organization of the attitudes of members of all communities and cultures both present and past, but it would still be a human perspective entertainable and sharable by individuals.

Mead developed the theory that language is a phase of the social process inseparable from action, from role-performances. The primary function of language is to incite action. All other effects of language are parasitic on its perlocutionary force. To designate, to appraise, to emote, and to construct meanings of things are all dependent upon this primary function. The meanings things have for us can be stated in terms of our reactions to them and their reactions to each other. To point to or to indicate an object to another by gestures involves also an attempt to elicit some kind of response by the other, etc. It is by gestures, language gestures, that we communicate meanings and attitudes, and when communication is effective, i.e., when the addressee understands the addressor, only one meaning is communicated and the same (functionally identical) meaning is had by both. Mead did not believe that a private language is possible. Language is necessarily social and requires that language symbols have shared meanings. Consequently, solipsism is impossible. Even if an individual makes marks on, say, blueprints that have meaning only to him, they are parasitic on a public language.

Mead says "morality is constituted where a person has in his own conduct the universals that govern the whole community." In this way the behavior of the group as a whole enters into the conduct of the individual. The universality of which Mead speaks is identical with the generalized other, the rational other. It consists of attitudes and commitments shared by members of the group. Thus morality for Mead depends upon role-taking and being in the perspective of the other. Although ethicists in the past, especially of the eighteenth century, have tried to establish a basis for ethical conduct on the feeling of sympathy, conscience, and a sense of duty, no one before Mead explained that these notions depend upon role-taking. Recently sociologists have rightfully argued that such emotions as shame, embarrassment, guilt, conscience, etc., have powerful control over the moral behavior of the individual. None of these emotions would be possible apart from language and role-taking. They all emerge within a social context. No doubt much more will be done on ethical theory and social control based on Mead's contention that role-taking is essential to moral conduct.

Mead's conception of freedom is also based on his theory of taking the role of the other. The organization of perspectives leading to the integration and coordination of the behavior of individual role-performers does not lessen the freedom of the individual. Rather, it increases human freedom and, in fact, is essential to it. Thus humans, due to social organization made possible by the generalized other, have a different kind of freedom from that of lower animals. Organizations, institutions, and government and civilizations do not restrict one's freedom but make it possible.

All of the above-mentioned topics are discussed in these lectures. Their full implications for philosophy and the social sciences have still to be worked out.

Consciousness, Mind, the Self, and Scientific Objects

In this essay Mead is concerned mainly with refuting Cartesian dualism and with defending his own claim that neither consciousness, mind, nor the self can be separated from action which involves a relationship between the organism and an environment. Just as we cannot separate sensations from organisms functioning in an environment, so consciousness cannot exist apart from a functioning organism. "Consciousness has no other meaning here than that the organism is functioning normally" (p. 177).

Mead, in refuting dualism, does not reduce consciousness or mind to material, mechanical action. Consciousness is an emergent, as is mind, and both are qualitatively different from what is found in a purely physical world, though necessarily functionally related to the latter. To reject dualism does not commit one to a monism, to either materialism or idealism, say. Rather Mead is saying that mind, the self, and the symbolic process, though dependent upon a physical environment as well as a social environment, and necessarily functionally related to the latter, are also real and objective. Here Mead invokes the principle of objective relativism. Secondary qualities such as colors, sounds, and odors are real and exist in the objective world, though only in relation to living organisms. So minds and selves are real, but only in relation to a physical and a social environment. In this sense Mead is a pluralist. Hence there are different levels of reality. Matter seems to be primary. No other items are ultimately separable from it. Living organisms with sense experiences had in direct contact with material objects, are next in the scale of evolution. But these feelings, say of pressure, are not separable from matter. They are what Mead calls contact experiences in which physical objects are experienced directly and immediately. The distance senses are next. In vision and hearing we experience the physical thing at a distance, and these distance experiences, through perception, enable organisms to be in readiness to react to the things sensed when they come in contact with them. Distance experiences are intelligible only in relation to contact experiences and the manipulatory phase of action.

Minds and selves emerge out of the manipulatory activities whereby we use physical things as means to ends. Prior to the emergence of minds and selves, animals are conscious in that they sense objects in the environment; they are stimulated by objects and normally respond in a way conducive to their individual well-being and especially to the welfare of the species of which they are members. But in such cases the organism lives in a present; it responds to items in immediate sense experience. It is not aware of itself and does not indicate to itself anything beyond what is in immediate experience. Minds arise when, in the experience of the organism, they break out of a present, and this is done when the organism becomes an object to itself. This is called, not merely consciousness, but self-consciousness. Hence, not only are others and other things objects to the organism, but it is an object to itself and therefore a subject. This is done through role-taking.

Several things happen when the individual becomes aware of itself or becomes self-conscious. Not only does the mind and the self emerge at this juncture, but also the symbolic process arises, for the reason that role-taking, reflecting back on the self and indicating things, not in immediate experience to oneself, requires that the individual be aware of the relationship of his own personal role to the roles of others who are participants in the same (social) act. At this point social objects arise.

A social object answers to every phase (every role performance) of the social act, such as a baseball game or a heart transplant, say. For the individual to have, within his own experience, the entire social act is to take the attitude of the generalized other. The generalized other consists of an organization of the roles of individual participants in the social act. The individual can have, within his own experience, the roles of the other participants, but not by actually performing their roles. Role-taking does not mean role-performing. Taking the role of the other, including the generalized other, is a conceptual affair. It requires an abstraction from the particularity of the situation at hand; it requires universals. "The effect of taking the role of anyone is to eliminate the peculiarity of the environment of any one individual, and to substitute for any concrete individual an abstraction—a generalized individual—the thinker" (pp. 178 below). A generalization of the environment and of the individual happen together and simultaneously with the emergence of the generalized other. The process of role-taking requires symbols whose meanings are shared by the various participants in the social act. This is done by abstraction (by use of significant symbols) from concrete situations and from particular individuals.

Mead argues against Cartesian dualism as well as against the monism of Berkeley, which resulted in subjective idealism and finally in Hegelian absolute idealism. This monistic view holds that the real is ultimately mental or spiritual, and, according to Berkeley, what we call matter is nothing but a collection of ideas which depend upon a perceiver, a mind. If this were true, clearly Mead's claim that mental phenomena, minds and selves, emerge in time and are not in a world that is there prior to their emergence, could not be defended. This is why Mead is concerned with the distinction between primary and secondary qualities, indicated by Galileo, Descartes, and Locke. All held that the secondary qualities—colors, tastes, sounds, odors—depend upon a perceiver for their existence. For Galileo, Descartes, Locke, and many others, this meant that secondary qualities, since they exist only in relation to perceivers, are subjective. They are transitive, they come and go, and are, so they argued, less real than the permanent primary qualities of material objects, namely, their inertia or mass and their continuous occupation of space and time. Mead, by invoking the principle of objective relativism, contends that, although secondary qualities exist only in relation to perceivers, they are nonetheless as real and objective as are the primary qualities of matter dealt with by the physical scientists.

But how can Mead refute Berkeley's claim that the primary qualities of matter also depend upon a perceiver for their existence, that all we can mean by the inertial resistance of a body is the experience (the idea) we have in muscular kinesthetic sensations? Furthermore, Berkeley argued that motion is not a property of a body per se, but rather the motion of any body depends upon its spatial relation to some other body. If we can correctly say the sun moves, it is only in relation to other celestial bodies. John Locke, who held that all knowledge about matters of fact comes from sense experience, believed we cannot sense that which is the cause of sensations, these primary qualities of matter itself. Hence he resorted to a metaphysical postulate. He believed we can know about matter only by its sensed effects, but in itself it is something we know not what. Locke's metaphysical speculation went beyond and was in violation of his thesis that all knowledge about the world comes from sensations. He by no means gave reasons or evidence against Berkeley's later argument that, since sensations are mental, their cause must be mental or spiritual.

Apparently no one prior to Mead had answered Berkeley and the other idealists satisfactorily. Kant subscribed to the *ding an sich,* which he posited as a physical cause of sensations, even as he spoke of the self as being beyond experience and as unknown in itself. But Mead wants to do four things. First, he wants to avoid metaphysical speculation about matter, or the physical thing. Second, he wants to justify a knowledge of the physical thing by resorting to experience. Third, he wants to evade Cartesian dualism and Berkeleyan and Hegelian idealism. Fourth, he wants to escape positivism (including logical positivism), which holds that terms in physics and all other sciences, if meaningful, must refer to sensations or sensibilia, or sense data only. Nor does Mead subscribe to logical atomism, a view that implies that the real is built up out of isolated atomic parts, each being what it is apart from the others; i.e., all relations between them are external.

Mead's account of how we come to know, by experience, the nature of the physical thing, or how we arrive at the concept of it, is new and ingenious. His success in accounting for this knowledge lends support and justification for his theory of the genesis of the self. We experience the physical thing directly by the muscular kinesthetic sense, or the haptic experience. In contact experience with the physical thing we not only have the sensation of pressing, pushing, or pulling on it, but simultaneously we have the experience of its inertial resistance, its pushing or pulling on us. Included in that experience is the experience of its acting at a place and, of course, at a time. Furthermore, the force and resistance of another body on us is simultaneous with and numerically equal to the effort or resistance we offer to it. Action and reaction are simultaneous and numerically equal. "Color, sound, taste, and odor cannot be identified with the responses which they elicit, either in organisms or in other objects; while the experiential inner content of matter is identical with the responses which it calls out in things" (*The Philosophy of the Present,* p. 123). Since one's effort and the resistance an object offers to that effort are simultaneous, we cannot argue that the individual's experience is projected into the object. Rather we have a direct experience of the physical thing.

Now this direct experience, which no doubt is also had by lower animals, still does not give us the concept of the thing. To have a concept of the physical thing requires taking its role. This means anticipating the resistance of the thing at a distance from it and prior to reaching and acting on it (manipulating it). This means that the implicit response we make to it, prior to the contact experience, is numerically equal and of the same kind as the response (or reaction) it will make to us when we handle it. The concept is an inhibited, implicit, or covert response. It is a (mental) response to a later response. Through linguistic symbols only can we respond to our own responses. Although lower animals respond to objects in their immediate environment as well as to bodily states such as pain, thirst, and hunger, they cannot, according to Mead, respond to their own responses. This requires role-taking and the use of linguistic gestures, significant symbols.

Mead accounts for the difference between primary and secondary qualities by the difference between distance experiences and contact experiences. We do have a direct experience of the physical thing, its mass and inertia. What one experiences in contact is not confined to the organism—it is not wholly inside the organism, as Locke would have it. Rather, we experience something outside—a resistance, a pulling or pushing. No secondary quality is finally separable from the primary, provided we have veridical perceptions, neither illusory nor hallucinatory. Furthermore, the imperceptible, unobservable scientific objects such as atoms and electrons, are, according to scientists, of the same logical structure as are objects of contact experience. They have mass, inertia, and occupy space and time. They are not transcendent, spiritual entities. The qualities of matter are primary in another sense. The principle of the conservation of mass-energy justifies the claim that all newly emergent forms, such as plants, animals, minds, and selves, arise from a material world as a necessary condition, and this world is required also for supporting and sustaining these forms. Furthermore, the process of emergence itself may be expressed in general terms called by Mead "the principle of sociality" (*The Philosophy of the Present,* pp. 65ff). "I have wished to present mind as an evolution in nature, in which culminates that sociality which is the principle and the form of emergence" (ibid., p. 85). Mind appears when, "in social conduct of the deliberative type, the self as a social object enters the field of adjustment on the same basis as other objects" (p. 184 below).

Finally, from this essay we can see that Mead was wrestling strenuously with problems in epistemology and metaphysics in order to defend the conclusion that we live in an open universe of open selves. He is neither a materialist nor an idealist. Still less is he a reductionist. Rather he believed in emergent evolution, and held that the effects of natural processes are novel, unpredictable in fact and in principle, and that they cannot be assimilated to their causes. So, finally, the self is an emergent whose influence in determining the behavior of the individual and that of society is not fully determined or predictable from its prior relation to society. Thus the individual can choose on the basis of reflective intelligence and is a free moral agent insofar as his choice is sustained by his social and physical environments.

Functional Identity of Response and
Functional Identity of Stimulus

The two essays in the Appendix, "Functional Identity of Response" and "The Functional Identity of Stimulus" have been in my possession for several years. I am by no means certain about who wrote them. After much consideration about who might have been the author, I have eliminated several who were Mead's students or colleagues. It is clear that the essays were written after rather extensive use of radio and before television. I judge they were written about 1925.

In these essays the author is concerned with clarifying Mead's greatest insight: The language gesture or the significant symbol arises when an individual evokes in himself, by his gesture, the *same* response that he evokes in an other.[1] Possibly many readers have been puzzled over what the word "same" can mean, or did mean, for Mead. After all, X's response is made by him and Y's response must be a different response made by Y, and here we have two responses which are substantially and existentially different, not identical. What can be meant, then, by saying they are the same? In the essays the author makes a clear distinction between substantial or existential identity (when X is identical with itself and not another thing) and *functional* identity. A significant symbol (or a language gesture) is one that evokes the same *functionally*

1. See David L. Miller, *George Herbert Mead: Self, Language, and the World*, pp. 12ff., for comments on this problem.

identical response in the one who makes it as it evokes in the other. The concept of functional identity is essential to a clarification of what Mead meant, but it also has far wider implications for Mead as a process philosopher.

Here I will only hint at a wider implication of the meaning of functional identity in connection with a substance philosophy and in contrast with pragmatism, functionalism, and process philosophy. In what sense can any two things, though numerically and existentially different, be said to be alike, the same, or similar? It is not the case that two things are the same because each is a substance having an identical attribute in common. This would assume that a single attribute, say blue, is a universal, a sort of eternal object that can be in different places at the same time, that there is only one universal and that it is numerically the same though in different places. Rather, two things, such as two BB shots, though existentially different and distinct, are nevertheless the same in the sense that they function alike in a context. They are functionally identical. In general, any two or more things that can be subsumed under the same law (things that follow a given law) are functionally identical. This implies that the locus of universals and universality is not in particulars, but rather in laws, in how particulars interact with each other. Also, only by laws do we understand what particulars are like. Our only *knowledge* about particulars is found in how they function, and this functioning takes time. Process philosophy maintains that a thing cannot be what it is without including the temporal factor. Mead's system is a breaking away from Platonic-Aristotelianism as well as from realism.[2]

These profound and succinct essays have further implications for the meaning of "the generalized other," which at present, I believe, needs further clarification. Just as Mead holds that the meanings of things (particulars) are in transactions, in laws (Peirce's *Thirdness*) involving time, so the generalized other, which represents the rational other, is found in the organization of perspectives or in the organization of roles, and this organization involves the performance of organized roles taking place over a period of time. The generalized other, or an organization of roles, belongs, Mead says, to the "me" component of the self. It is expressed in such things as rules of the game, in shared (institutionalized) habits, and is a universal factor communicable from one person to another. This communication depends upon responses or roles that are functionally identical, and all meanings about particulars must be stated

2. See David L. Miller, "The Meaning of Sameness or Family Resemblance in the Pragmatic Tradition," *Tulane Studies in Philosophy* 21(1972):51-62.

in terms of universals, in terms of how the particular interacts in a functionally identical or lawful way along with all the other particulars belonging to the same class. The locus of universality and generality is in the process.

There are many significant implications these essays have for epistemology and metaphysics, and a clarification of the distinction between existential or substantial identity and functional identity is essential for a clear understanding of Mead's theory of mind, self, and society.

1   1914 Class Lectures
in Social Psychology

We approach this subject from the point of view of the psychology of perception. The social object is the self. What are the conditions under which we perceive selves? Review the chapters on perceptions in some psychologies. This treatment deals with physical objects rather than social. We shall discuss this distinction later.[1]

We approach the problem from the point of view of the act, involving all the states of consciousness. We conceive of the act as the primitive unit. We consider consciousness as activity, and the different phases of consciousness as parts of this activity. Consciousness as such is connative, attempting to do something. There are two poles of the act: stimulation and response. Herbert Spencer conceived of protoplasm as sensitive to stimulations which led to reactions, some of which were perpetuated. He thus conceives of the act as arising. From that point of view, it does not seem important to make the act the primitive unit.

If, however we take such an act as eating, we find that there is something besides stimulation and reponse. There is the precondition of hunger, which tends to select the stimuli. In the laboratory we can build up an act in a perfectly arbitrary way, and all sorts of responses can apparently be combined with all sorts of stimulation. But a normal act grows out of the condition of the system.

The question is, Can we conceive of all our activities in such a way as that? Can this point of view be applied to the acts that seem to be arbitrary and under control? The further down the developed mental series we go, the closer we come to the case represented by hunger. Imagery which we have of what we are going to do renders us more sensitive to the stimulus as well as more ready for the response. Even in the arbitrary acts we do find something which corresponds to hunger. It is the third element which we must take into account in the act.

1. James Rowland Angell, *Psychology*, chap. 6; G. F. Stout, *Manual of Psychology*, bk. 1, chap. 2; bk. 3, chap. 2; William James, *Psychology*, vol. 2, chap. 24; L. T. Hobhouse, *Mind in Evolution*, chaps. 3 and 4; William McDougall, *Social Psychology*, introd. sect.; Charles H. Cooley, *Human Nature and the Social Order*.

The act is, then, a stimulus and response on the basis of an inner condition which sensitizes the system to the stimulus and quickens the response. The neural counterpart lies in a certain structure of the central nervous system; certain paths are inherited. In such a case as hunger, the condition of the blood and of the various organs, the presence of certain glands, etc., enter into the sensitizing of certain tracts of the central nervous system. We have to take into account not only the central nervous system, which we are apt to regard as something separable and independent, but the body as a whole, the relationship brought about through the blood and the lymph.

From this standpoint we conceive of the stimulus as an occasion or opportunity for the act, not as a compulsion or mandate. The animal seeking for food is looking for certain stimuli which will set free the tense reaction which is ready to go off. If our process is very simple, we have a reflex act; in the more complex act, however, the early reactions affect the form in its relation to the later stimuli. The result of the first part of the act becomes essential to reaction to later stimuli. It brings one in contact with the stimulation which sets free the next part of the act. We find it in the relationship between stimulus and response, e.g., in the carpenter's rise of a saw in sawing to a line; sawing keeps the eye to the line, and the eye keeps the saw to the line. Any professional musician's fingers take care of themselves. Such processes in man correspond to the instinctive actions in animals. The result of one step is the precondition for the next; the precondition is essential to the stimulation and must be taken into account if we would reduce conscious life to the act.[2]

We find the precondition of the act in imagery, the sense imagery which controls the selection of stimuli and motor imagery which facilitates the response. Sensations may be centrally excited by a disturbance of nerve fibers, which were formally disturbed by corresponding peripheral excitation. That imagery is more or less dependent upon such tracts; e.g. if you disturb certain tracts, the imagery which is the signal for speech fails to appear and aphasia results. Imagery plays just the part in the act that hunger does in the food process.

Perception and Conflicting Responses and Inhibitions

What is the situation out of which the perceptual relation arises? Conation arises out of certain disturbances of the balance of the system,[3] which reveals itself in the consciousness of dissatisfaction, discomfort,

2. See Dewey, "Reflex Arc Concept," *Psych. Rev.*, vol. 1.
3. See G. F. Stout, *Manual of Psychology.*

and more or less effort to remove the discomfort. Sometimes we do not know definitely what we do want. Stout assumes that there is inevitably some effort to overcome discomfort, and if the want is not satisfied, some other effort will be made, and so on until the discomfort is removed. If we know what we want we seek to obtain it instead of making random movements. (Cf. E. L. Thorndike's experiment with the cat.)

This dissatisfaction is the precondition. How does that experience of the cat differ from the conduct of a man shut up in a room? That situation brings out the distinction between random movements and perception. Animals do not give attention to the objects about them. You cannot get the cat to see the object by means of which it can secure release.

Perception is a grasping of a stimulus which sets free the response. Two characteristics of perception are: unity and the presence of imagery from past experience. A third is the response to actual stimulation from the outside world. Fourth, our imagery fills in what we do not actually see, hear, etc. In reading, there are perhaps only two or three points in a line which we actually take in. A word may be incorrectly spelled and we may actually see it spelled correctly. Past experience is present in the perception. The past experience which comes in is one in which we have acted upon the same or a similar stimulus. Familiarity with the style of an author enables us to anticipate that which is coming after. If we see a singular noun, we expect a singular verb, etc. There is imagery of a past experience which has been carried out under the same or similar stimulation. A perception is what we call a collapsed act. A cat is not able to put into the stimulation what the human individual can put into it. This gives us the value of past experience. Where one can find out where he gains his skill, he can work out a theory of it. This imagery gives us the result of the act before we carry it out.

The unitary character does not belong simply to the percept. The object is only the center of the perception. Unity is not a unity belonging to that single object, e.g., chair, but to the entire field, to the situation in which the object occurs. Unity involves the perceiver as much as the thing perceived. Unity is of the object in its place in the field, and in its relation to the person perceiving. Attention moves from one object to another, e.g., from the chair to the clock, etc. The things in the room all enter into the perception, though the chair be the center. We always have the so-called percept at the center of the field. What we have with reference to the past is that which is necessary to start a response and a feeling of readiness to respond. The character of the disturbance of balance is not very clearly brought out by Stout. If a person feels an impulse to which he can give expression, a desire which he can satisfy, he can do it without definitely perceiving what he is about. It is not then merely the presence of a need, which is the disturbance; there must be an obstacle, a conflict between different tendencies to act. Even such a situation as that does not necessarily lead to perception, e.g., the dog with reference to receiving meat from a stranger may not present the situation clearly to himself; there may be a conflict between tendencies without reaching a definite perception; but such a conflict is essential to perception. When one stands before a chair he has many stimuli tending to call out many different responses or possible actions. If we perceive anything, that is tantamount to acting with reference to it. There has to be an open path in order that our senses may be effectively influenced. Many possible tendencies are inhibited by others. It is characteristic of the child that it does not inhibit but follows the first current that opens. These stimulations coming in from all sides enable us to maintain our balance. It is this sensuous material, tending to call out certain responses, that affect us, and they must be images from the past, from the result of the act. We have, then, disturbance, necessity for action, conflict of the different tendencies to act, and the result of experience. These are the elements that are essential to perception. We are not very conscious of motor imagery ordinarily, of the motor part of the act. We are aware of the beginning of the act and of the end of it, rather than of the motor part. It is highly probable that kinesthetic imagery is more important in the lower animals.

When we speak of a physical object, as such, we usually translate auditory, olfactory, and tactual imagery into visual imagery. On the other hand, the result of the activity we tend to put into the form of contact experience, even though the contact be not or even cannot be carried out. In a person born blind the place of vision is taken by a combination of sound and contact. A certain sense, such as vision, is that into which we translate the experience of the act; another sense, as contact, is that into which we translate the result of that act.

If we take the field of physical conduct as that within which percepts lie, there is still another element of sensation and perception, viz., unity. Some influence is going to determine the response. It sensitizes the man to certain stimuli. Interest, which he has, helps to select the particular stimulations to which he will give attention. Back of this interest lie his tendencies to act. The unity of the object is unity of that tendency to act, that which assures the individual that the object is one toward which he can move, or put in his mouth.

The Relation of the Object at a Distance to Other Objects

In perception there are other objects besides those that are central, and their paths move in other directions. But one's attitude toward them is essentially different from the attitude toward the central object, e.g., apple. They are in one's background, and have a certain necessary relation to the apple: the apple is perceived with reference to them. They go to make up the field within which the act takes place. Perception includes, then, not only the end toward which the act is moving but also the means by which the individual can reach the end. The perceptual world is made up of ends and means. All of the objects are organized by means of that particular act. In a sense there are obstacles to be overcome, but they are also the field of the act and the means of carrying it out. Each object has both positive and negative aspects.

The percept is a field of activity, with the goal as its center and other objects as obstacles and means of its attainment. The goal of activity is there as imagery of the result of the act. Perception always involves such a complete field and has behind it an act.

The Gesture

Analysis breaks up, for the time being, this organic unity and these relationships. Our social objects are for the purposes of conducting physical objects, but they are more than that.[4] We take up next social conduct from the standpoint of the gesture.

The act is that within which the percept occurs. The percept is the psychological term for the objects which exist for us. We are going to discuss social objects. The act in its simplest form may take place without perception of what the object is. It does not exist for us as an object in such acts. Subconsciousness is frequently part of our conduct. Stimuli occur in that field, the act follows, but there is no percept. There must be conflict. This results in inhibition, the throwing up in consciousness of past experience. We cannot act with reference to all tendencies, but they represent the field and the means of action. The distinction between the percept and the concept is only a matter of degree.

There is another field of conduct which is not purely and simply physical. If we go into the life history of children and primitive people there is no sharp line, practically no line, drawn between physical objects and social objects. Myths socialize physical objects. The line of

---

4. Wilhelm Wundt, *Völkerpsychologie;* Charles H. Judd, *Psychology,* chap. on Language; Charles Darwin, *Treatise on the Expression of the Emotions;* Herbert Spencer, *Psychology,* chaps. on emotions.

abstraction has not been drawn. It is with something of an effort that we make the abstraction, e.g., restrain from objurgating chairs. Our aesthetic appreciation of nature is essentially a social experience. We find also in situations of great stress that there is a social attitude and act. One who has no belief in gods, in such cases, may pray. This is the outcome of an instinctive social attitude toward nature. Thus there is a merging of the field.

The process of thought is itself social. Thought is an inner conversation. We find children doing their thinking by conversation with imaginary persons. This distinction we have to carry out with some vigor. We look for a social act that will answer to a physical act. A physical act arises out of tendency to act, which renders us sensitive to stimuli from distant objects. Is there a corresponding social act? Are there tendencies, stimuli, and results that are social? We are discussing this from a psychological, not a metaphysical, point of view. From this point of view the soul does not exist any more than matter does. The social object is a self. Our psychology takes the field of consciousness and finds in it objects. Instincts are essentially social, and lie behind the act.[5]

Social conduct means conduct that takes place under the stimuli of some other form that belongs to the same group, "group" being used in a very wide sense, e.g., man and totem, animals of the barnyard. This is a temporary definition, however. Each form acts with reference to the other form. We must assume that the stimulus is not the cause but the occasion for the act.

Some instincts are distinctly social. Certain forms move and act together, thus securing protection. Frequently animals are uneasy unless in the presence of other forms of the same sort. McDougall refers to this as gregariousness, F. H. Giddings as consciousness of kind. Sexual and parental instincts are distinctly social; the parental instinct is probably the most important one for human society. The parent may be satisfied with dummy forms, or may devour its young, without being devoid of parental instinct. Attack and defense are founded on inbred characteristics of the nervous system, and are social instincts. Certain types of hostility are social, for they are set free by other forms of the same group. McDougall refers to subjection and self-assertion as instincts, but it is doubtful if these can appear before there is a consciousness of self, which is more complex. The dog cringing before a master does not require this instinct for its explanation. It rests on the dependence of the animal on man. The dog is accustomed to live with a being who both

5. William McDougall, *Social Psychology.*

feeds and strikes him. McDougall also finds something that answers to rivalry. This is a field that has not yet been adequately analyzed; for example, when puppies play together, a certain superiority is sought without the intention of carrying out hostility. Whatever the list of instincts may be, there are certain social tendencies, i.e., tendencies to act with reference to other forms of the same group. We shall turn our attention first to the stimuli to which social instincts are adjusted. They are the so-called expressions of the emotions.[6]

The stimuli which set free social instincts and habits may be visual, auditory, olfactory, etc. The expression of the emotions is another type. This was first brought to the attention of psychologists by Darwin. The study of physiognomy led to interest in this subject. His point was, Why have certain gestures maintained themselves after they cease to be of value to the form and after the purposes they once served have vanished?

Darwin held as principles (1) certain number of acts originally had a value for the form. Darwin says they have remained even where they have not served such a purpose, e.g., in the grinding of the teeth, the clenching of the fists. It would be difficult to be very angry with an innervation of the muscles that cause grinding of the teeth. These acts are "survivals." Such vestiges are of great value to the evolutionist, as indicating the form from which we are descended. (2) Darwin found a number of expressions of emotion which he thought could not be brought under this head, e.g., the dog's approach to the master. Darwin thought he found the exact opposite to that in joyous romping, and the opposite of attacking. As the dog found itself in an opposite emotional state, he assumed an opposite physical attitude. (3) Since emotions represent a high degree of nervous excitement, it is natural that this should flow out through the entire system, resulting neither in valuable actions nor in their opposites. A great overflow of nervous energy might cause a trembling of the body, the expenditure of energy and movement.

The first of these principles alone has a great value in the study of gestures, the third has a certain degree of value. Still if we should go back to the beginnings of these emotions that appear so violent and inappropriate, we should find some purpose served by them. The structure of the nervous system is purposive.

Spencer tried to get at this from a physiological point of view. He assumed that nervous energy, when stored up, flows out. Nerve cells were regarded as explosive in their nature, and Spencer undertook to explain the expression of the emotions by the structure of the nervous

6. Wundt, *Vökerpsychologie;* Berthold Delbrück, *Grundfragen der Sprachforschung.*

system. The weakest muscles, those in the face and the ends of the fingers, would be the first affected, then the muscles of the limbs and trunk. This mechanical explanation does not correspond with the facts; e.g., some of the face muscles are among the strongest in the body. Thus the elaboration of Darwin's third principle breaks down completely.

A psychological explanation was set forth by Piderit.[7] His point of view is represented by metaphors, such as bitter, sweet, etc., with reference to social situations. This does not explain it, and the analysis has been vague and unsatisfactory. But they explain that there is a certain identity of discomfort in taking quinine and in being under social pressure; or of pleasure in tasting honey and hearing music—the pleasures experienced are alike. If that is the case, the expression of the countenance would be symbolic of the attitude of mind. The individual who was thinking of a sweet strain of music would tend to take on the expression he had when eating honey.

Wundt says that this can be a symbol only for the observer, not for the person experiencing the pleasure. This is an aesthetic explanation rather than a psychological one, representing the attitude of the individual who stands outside looking on. It does not explain the gesture as it arises in the experience of the individual.

If a man could strike at once when he clinches his fist there would be no emotion, for there would be no checking, no inhibition. Darwin's third principle fails to realize that all acts arising are purposive, at least normally. If Spencer's account were in accordance with the facts, it would still be necessary to account for the relation of the acts to the structural system. Piderit assumes that there are certain identities when a person is under different stimuli. It is the business of the professional actor to symbolize anger; their theory is built up out of the actor's technique; they tried to explain all gestures on the same basis. All our ideas are objects to us and we stand over against them and symbolize our emotional attitudes toward them by our gestures. Wundt criticized this.

Wundt's Psychophysical Theory

Wundt uses Darwin's principle. Every attitude of consciousness is accompanied by certain physiological parallels. We have a state of consciousness and at the same time there must be excitement of a part of the nervous system. When we have a motor image of clenching the fist, there is excitement of motor tracts. The expressions of the emotions are

7. Theodor Piderit, *La Mimique et la Physionomie,* 1888.

simply physiological accompaniments of effective states out of which the emotions arise. The emotions are combinations of certain courses of feelings, following after one another. Wundt speaks of them as having three dimensions: excitement and depression, tension and relaxation, pleasantness and unpleasantness. This is a parallelistic theory—for every psychosis there is a neurosis. He undertakes to find out the neuroses and their results. He starts with the analysis of the psychical affective conditions, dividing elements of feelings named above. He treats these not only as elements but also as dimensions. His theory of analysis cannot be followed out either introspectively or by experiment. He held that if you take a like feeling you will have a like expression. He differs in this from Piderit, who has the actor assume an expression. Wundt's theory implies that you can divide psychological states into elements, and that the psychological states correspond to these elements, that there are identities of feelings which can be associated. Thus far, he does not make use of Darwin's principle. His position is mechanical, and he abandons the physiological principle used by Darwin. But he makes use of Darwin's mechanical treatment of communication, language as it developed out of gestures. The earliest uses of the voice are expressions of emotions as definitely as they are of these attitudes. Language is made up of sounds, which were originally expressions of emotions which are teleological. You start off with psychological compounds and their corresponding physiological attitudes. Given these elements, purposive intelligence can make use of them in building up an artificial langugage.

There is opportunity for another type of theory. It is conceivable that these various expressions of emotions have a functional value, which is responsible for their selection and persistence. Darwin uses his theory only with reference to vestiges, indicating descent. That is, he recognizes that they have a purposive character but not one that is still functioning. It may be that they have a function that is responsible for their selection, and the point of view here is that the gesture is a means of social intercourse, having a functional value in the social act which is the reason for its selection and preservation. Wundt has not analyzed the gesture as such as part of the act. He has treated it as an anatomist, not as a physiologist. We do not see the purposive relations of expressions and the emotions. We must see how they are related to the conduct of the individual without bringing in a mere association of psychology and physiology.

Most of the expressions of the emotions represent a truncated act— clenching the fists, dropping the jaw, and opening the eyes, are attitudes assumed by the individual which represent the beginning of acts. They represent preparations for activities which may be carried out or inhibited. The attitude of surprise exposes the organism as completely as possible to the new type of stimulus, and it has, of course, a value in judgment of the new situation. It also facilitates the act, e.g., jumping when you hear a loud sound.

Various expressions of countenance represent vasomotor adjustment of the system to sudden activities. Adjustment of sense organs and a certain set of stimuli and adjustment of the system in respiratory and circulatory parts to acts are represented. Back of it all are tendencies to act. We would not hold the head tense at a sound unless the whole system were ready to act in a certain way. The heart would not beat more rapidly unless we were ready to perform some act that required higher blood pressure.

Back of all gestures, then, lie tendencies to act. Gestures may be regarded as the beginning of acts. As Darwin pointed out, some of these acts are never carried out; the gnashing of the teeth does not go any further than that. Why then have they persisted? Darwin dealt with them simply as vestiges.

From the point of the observer and the actor, they have a present value. If you see signs of anger, it is important to take them into account. It is of great importance to other individuals to recognize gestures. The beginnings of social acts are the most important stimuli for members of a social group—not only from the standpoint of the individual but of the group.

Gestures are the natural stimuli to other social forms, even if the act of which they are the beginning is never carried out. We have to conceive of language not only from the point of view of sound but also of sign language, or the gestures of little children before they make use of articulate speech. So that language is a much larger field. When the child points at food he is doing the same thing that he would be doing if he asked for it, and this is a different thing from the whining of a dog. Animals give signs of hunger without stating that they themselves are hungry. The parrot makes articulate sound, but he does not speak.

Language is a social process and grows out of gesture. It might grow out of any set of gestures, but seemingly it has chiefly grown out of the gestures of the voice. Wundt speaks of a *Vorstellungsinhalt*—intensity, ideal content, quality. Quality is expressed by the gesture, intensity by the physiological change. Every feeling has its relation to some idea. It arises out of the presentations of objects or has in view the presence of objects now absent. The gesture as the origin of language grows out of

this *Vorstellungsinhalt.* One calls out in the presence of dangerous animals. The cry indicates the character of the object and, because of that,
may come to represent the object in language. A gesture of the child
may represent the presence of the object. All of these characters of the
gesture which are related to the character of the object are the basis for
the indication of the object, and language may grow out of them.

Wundt says that there is not only this indication of character but also
a tendency to imitate the objects. To account for this, Wundt speaks of
the imitative tendency in all forms. He assumes this imitation as a tendency to act somewhat in the same way. But seeing an animal of one
form act is not a stimulus to another form to act in the same way. The
nervous system could not be loaded up with such a weight of possible
actions. Seeing another form run may be a stimulus to run in the same
way and at the same rate, but not necessarily, however. I cannot see
what the mechanism would be which would make this possible. Any
social stimulus will lead to some sort of a response, but it may or may
not be a response similar to the stimulus; e.g., a response to a loud
sound is not similar to it.

Wundt deals with the expression of the emotions as being a psychological parallel of certain conscious states. He would put together the
different physiological elements. He carried these back to certain expressions of countenance associated with taste, to be explained on the
basis of an act of tasting. You have to get a whole act in order to understand this expression of bitterness; you cannot take it by itself. Wundt
assumes that the social process is simply superinduced upon such an
association of physiological expressions and psychological states. The
social process is possible only through this association.

Wundt does not assume that where you have like impulses, where
you can see an act in another animal of the same form, you will be stimulated to carry out the same act, if you have the tendency already in
your nature, e.g., the child sees the mother crying. But Wundt does not
assume there is an instinct of imitation. The expression of the emotion
is associated with the emotion itself. Tears are associated with unhappi-
ness; they arouse unpleasant experiences that we have had in the past;
it is an association with an affective state rather than with an idea. This
idea of the emotion being associated with the emotion thus tends to
arouse the same emotion. If the conduct of one bee is associated with
an impulse to the same conduct in another bee the sight of the first bee
is a stimulus to act in the same way.

There must be a limit to this imitation. You can sympathize with
great losses, but it is hard to put yourself into the same small irritations

seen in the expression of someone else. We find ourselves unable to have a sympathetic attitude. We find it easier to sympathize in small delights than in great delights. The principle of simple association makes it hard to see why we should have these different sorts of association. It does not seem to get into the facts of our sympathetic relation with other people.

The expression of another person crying is not the same as your expression of crying, but there is a relation. The response is direct and immediate. The stronger the association (with the passing years) the less immediate and direct the response. The fact that another person cries is not associated with our own past experience of crying; it is unnatural to give attention to our own action and expression under such circumstances. Moreover, the young child responds very readily.

What we do seem to find are immediate responses to the expressions of others. They may be the same or they may be different kinds of responses. They have their place within social acts, and are to be explained within those acts. It seems much simpler to see what the social relations are within which the expressions of the emotions occur. In all social forms as such, the attitude of one form becomes the stimulus to the other form in its response. As soon as form A begins to act with reference to form B, the action is a stimulus to form B to respond. The child cries and the parent picks it up. The parental instinct and the stimulus are enough to start the reponse.

In your relations to other persons, it is your own hostile attitude to the other person that is your evidence of his hostile attitude toward you. Change that takes place in yourself is an indication of the attitude in the other. It is of immense importance to the form that he respond readily to those indications. So that the beginning of the social act becomes of the very greatest importance to the group. Whether we can refer to this attitude as instinctive or not, there is no question that the young child responds readily long before his own experience can help him. The tone of voice and the expression of the countenance are particularly effective in bringing about certain responses.

The child finds itself in a situation in which those about it are unhappy and it is itself unhappy. The child's social weapon is its cry. It is advantageous for the child to cry when it is in a situation where others are unhappy. This situation in the surrounding company is one which is dangerous to the child, and we have the response, the natural explanation from the evolutionary point of view. The suckling process is the natural response to the cheerful attitude. You have a series of attitudes which call out responses. These so-called expressions represent the beginnings of social acts, not merely the physiological accompaniments or merely a mechanical physiological reaction. The attitude of one form becomes the stimulus to the other from in its response to the social stimuli. Only in the human face do we have the expressions of great significance. A man's expression of countenance and tone of voice are of great importance in revealing his meaning. We shall attempt to identify expressions of the emotions with the beginnings of social acts and to account for their value from this point of view.

We go back to the act in order to interpret these expressions of the emotions. Piderit does not account for the function of the observer within the act. For him symbolism did not arise out of the act itself. It is quite another thing to respond immediately. Our position implies that these expressions have arisen out of social contact and are in a sense created by social conduct. Wundt makes the social functions of the expressions of the emotions a later matter; at first he considers them merely as parallels of psychological processes.

The expression of the emotions is the beginning of an act. The person in a merely physiological act has a different attitude from the person in a social act. We recognize this when we give attention to the social attitude toward things, e.g., nature. As soon as one takes another person into account, his expression and action are different. Wordsworth has called attention to the social relation toward nature. The social attitude is expressed most clearly in the gesture—mimetic, pantomimic, or tone of voice. The moment we enter into relation with other selves, we find ourselves in a totally different attitude.

This social attitude is more definitely emotional in its character. This is shown by the fact that these gestures are spoken of as expressions of the emotions. Is there a reason for this peculiarly emotional character of the gesture, as stimulus to a social act? We do not conceive of other stimuli as having a peculiarly emotional content. Wundt makes them simply the parallel of certain affective states and takes the question beyond the possibility of an answer. We have another view in the James-Lange theory of the emotion; when we have certain physical conditions, there follows a certain emotional condition. If a person clenches his fist, grinds his teeth, and increases his blood pressure, he arouses the emotion of anger. James later modifies this extreme position.

Another theory will give us more of an explanation.[8] This theory does not regard the emotion as a simple result of a series of feelings as Wundt does. He makes an emotion a series of feelings, accompanying an

8. Angell, *Psychology;* Dewey, *Psych. Rev.,* vols. 2 and 3, articles on emotions.

act, a successive complication, the affective stream. The point of view of Dewey assumes that the emotion as such arises through the inhibition of a tendency to act. There is of course an affective side of all consciousness, but this does not appear as an emotion unless there is an inhibition of a tendency to act. We see an object in many different ways and have as many different tendencies to act toward it; the inhibition or checking of some of these gives the emotional content. Inhibitions are not well worked-out in the case of the baby. He cannot stop himself. He must grasp something. When that objective attitude has arisen, when inhibitions are beneath the surface of consciousness, emotional content is reduced to a minimum. But if there is a checking, we feel its value, e.g., if there is danger of an object being stolen.

If the emotion is to be regarded as a function of inhibition, we cannot accept Wundt's theory or the James-Lange theory. The clenching of the fist does not cause the emotion, but the inhibition of the act of striking does produce the emotion.

Our attitude toward physical objects does not as a rule permit any high degree of emotional content. We are pretty well adjusted toward them. In social relations, however, there is more or less continuous inhibition and readjustment. Our attitude toward another individual depends on what he is going to do to us, which is expressed in gestures. We respond to his gesture and take an attitude which indicates our response, and put him in a different position from the preceding one. Then the first individual prepares to act in a different way, producing another response in the second individual, and this may go on for some time, e.g., two persons fencing represent the play back and forth by the gestures, which is simply an illustration of the normal social act. Social conduct involves a conversation attitude. This is a very conscious adjustment of the individual which is different from that which we assume toward physical things. They do not change for us but remain about the same, but if we are going to act in cooperation with another person, we have to converse before we act. He replies to my suggestion in a way that makes me change my suggestion. I am sensitive to the manner of his handshake, etc. There is a constant adjustment when we have to adjust ourselves consciously to physical objects, e.g., waves; we inevitably assume a social attitude toward them. If we can let a series of acts, previously coordinated, go off, we act as toward the physical objects; if not, we act toward people. Social conduct involves continuous, conscious adjustment and inhibitions. These gestures are then the natural expression of the emotion which arise from these inhibitions. Gestures

are the attitudes of people who are going to act but are not yet acting.[9]
It is a very distinct advantage to a group that gestures mediate the social
act, for it helps in the group struggle for existence. Many social acts are
not immediately for the individual's good, some are primarily for group
welfare.

We return to the background of social acts—instincts. Every act involves not only stimulus and response-gesture—but also predisposition—
impulse, instinct—which is responsible for the sensitiveness to a certain
type of stimulus and readiness for a certain kind of response.[10]

Conditions of the Social Act

What are the preconditions of the social act? They are rather a curious
group according to McDougall. On some of them we can all agree, e.g.,
flight, pugnacity, parental instinct, something corresponding to acquisi-
tion, and the sexual instinct. But when we come to "curiosity" we have
a more delicate case. It would be natural to ascribe this to other grounds.
"Self-assertion" and "self-subjection" are also questionable. McDougall's
instances belong definitely to the natural process of wooing, and can be
classed under the reproductive instinct. How about the evidence for
these instincts in the behavior of the dog? We seem to have here simply
the combinations of different tendencies. First, to withdraw on the
account of fear of a large animal, and, second, dependence on man for
food. I think there is no justification for these so-called instincts. Mc-
Dougall himself admits that we cannot assume self-consciousness in
cases which he illustrates.

There seems to be no basis for an instinct of construction. Gregariousness belongs to the lower social forms and implies a willingness to
adjust. It is not to be identified with the parental or reproductive processes. Forms that flock together indicate a readiness to adjust their
own individual conduct on a basis different from the parental or reproductive processes. Gregariousness is of great importance for protection
and attack, though it is more than this. We seem to have good evidence
for the existence of such an instinct and for it underlying "neighborliness," which is so important for human society.

McDougall assumes emotions to be connected with the instincts, and
his whole theory of instincts is bound up with the emotions. For him
the emotion is simply there, and he does not seek to find out how it

9. See McDougall, *Social Psychology.*
10. Dewey: *Psych. Rev.,* 1:553-69; 2:13-32.

arose. But we have no right to assume that emotions are always accompaniments. His doctrine of sentiment is also unsatisfactory. It is unfortunate that he tied up his doctrine of instincts with these other two theories. There is one very interesting discussion, of the tender emotion as corresponding to the parental instinct. He holds that the two always go together and that a large amount of the sentiment of love is taken over from the parental instinct. It also appears in the attitude toward the young forms of all species, and goes even beyond the living forms. There is a certain tenderness in the use of the diminutive as a term of endearment. Alexander Bain reverses this, making love develop out of the pleasure of contact with the young forms; the fondling of the young grows out of the protective impulse. In this discussion McDougall has made a distinct contribution. It is perhaps the maternal instinct, but both elements of sex always appear; it finds expression in the human male, though differently in the female (cf. Cooley's discussion of primary groups and ideals).

The list indicated can be approved but may be subject to modifications. We cannot be sure there are no others. James holds that man has more instincts than any other animal. They are subject to change and reconstruction; this change in man is more rapid but not different in nature.

By an instinct we mean a certain definite cogenital tendency to act. The attitude is that of acting and finding out later what we have done, or even of an impulse to act contrary to the judgment. Certain social stimuli call out the instinct of flight. The baby withdraws from persons with certain expressions of countenance without any previous experience of that sort. All of these indicate social stimuli and responses, modes of conduct which are cogenital. Courtesy, constructiveness, etc., are combinations of such tendencies to act.

What we imply, then, in social conduct are tendencies to act because of social stimuli, with reference to other individuals who are responsible for the stimulation. There are certain attitudes or stimulations which are the occasions for the expression of social acts, and responses to stimuli have their relations to forms that are responsible for the stimuli. Instinct, stimulation, social response. This does not imply in itself any self-consciousness. The self arises in social conduct and presumably does not arise except in the human form. There may have been long periods of human conduct before self-consciousness was attained. We stress especially the conversation of gestures, which indicate such difference between what we call social conduct and physical conduct. Physical conduct implies relatively stable objects with reference to which we are acting. Adjustment is apt to lie below the threshold of consciousness. Our movements with reference to physical objects about us do not usually involve conscious adjustment. But the social object with reference to which we are acting is changing just because of our acting. That change calls for a change in our own attitude. The mechanism of the physical object is an adjustment made once for all, when we gain acquaintance with the object. When change takes place in the physical object, we discount it.

The implication is that there are social instincts and habits which account for the sensitiveness to social stimuli. Early social conduct does not involve social consciousness. It is only in the last century and a half that physical science has eliminated the social content from its material. Also this holds for the everyday consciousness of the average man. The physical world is full of spirits. The average individual is not able to get rid of that social content, at least in uncritical thinking.

One of the differences between physical and social conduct is the emotional content, which is much more vivid in social conduct. As a rule, the so-called physical stimulations are not expressions of the emotions and do not call out responses that we call expressions of the emotions. Emotions arise under tensions. In social conduct there is constant adjustment and readjustment, hence emotion. Conventional conversation, however, approaches physical conduct, but even here there is anticipation of change. It is legitimate to call these the expressions of the emotions, though they are not there for that purpose, not for the person himself. Many objects are social objects for the child, but the child is not adjusted to them.

Process of the Development of Language[11]

A conversation of gestures consists simply in the continued readjustment of one individual to another. The acts which have been started have to be checked and started again, but the stimulation has changed. Articulate speech is the development of one kind of gesture, and its development is a matter of convenience. Some forms use articulate speech and yet do not speak in the human sense. This represents the type of intelligence shown by the trick dog or horse—catching the expression of the eye or other signs of which the person who gives the sign may not be conscious. The problem is that of articulate structure of words.

In language, what we have reached is the consciousness of meaning attached to a gesture. Such a consciousness of meaning is not necessarily involved in a conversation of gestures, e.g., the child adjusting itself to the mother's arms without consciousness of meaning. What we have

11. See Wilhelm Wundt, *Völkerpsychologie;* Berthold Delbrück, *Grundfragen der Sprachforschung;* William James, *Psychology;* C. H. Judd, *Psychology.*

to discover are the conditions under which the consciousness of meaning attaching itself to certain gestures arises. Stout takes us back simply
to an anticipatory attitude of that which is to take place. There is a
great difference between a mere adjustment to what is going to happen
and a consciousness of the meaning of what is going to take place, i.e.,
an indication of what is going to happen. The words "familiarity" and
"recognition" imply this distinction. These two attitudes are, in a sense,
opposed to each other. In recognition there is something unfamiliar
that calls for recognition. If there is complete familiarity, there is no
conscious inhibition; the adjustment is immediate and unreflective. That,
however, is not a situation in which we recognize an object and are
familiar with its meaning.

When we are not conscious of the signs that stand for the meaning,
if we are uncertain, we hesitate and compare and seek something that
enables us to identify the object. When we are uncertain, we are not
able to act at once with reference to the object. Stout's treatment of
the consciousness of meaning is not adequate. From his point of view,
meaning accrues to any experience that is anticipatory of a later experience. But a consciousness implies that the action which carries us from
one moment to the next is inhibited and a readjustment is necessary,
e.g., each note of a song is anticipatory of all to follow, but if a familiar
song is sung, we are not conscious of the meaning of each note. Consciousness is not simply adjustment, so that an action can go on, but a
situation in which adjustment must take place, and in which we are
looking for those signs which will enable us to make that readjustment;
it is not simply complete familiarity, but a situation in which action has
started but has been stopped and cannot go on for the time being, and
we are looking for the symbols that will enable us to go ahead, which
will serve as stimuli to set free the activity and to enable us to complete
the action. A state of consciousness, then, in which we are picking out
different stimuli, which enables inhibited activity to go on, is one in
which we have an awareness of meaning. In some instances we respond
to a situation without being aware of what the stimuli are, e.g., in playing a game, and we cannot give a theory of our acting. We cannot carry
out our theory of singing far enough to indicate just what the stimuli
are that give rise to an adequate expression of voice. Each person has
to depend, to a large extent, upon certain kinesthetic sensations. This
familiarity may take place gradually and without consciousness of meaning. We do not have the consciousness of meaning except when we can
indicate the stimuli, the symbols, to ourselves.

We find that our consciousness of meaning has passed over in part
into articulate speech—a readiness to describe an object corresponds to

our consciousness of what it is. This is a social attitude, for the words are symbols whose meanings are shared. Thus the words are social symbols.

We have a situation in which the beginning of an act of one individual must be interpreted in terms of our response to it. But the situation is constantly changing, so we have to be continually on the outlook. We have to adjust ourselves first of all to the changes, but we find in our own attitude of instinctive defense the value of the gesture, the value of the other person's attitude. We find in our own hostile attitude evidence of the fact that the other person is hostile.

First of all, there is that checking of activity which is essential to reflective consciousness; the necessity for adjustment to the changed situation. Further continuation of that process is one in which we ask ourselves what the completion of the act indicated in the gesture will be. If we are in doubt, we have several tendencies to respond, which mutually check one another. What is present in consciousness are these tendencies to respond in different social ways to the gestures of other persons. Interpretation takes place in its simplest form in our tendency to respond. We adjust ourselves before we can act.

In the consciousness of meaning there is more than the familiarity and adjustment, even with relation to an ongoing act and anticipated stimuli. The material is there, but not a consciousness of meaning for us, meaning that is itself present. In contrast with the animal, we can see the meaning of its action, but that meaning is not present to the consciousness of the animal. We have in mind a definite consciousness of meaning. Under what conditions may such a consciousness of meaning arise? In the act we have necessity for conscious readjustment with awareness of change in stimulation and of our own response to the changes taking place. One is more aware of his response in conversation than of his walking around the room, avoiding chairs, etc.

Control takes place, then, by directing attention to characters in the field of stimulation, not to the motor reply. There is a consciousness that answers directly to incoming stimulation. To this is due our consciousness of what we are doing. There is no awareness of the outgoing current, and no direct consciousness corresponding to the motor response, e.g., in learning a game all attention is given to the field of stimulation. In the social situation there is a great consciousness of meaning. We are much more immediately aware of what we are saying and doing to other persons than of what we are doing to physical objects.

One phase of this is that we frequently become aware of the attitude of the other, rather than becoming aware of our own response to that person. This is due to continued inhibition and readjustment. This is, however, due to another kind of gesture not found in any degree in the conversations of gestures in the lower animals. A dog may frighten another dog by his attitude, but there is little evidence that the animal is aware of the changes that he makes, and the adjustment takes place with little consciousness of the adjustment itself. The same thing takes place in a person who is terror-stricken. A person going into a fight is relatively unaware of his responses. When we reach higher means of communication, these gestures can be distinguished from other gestures. One sees movements of his hands, or hears his own voice. In a normal condition the individual is affected by his own responses to the stimulation of others in much the same way that the other person is. In this respect these two types of gestures are quite distinct, e.g., from the expression of his countenance. Awareness of the latter is difficult to attain. A person is aware of his own response under these conditions. In that sense he is talking to himself as to others. If he cannot hear his own voice, he is confused. The deaf and dumb have a system of kinesthetic images. A person must be aware of what he is doing in order to talk intelligently.

Self-consciousness involves an awareness of the self in relation to others. The situation in which we become definitely self-conscious is the situation in which speech or hand movements appeal to our eye or ear as well as to others'. Given self-consciousness, one is not awkward in conversation, just in being aware of what one is saying. But in physical conduct this awareness, if abnormal, produces awkwardness. Control over physical objects consists of being very delicately aware of all the elements in the situation to which we must respond, but in not being aware of our own response. But in social conduct, self-consciousness is the normal thing—when there is communication of the hands or articulate speech. I am influenced by my own conduct and can respond to it; the "I" of conversation never gets into the field, only the "me." It is the function of language that one does and should become aware of responses. It is there that the conscious self arises. One's own responses become stimuli to himself, and he sets himself up as object, just as he sets up other people as objects. He has a tendency to reply to himself. Thought is a replying to self, a conversation. The thinker has become an object to himself just as have other people. When you carry social conduct to the level of language—a gesture or speech—man becomes aware of himself as an object. It is normal that consciousness should be centered in the response to physical objects, as it is toward social objects. How could a baby build up a consciousness of a physical self? This is built up on a basis of a social self. The subjective experience of a self gathers about the objective self.

Wundt's account of languages is based on his theory of the association of expression of emotion and the *Vorstellunginhalt,* which goes with emotional experience. Wundt holds that when a person is in the presence of another person expressing an emotion, he has the emotion aroused in himself. This has been seen to be an unsatisfactory account. The *Ausdrucksbewegung* is a stimulus to an appropriate reaction. We find sympathy, so far as we know, only when we have self-consciousness, though there is a parental attitude in the lower form. All that the parent requires is a response to the stimuli which the instincts require, e.g., the cow is satisfied to lick the skin of the calf which has just been killed. The characteristic about sympathy is the definite consciousness of putting one's self in the place of the other person; it is not a mere impulse to help. When a child tumbles down, my immediate impulse is to pick it up and not be sympathetic at all. Except in the most universal things, the child cannot sympathize with the adult. What is the mechanism by which the expression of sympathy calls out the same emotion in another?

Wundt says individual experiences differ and the emotion is a complex of feelings which vary in individuals; and especially does the *Vorstellunginhalt* vary. There will be a corresponding variation in the expression of the emotions of the second individual, and this will change the emotional content of the first individual. This play back and forth is not that already described, but a copying process. The ideal content, the relation of the experience to the objective world, involves a new group of gestures, the pantomimic, especially of the arms; *hinweisende Ausdrucke* arise out of the *Reifende.* There are many other gestures; when you stand on a lofty cliff, or tend to follow the cliff with your eyes or even draw the objects with the movement of the hands. Out of these varying gestures have developed the primitive sign languages. The gestures have reference not only to the emotions but also to some extent they mirror the ideal content. They bring new elements into primitive conversation, and make the process more extended. The statement seems somewhat artificial but can be presented very effectively. But a better explanation can be found in the response that gestures call out rather than in the association of gestures with emotional states. According to Wundt, language developed in gesture, as commonly understood, more than in articulate speech. But they probably went along together. Vocal gestures may have had an earlier part than the pantomimic.

Divergence from this view lies in Wundt's belief that the association is an adequate explanation. This somewhat farfetched explanation seems unnecessary. The reason for the expression of the emotion in a somewhat extended act is that it is a social situation. Wundt makes a distinction between the affective and the ideal contents. Wundt assumes that it is through the display of one's ideas that languages arise. We have the gesture representing the attitude of the individual. The meaning of the gesture is revealed to the other by the latter's response. Experience from the past comes to fill out the tendency to act and respond. This will give him that which comes to be the meaning of the act, as in the perception of the object. The ideal content is one that belongs to the act from past experience. There arises the image of the act carried out.

Consciousness of meaning in its relation to communication arises out of a conversation of gestures. Wundt assumes there is simply association between certain affective and ideal contents of consciousness on the one hand and certain gestures on the other, and that this leads to communication. These, he believes, are relatively independent; he puts no limit on the process of combination.

There is a normal relation between the elements. It is not simply that we have had these experiences in succession, but they fuse into an object. There is the beginning of the act and its completion, a connection between stimulus and the response, not simply that they take place in succession or are together, but it is their relation to the act. This is another way of getting at what is meant by attention.

There is a relation of these elements to each other in the consciousness of meaning. To say that a certain shade indicates the projection of a building is a consciousness of meaning, but to avoid it in walking is not. The latter may not involve consciousness at all. The distinction between the intelligence of lower animals and man is that there is no evidence of the animal being able to recognize that one thing is the sign of something else and so to make use of that sign; the stimulation that comes to the eye is an indication of what the result of the act will be, e.g., in making use of a rake to pull things toward one or pulling a string to open a door. It is a trial-and-error process and for man brings back not only the result but the result as a meaning. Consciousness is a definite recognition of the relation between the stimulation to act and the experience that follows upon the completion of the act. L. T. Hobhouse thinks he finds in higher animals an incipient consciousness of meaning. According to his point of view animals have a feeling of the relation but cannot pick out the separate elements. His observations do not bear out his statement, but it is an open question. When we separate these two contents, we get just what we mean by a consciousness of meaning, namely the stimulus stands for a certain result, and we know from past experience what the result of the act is going to be. The animal has experience which leads to "stamping in" the right sort of activity and stamping out the wrong but, so far as we can find, without conscious meaning. We can generalize this. An object of thought is a question and answer—the question as a part of the whole body of discourse and the uses to which that body is put. There is a consciousness of the two elements that go to make up the object. We are able to separate and bring out the elements and relate them to each other. Question: What are the conditions under which we accomplish that separation? The tendency is to fuse these two elements. Ordinarily it is abnormal to distinguish them. The more closely the result of an activity can be fused with the stimulation, the more perfectly the act is carried out. Where there is doubt we have to pick them apart. Can we deal with those freely under conditions where we can pick them out? Yes, there is inhibition, when the stimulation brings out opposite responses. These different responses that we had in past experience do tend to arise separately from the stimulation. The stimulation is presented in an impersonal way, e.g., when the stimulus is a man of whose character we are not sure. If you look at a dog that is in doubt whether to avoid or approach a man, you find him not questioning whether the man will strike or feed him. He accepts the man as a possible enemy and starts to run; then he takes him as a friend and approaches. The two tendencies conflict, but we do not find that the object is so broken up that the dog can deal with the *Vorstellungin-halt* as a man does. The objects in his consciousness are whole objects. They are complete. We have no evidence that the animal is able to take his percept to pieces and get the meaning out of them.

The way in which we separate these conflicting tendencies to act is by analysis of the stimulation. There is something in the man that leads him to give way under certain circumstances, and you cannot depend on him. It is a definite problem. We have to account for this separation of these elements. We have to find a phase of consciousness in which they are separated. It seems to arise in the process of communication.

The Development of Self-Consciousness and Its Relation to Social Conduct

We found that the passage from perceptual to reflective social consciousness and conduct takes place through the consciousness of meaning. Under what conditions does self-consciousness arise? When or where there is a stimulation, a gesture, made by an individual, it affects him in the same way it affects other individuals of the group. Where the individual responds to his own stimulation, where he becomes an object.

This is also the condition of passing from perceptual to conceptual consciousness. The child knows how to respond to all the different selves in the group, and has the imagery of the result of the response. We find also the child referring to himself in the third person. He becomes aware of himself in an external way. He is one of the individuals of the group and stands on the same plane. He seemingly stands outside of himself. The self has not been *verinnerlicht,* but it is an object. He talks to himself and is aware of his own responses and what he will do under certain circumstances. But it is not a subjective self. It has only a perceptual value. He has not yet reached the point of thinking and of lodging that thinking within himself. He carries on his thinking in an external way—as conversation of persons.

The process in which the self appears is that out of which thought arises and it serves the purpose of separating the meaning of the object from the object itself, the stimulus from the response. Our thinking is a tearing apart of these elements. When we do this, we have commenced to think, and we do this in judgment, e.g., the chair is made of wood, the chair is to sit on. This process of separating takes place through the relation of the self and other selves, in that we get consciousness of the response as isolated from the stimulating objects, the perceptual object as such. Social intercourse as such is adapted to this, but our consciousness of the response to the stimulation is more vivid than in the case of physical conduct, and our response to another is a stimulation to ourselves. In the case of physical stimulation we are apparently aware of our response.

We interpret what is in our immediate consciousness by saying that we know what we are saying or doing to one another. If action takes place at once, without any opportunity for reflection, it approaches an instinctive or highly habitual response. It is in the social play back and forth where there is no immediate action that I become aware of my response, set myself up as an object, and thus become self-conscious. If you could talk without knowing what you say, you would have no consciousness of the meaning of the social stimulus. It is only because we hold our own responses in consciousness that we become aware of the meaning of the stimulation. The meaning of the stimulation is the response, e.g., I am insulted but I feel resentful.

In the process of social intercourse, we are isolating the stimulation from the response, but we do not do so in our physical conduct. This distinction is not absolute; but only where we affect ourselves as we affect others. That is the only situation in which we are definitely aware of the meaning of the object.

Assume a person to have grown up without social contact. Would there be present the basis for primitive thought, as in the case of persons who grow up in society? Would the person see the signs of the weather? Would he be able to separate the object from its meaning? We must find a situation in which this meaning can arise in conduct itself. What is essential is not that he says this means rain, but that he have a tendency to go to the cave. Birds respond to stimulation and fly south, but there is no consciousness of meaning. The elements of meaning do not have a function to perform in this conduct; the response tends to fuse with the stimulation. We must find a situation in which the response is isolated, in order to find a consciousness of meaning. This is found in communication.

We found in the individual's own stimulation of others the beginnings of self-consciousness and with that the consciousness of meaning. We found in this process the consciousness of meaning, but the meaning of an object lies in our response to it. It requires an active analysis in order to respond to it. In the human social environment the response is isolated and we stimulate ourselves, we are self-conscious of what we are doing. The self-consciousness is in the relation to other selves, i.e., in social conduct. Our own selves arise in this conduct. With the tendency to respond to our own stimulation comes the consciousness of that tendency and of its meaning, as the result of the response. As a rule, we are aware of little more than the tendency to respond, and the imagery is very vague. Some psychologists try to show the state of consciousness in which there is consciousness of meaning without imagery. But they have evidently ignored the imagery of language. We find in our everyday experience the presentation of social stimulation; it may be in the form of a question. What we have in consciousness when we say that we know what a thing is, is a readiness to respond to it, to describe it. Self-consciousness is a stream, as it were, which flows parallel to our consciousness of others. When a problem appears, first of all in the social experience, the mechanism I have been describing becomes the mechanism of thought, and the problems of a young child are essentially social in character. Because of this dependence he must be in suitable social relations with those about him.

The life of the infant is regarded from two points of view. He is interested in material things just as in social objects. He acts toward physical objects and persons in very much the same, if not exactly the same, way. But important responses are essentially social. He is depending, whether aware of it or not, on social responses as his means of control. He isolates certain social stimulations in the countenances of others, and comparatively early he forms satisfactory responses to them. He thus forms social objects before he forms physical objects. His mechanism is essentially social. He talks to things and has emotions with reference to them, which adults have only with reference to other persons. His whole control of his immediate environment is very definitely through a social mechanism. We have carried the attitude of physical science into psychology, so that we have lost sight of the social nature of early consciousness. Our metaphysics of self, as well as our psychology, has talked on the subject-object relation, assuming that the object is not a self, while the subject is. Historically the first objects have been selves. It is only afterwards that the inner self, the subject, has arisen.

The little child gets his first control by his cries and by reaching out his arms. Later he gets control of physical objects. The orange color and the taste of the orange are things with which he enters into a social relation. But this is not the whole social relation. What is true of the child is also, so far as we can find out, true of the race, as seen in the attitude of primitive people. The method of control over the world is a social technique. It may be a hopelessly inefficient technique, but it is simply carrying the social technique into this larger world.

The mechanism by means of which we do our thinking when we face problems is inevitably a social mechanism. The dog, in alternatively remaining and approaching, is responding to two separate stimuli. Men construct and separate these two objects which include both characters. As long as we have entirely different responses, we have two objects, e.g., the child who gets his hand into the flame of the candle. His analysis enables him to bring out both of its characters—plaything and object that burns—into a single object, and to act in a way that enables him to play with it and also to be burned.

We get ways of dealing with our difficulties which enable us to force contradictory elements of the stimulation and the response together.

What is the mechanism by which a person consciously reconstructs objects? It is not the trial-and-error process, for that is presumably not a conscious process. How do we learn a game? That does not take place in human beings as in lower animals. Rather there is a conscious construction which men carry out that we do not find in the lower animals. There is an ability to hold in consciousness the conflicting stimulations and tendencies to respond in a conflicting fashion. And then we can suggest a hypothetical way which will include all the elements with all these tendencies to respond. Scientists present to themselves data and construct a hypothesis which will explain apparently conflicting data. This is a refinement. Where is the mechanism that makes this process

possible? The suggestion is, in our conscious, subconscious, social conduct. It is that social conduct in which we are aware of our responses
to others, responses that have a meaning to ourselves, and we tend to
respond to the things we say to others. These responses become not
simply bare elements of sensuous experiences or images but sensuous
experiences to which we ourselves respond. Then they become a *Vor-
stellungen*. It is through self-consciousness that we are able to get hold
of our material, so as to deal with it; e.g., a person who in other respects
insults us, we tend to respond to in different ways. What is characteristic of reflection here is our own responses to our own replies to these
conflicting stimuli. There is a feeling of strangeness about his act, still
I have a tendency to reply as in the past. How is it that this friend acts
thus? I myself reply to my own tendencies. I set up his act and his former nature as an object. I have thus the material I can use in reconstructing, but I get the material in my inner response to my tendencies to
react to his stimuli. It is not the response alone, but our response to the
response, with a locus in self-consciousness, that has arisen. The meaning is found, then, in our response. That meaning becomes a concept
with which we can deal when it has a different meaning for us. Our consciousness of meaning has arisen within social conduct. The whole field
of thought is a field of discourse, a social field. Our so-called laws of
thought are abstractions from social intercourse. Our whole process of
abstract thought technique and method is essentially social, and, e.g., in
identity we are coming back to the fact that all persons in a group agree
to deal with a certain object.

The Development of the Self

We now turn more definitely to the development of the self and its relation to other selves. We are sometimes afraid of our own anger. This is a
case of consciousness of our own response. We sometimes work on our
own sentiment. The child may center his mind on his wretched condition and how little sympathy he gets from others. We are aware of day-
dreams. Thus we find ourselves replying to our response—we fear, admire,
sympathize with ourselves. It is largely in the field of language that we
do this.

Social consciousness is organized from the outside in. The social percepts which first arise are those of other selves. In adjusting himself to
gestures, the young child probably forms his first objects. It is only after
he has reached the point of communicating with himself that his own
self-consciousness can arise. This process largely takes place through
vocal gestures. A child which the child hears calls out a response, an-

other vocal gesture. In the bird this has a function in the process of mating and the care of the young. Cf. Craig's study of pigeons.[12]

We have also the bird stimulating itself by its own notes when in confinement. The child, similarly stimulates himself; he talks to himself, on the whole, more than to others. This is important in his learning to speak. This provides a mechanism which can lead to the formation of a self over against other selves.

In order that the self may arise it must have a definite functional value in the conduct of the child over against others. The child fashions his own self on the model of other selves. This is not an attitude of imitation, but the self that appears in consciousness must function in conjunction with other selves. The child's consciousness of its own self is quite largely the reflection of the attitudes of others toward him. Of course by no means all of the child's consciousness is within the self. A great deal of it is impulsive. In sudden outbursts of anger or joy we are not predominately self-conscious. Legally, persons who act thus are not held responsible, as they are when they are self-conscious. Before the child's character is formed a great deal of his conduct is not regarded as his own. Gradually an organization of the self takes place. More and more impulses are brought within the self. What is the self that the child recognizes? It tends to appear as a third person. He takes that form of the self which appears in the speech of others. He is good or bad. That becomes the model for the child in building up his own self.

Some have held that organic pleasure-pain changes are that out of which the self is built, but there is nothing there which would lead to the construction of an object. Still, pleasure and pain are important in the child's conduct. That material has to find its place in the self-consciousness which arises, as we have indicated.

C. H. Cooley (chap. 2) stresses an abstract sociability which does not involve for the time being a self-consciousness on the part of the child, whereas the recognition of the self arises in the instinct of sociability. There seems to be there only the tendency to respond to social stimuli. So that it is normal for the child to depend on them. Cooley brings out the essential sociability of the child in his own imagination, building up imaginary comparisons and talking to himself. This essential sociability is that out of which personality arises. There is a difference between this thesis of Cooley's and our point of view.

12. Wallace Craig. "The Expressions of Emotion in the Pigeons. I. The Blonde Ring Dove *(Turtur risorius)*." [Granville] (Ph.D. thesis, University of Chicago, 1909 [reprinted from the *Journal of Comparative Neurology and Psychology*]); "The Song of the Wood Pewee, *Myiochanes virens* Linnaeus: A Study of Bird Music" (New York State Museum Bulletin, no. 334 (June 1943).

We have a social consciousness which is organized from the periphery toward the center. In the animal, if it has a percept, there is nothing but the center. He cannot be conceived of as an object existing to himself. This conception of the self at the center of the field arises in social conduct. We do not have subject-consciousness but object-consciousness. So far as psychology is concerned the self is always an object. The subject represents that point which is assumed to be at the center of the animal's conduct. The bringing up of that object follows the bringing up of other objects, other selves in consciousness. This "me" which arises in consciousness arises as an object in the same fashion that other selves have arisen. But it is definitely related to the "I" as the others are not. They are put into relationship with the "me." There is the grand vizier which represents the "I" over against the other selves. The "me" is an object in just the same way that the others are. Solipsism is an absurdity. The self has reality only as other selves have reality, and comes in fact later. C. Lloyd Morgan has reversed this (in *An Introduction to Comparative Psychology*).

Cooley's contention is that other persons are made up out of our sentiments of those emotional and intellectual contents that answer to their gestures. He believes another person for us is the expression of the facts with which we are familiar and the various sentiments which that stimulation arouses. The persons are the results (constructs) of our imaginations, answering to these particular stimulations. Cooley would distinguish between social objects and physiological objects. The latter are exclusive of each other, social objects are not; i.e., the same elements may enter into the characters of Aristides and Washington. This position makes a different type of objects out of social objects, so far as the stuff out of which they are built is concerned. It seems as if Cooley were on the wrong track there. I doubt if there is any more identity of material for Aristides than for two chairs. Where we get an identification of content under a general term, we have exactly the same situation with physiological objects as with social objects. If we reduce them to psychological content, they will be just as identical in both cases. All objects as such arise through our reactions, and our experience of the past enters into perception. One is built up out of the material that has to be used over again, the other is not.

Other selves, as distinguished from physical objects, have a greater emotional content on account of the emotional nature of social conduct. Where there is no emotional tone in our converse with others, we speak of it as mechanical. There is less of the person there. There is relatively a difference in physiological and social objects in regard to emotion, but no difference in reality. I.e., what we associate with the grasp of the hand differs from the holding of a muscle at the butcher shop. But it is not correct to hold that persons are constructs of the imagination, while things are somehow just there.

But there is a difference when the self comes in as a percept, and when we take the objective view of the self. There, also, it is true that the situation is the same for the physiological as for the social object. So far as we assume that our self belongs to this "me" just so far is it possible to fall into solipsism, but we take that attitude just as truly toward physiological as toward social objects. The possessive as well as the personal pronouns belong to the "me"; the self is secondary. Others come into existence first of all, and later one becomes aware of one's self. The reality of one's self is just as genuine as other selves, but it has no superior reality. I am no surer of my self than of any other self. However, I may take the point of view of that self and relate every thing simply to that self, overlooking the fact, as the solopsist psychologist does, that the self has arisen later. Or I may relate it to other selves as the Hindu religion does in all dreams of God. If a person takes the solopsist attitude toward himself, he must also allow others to take it. This overlooks conditions under which consciousness of self has arisen. It never occurs to us to assume that our own selves are any more real than any other self. This is the commonsense view. We know that if other selves should disappear from consciousness we should lose our own selves.

Cooley is taking a secondary point of view—not an immediate point of view out of which our own selves have arisen, but the point of view of the "me." We take a secondary point of view when we speak of a star as being a construct of a certain sensation of light, etc. That position is to be identified with Cooley's view of the social world. We are not more in social than in physiological conduct. The self arises as a self on the social side. A physiological self also arises. We somewhat naively state the external world in terms of states of consciousness, and inner consciousness in terms of the nervous system, forgetting that we must state the nervous system in terms of inner consciousness. We state the whole external world in terms of the nervous system. In a sense everything is mirrored in us. We build up the physiological self over against other physiological selves.

The Other and the Self

We take up now the statement of the other in terms of the self. The mechanism for social conduct is conversation, language. A talking bird learns the song of another. This process is the same as that which is so important for human beings. Talking birds stimulate themselves and respond to their own notes. The talking bird can be trained to make use of articulate speech, though there is no evidence of a grasp of meaning. In all these cases we have an individual influencing himself when he is responding. This tendency to reply is in itself an organization, an impulse or instinct, which will tend to bring out such responses, e.g., the attitude of little children dependent on parents. We know that with the very beginning of the child's awareness of objects about him, the parental as well as the filial attitude appears. We see in this situation the tendency to occupy the attitude of the parent toward the child. The child's responses to the parent tend to arouse in the child an attitude similar to that of the parent. The child's own response to his response to the group that is parental toward him leads the child to act in a way that is parental. His behavior has the same effect upon himself that it has upon the adult.

How may this take place? I am quite unable to accept the statement in terms of imitation. Wundt attempts to get out of it by assuming different instincts in different individuals. If an animal has an instinct of running, the mere sight of another animal running is a stimulus for him to run. Why should this happen even if he had the instinct? There is no implication that the response will be the same as that of the form stimulating it. Another method of reducing imitation to the lowest terms is in appealing to the motor character of the idea. But the motor character does not make us do what we see another person doing or to say what we hear another person saying. That would be the case only when the child himself has use of that note, and then the hearing of it on the part of another would induce the use of the same.

The difficulty is this: How are we to explain that different individuals take on the conduct of other forms if there is no necessary likeness between the stimulus and the response? When one form attacks another and the second runs, the stimulus and the response are not alike. We have in the case of the bird that learns the song of another a certain number of responses, vocal gestures. One of these vocal gestures calls out a response in another. The ground of this is to be found in the parental and mating processes. When the first bird, assuming it to be placed in the cage of another, makes use of certain notes A, B, C, D, E, they call out in the other bird a second series G, H, I, J, K. They are the responses and G, H, I, J, K, answer definitely to A, B, C, D, E, so that each note the first makes use of tends to call out a definite response in the second. We have to consider not only the relations of A to G, B to H, etc., but the relation of the whole to the other song. In so far, then, as we have this determination of the whole, the response which the second makes to the first will have been in some way determined by the stimulus, and the first will have a tendency to respond to himself. If A, B, C, D, E become like G, H, I, J, K, there must be a certain phonetic element common to both birds. Element A may not necessarily bring out G, but there must be identities there. It is the selective power of the second over the elements which makes its response tend to be like that stimulation of the first. There is a tendency to bring out the male note in the female bird. The male stimulates the female by uttering a cry. Then the female responds with another cry, which contains some of the same or similar vocal elements. But in responding to the male the female stimulated herself, and responded to her own stimulation. In so doing she tends to assume the attitude of the male bird. In the succession of responses, then, those vocal elements are selected which are similar to the vocal elements of the male bird, and thus their notes become alike. This is not a process of imitation, but an unconscious becoming alike, functioning alike in social conduct.

In considering the possibility of the form being so influenced by the forms about it that its conduct tends to conform to theirs, J. Mark Baldwin implies that there is a tendency on the part of the form to reinstate the sensation that has been agreeable. We find among other psychologists (e.g., J. R. Angell) a statement with reference to instinctive imitation, limiting this imitation of sound, but it is not indicated what this would be. But so far as I know, no psychologist has had the temerity to say that mere vision of the way another form is acting could not itself set up a coordination in the central nervous system which would result in the same sort of acting. Imitation has not been satisfactorily discussed.

The situation in which imitation takes place is much narrower than used to be assumed. Wundt still includes conformity of ants and bees. It is made also to cover conformity of the behavior of young forms to the parent forms. There is no question that the young takes up activities from the parent which are not instinctive. But these activities have not yet been analyzed with careful observation. There seem to be in the young certain plastic instincts, which lack perfectly definite stimuli. There are certain tendencies which have to be attached to certain definite stimulations. E.g., the young does not at first cower before the hawk's approach, but acquires this through contact with the mother. Instincts which have been assumed to be perfectly rigid have been found to be quite plastic and capable of development.

The instincts we have been discussing are those involved in the child learning a language and the talking or singing birds acquiring the song or words of another form. A form in responding to other forms stimulates itself. Response to the stimulation is selected; insofar as the form responds to that stimulation it has a tendency to respond to itself. Its secondary response will have a tendency to be like the response of the first form. The child-parent attitude is in human nature. The child instinctively assumes the parental attitude in response to its own child attitude. Frequently it is only a tendency and does not appear overtly. It is not so much the act of the other as the attitude of the individual himself which is directly responsible for it. We have a likeness of result which is due to the likeness of stimulation, in like forms. This does not necessarily involve self-consciousness, and it is just the process by which the parrot learns to talk.

All human individuals have the same phonetic elements. What does happen to the child is a selection of its phonetic elements in accordance with those which constitute the stimulus. It is not that you have a picture definitely before you and proceed consciously to copy it; but rather there is a direct response on our part to stimulations which other persons have called out in us. Stimulation selects a natural response, not necessarily identical. Speak to a person in an irritated tone and he responds in an irritated tone. When the child assumes the child attitude, it calls out the parental attitude which is a part of its own nature. When the child is playing, the emphasis has been on the secondary response.

There is a very marked difference between vocal gestures and other types of conduct in this respect. It is only in vocal gestures that we have anything which can be called imitation; e.g., in monkeys it has been eliminated under careful analysis. But the bird learning and the child learning are of the same sort.

That gives the basis for sympathy, for the individual has responded perfectly definitely to himself. The responses are the material out of which he builds up other selves. When he has built them up, he has other selves that are made out of the same stuff that he is made of, with the same tendencies to respond. The child plays at the characters that form his social objects. In this he is making use of responses to his own responses. These tendencies to act are already there and he is building them up into selves.

It seems that it is this type of vocal gesture which makes it possible to build up other selves and one's self. If this is lacking, some substitute must be provided, if self-consciousness is going to be built up. This other means of intercourse must have the same mechanics as that of speech, stimulations calling out responses to which the child can respond.

According to some psychologists the influence of the community on the individual has been expressed through a process of imitation.[13] They hold that the individual tends to do what he sees and hears others do. The first conclusions were that this is a definite copying. Later it has been seen that we are often unaware of the copy. In language, changes take place through long periods of time, without the change ever coming to the consciousness in the mind of the individual in whom it takes place. Persons are not fully aware of their submission to fashion. McDougall tries to get away from the mechanical statement of imitation by appealing to the motor character of the idea. The idea of the chair involves a tendency to sit down. The sight of another person yawning is a stimulus to do the same. This overlooks the relation of ideas to conduct. It leaves them relatively isolated. It belongs to the old associational psychology, according to which each idea is to a certain extent an entity in itself. This overlooks the organic character of consciousness, and that the ideas have their place in consciousness as parts of the act and must be taken with reference to these acts. In one case, a group of persons crowding along a street have little motor response; in another, watching a football game, it does. This psychology also fails to show how a person gets his first tendency to respond to the speech of another. An attempt was made by Baldwin to carry back this imitation to a fundamental biological process, a tendency on the part of the organism to reinstate a pleasurable sensation. This is an attempt to connect social development with autogenetic biological evolution. The mere process which is taking place tends to cause a certain amount of satisfaction to the form and hence the form seeks to repeat it. In the process of mastication, the very process reinstates the stimulus, brings back the flavor. Baldwin would call this self-imitation. This process, if it takes place at all, does not by any means meet the situation with which we are dealing.

Wundt presents another doctrine. Imitation is the setting free of an instinctive process ready to go off by sensing the other form going through the same process. What is the mechanism for this?

If we consider imitation as it is supposed to take place in the lower forms, it is confined to learning by the young forms, to the training of the young by the parents. Just what the nature of this training is, has not been made clear. What takes place in the ants and bees where the young workers must take on certain processes, we are in no position to explain adequately. Psychology has investigated such imitation as it appears in human beings. This has resulted in showing that most of it is not imitation at all. Cases which seem to be imitation are in doubt.

13. See Thorndike, *Animal Life;* Wundt, Morgan, and Hobhouse, articles on imitation.

But in birds, we have something analogous to the young child in vocal gestures. Under these conditions we have the form influencing itself as well as responding to other forms. It is in the identity of the stimulation that we seem to find the basis of the so-called imitation. Also this emphasizes the selection of the bird's response to the stimulation. Its own response tends to be like the stimulation of the field within which the response may occur. In the stimulation there is a selection of the response a man can make; e.g., the New Englander who is reserved in speaking English, but perfectly free to express himself when using the French language. The identity of stimulation in similar forms seems to be the basis of what is called imitation. The child's act stimulates his own parental nature as well as the parental nature of the parent. You find both sides of the fundamental instincts in all persons.

We are always affected by any process, but the affect of walking is not the same as seeing another person walking. This identity is to be found in the vocal and in the pantomimic gestures. Their importance lies in the fact that they have an influence upon the individual which is largely the same as that which they have upon others. Hence it is natural to find what seems to be imitation. Unconscious imitation is identical on the part of the individual and others to his own stimulations. This is to be distinguished from conscious copying.

One speaks in a certain tone of voice and that calls out the response in the other. The tendency of one to respond to his own stimulation is the material out of which he builds up consciousness of others and of self. When we recognize selves, there is a by-product of direct social responses. The by-product is the tendency to respond to one's self which is transferred and goes to make up other selves, giving them an interior. There is in consciousness the response to a social stimulation, out of which response one builds up other selves. There arises a social world which arises on all sides and before and after. The social world arises in the idea, and in that idea the stuff is the response of the individual to the physiological stimulation. It is identified stuff, that which goes to build up other selves and our own self. This gives the basis for the influence of the community on the individual.

In physiological conduct we found in distant stimulations that which was to make up certain responses, and the ideas which arose in these responses were those of contact, hardness, coldness, volume, etc. Those characteristics arose through carrying out the act occasioned by these different stimulations. What are the physiological objects which we see, hear, or smell? What is matter as it appears in our idea? It is found in the idea of contact; the stuff out of which things are made is found in contact-ideas as opposed to stimulations that come from a distance. In social conduct we speak of idea (or instinct) of response to our own gestures as the material out of which the physiological response constitutes the stuff of which physiological objects are made.

In saying this I am referring to the inside of selves—that which we speak of as subjective. Our own physiological selves are built out of the same material as the physiological objects about us. In the same way the social self is built up out of the same material as other selves; the same stuff is used directly and immediately in building up other selves in exactly the same fashion as the individual later comes to build up his own self. The other is there just as much as we are and exists as a being, before one's own self is organized and recognized. You can never get inside of a physiological object; you indefinitely create more outsides. In the same way the material which comes to constitute a social being is in its own character inner stuff, whether you have it in other persons or in the self. The idea of looking into the eyes of one who is suffering involves an inner idea. It is only when we reach the sophisticated stage that the problems of Berkeleyan idealism arise.

The other is a different person and, being different, his suffering is different from mine, but he is a suffering being to whom I react immediately. Other individuals exist for us as having inner ideas, which in a certain sense we can never penetrate.

It is because the material is the same that other persons have an inner idea of us. Psychologists say in regard to the conscious idea, for example, that the book has an inside for us because we project ourselves into it. There is the same mistake here as in dealing with social objects. The stuff out of which we and the book are made is the same. There is no conscious transfer. The difficulty is met in the effort to construct an introdermal self which can be projected. The child is conscious of the hard floor long before he is aware of the introdermal self that is injured by the hard floor. We use the same stuff in building up extradermal and introdermal objects. So in social conduct there is a response to our own gestures, which is the material out of which are built other selves and then our own selves. At first, the child accepts the judgment of others about himself; not all ideas that go to build up an organized self are brought together till after the self of the parent is organized. The child may recognize that the same parent may be loving or angry; but the loving child and the angry child are different partial personalities.

This gives us the basis for what F. H. Giddings calls consciousness of kind, and what social psychologists call sympathy. Cooley points out that sympathy is of two kinds: (1) feeling as another does, and (2) running to help. Taking the identity of material discussed above, we have the basis for sympathy.

This is the material which is lacking in the consciousness of the lower animals. The dog may save a child, or lick a suffering master's hand, but he does not have a response to his own action. It is a direct and immediate action. He is not aware of his act. He is not conscious of its meaning. There are varying degrees of response to our own gestures in different people. We must have an adequate response, a consciousness toward that which we are acting to make a charitable act a really worthy act. The comprehension of the other individual's attitude is built up out of the response to his own action.

The responses are simply there. Only secondarily may we deal with them reflectively as our responses. But at first they are simply responses out of which other selves and our own self are built up.

Sympathy, in the first sense, attaches to the direct relation of the self to others. Secondarily, we use that term to mean the structure, the common material, which is used for constructing others as well as one's own self. In a third sense, when the person is in doubt about another person, he transfers the part of his own self to the other person, e.g., where he himself suffered loss and deliberately recalls his idea, he reconstructs the other by transferring this idea. These ideas are not direct and immediate. We are trying to get something that is not immediately there. We have, then, those three stages in building up the self.

We can revert from the building up of social objects and get exactly the same results: (1) the habitual or instinctive action, (2) the construction of the physiological objects through contact with the idea, (3) deliberate analysis. First we move about without consciousness of the object—without the subjective idea—then the latter comes.

The response to the individual's conduct is in consciousness, at the center of which is the individual. Out of these responses are built up selves, both others and the "I." You cannot have consciousness of self without consciousness of other selves. Any self at the center of consciousness arises with other selves which make up social consciousness. The "alteri" arise earlier than the self, both in the child and the race. That is natural because the conduct of the child is determined first of all with reference to the field of stimulation. The objects in the field of consciousness are constructed by analysis of objects in the field of stimulation before the self appears. The self can arise only as a percept; the child must be an object to himself. He does not get that capacity before he is able to perceive his own social stimulations, gestures, especially vocal gestures. Then he perceives himself when he perceives his own social conduct. But he can perceive only as he reacts to it. Our perception of an object is a relating of ourselves to it with reference to a possible act. This is equally true of our gestures as objects. A person must be ready to react to these gestures in order to perceive himself as an object.

What, then, would be the difference between the "alteri" and the "ego"? The others can conceivably exist before the "ego" exists as a percept. G. F. Stout holds that animals may have consciousness of others. In self-consciousness the self is only the center of his social consciousness. Consciousness of others would be one stage in the development of the social consciousness. In the next stage we have the response of the individual to his own social conduct, and out of that response he will be able to build up his own self as a percept. That percept will differ from the other selves in this respect, namely, that he will give attention to his own responses in their relationship to himself, as he has not given attention to the responses that go to build up other selves. When he is aware of his own words he responds to them, but in this case he is able to exercise a control over this social process of stimulation and response which he does in the case of the others, e.g., a mother's countenance indicating displeasure. He may later by his own social conduct control others indirectly but not directly, as when both the stimulation and the response lie in the field of his own conduct. That comes out very clearly in the child's vocal gesture. He is more apt to be interested in talking to himself than to others, for there he can attain control.

The consciousness becomes a means of control over the stimulation. We give attention to the stimulation in the process of control. This comes out best in thought where we are carrying out both sides of the conversation. It is our response to our own stimulation that gives us control. The moment an idea arises in our mind, we are aware of our response to it, and our attitude toward the idea determines our social conduct toward ourselves. That constitutes the essential difference between ourselves and others. In the latter the stimulation lies outside our control. We select the stimulation with reference to its value to us. Only indirectly can we direct our conversation to some one else, but we can direct our own conversation so that the latter lies inside the same act. The fundamental difference between the "ego" and the "alteri" as objects lies in the control which consciousness of response gives the stimulation. When we are aware of the value to ourselves of what others are doing, our control can only be indirect. Our own response to our own conduct becomes a means to that control over our own conduct. We

get, then, the power of initiative. Here there are differences. Control of
the self is not complete. We know that our conduct is of the sort that
we can reprehend, yet the stimulation is so strong that we cannot control it, and we get the sense of double personality. This appears in moral
situations.

In conversation we must give attention to the gestures of others and
select out of them those that will give us control. Our attention is rather
to the stimulation than to the response. We control by means of selective analysis. We want to direct the conversation along a certain line.
The same is partly true of thought. A stream of images may be so strong
that we cannot control it and we have to give way, e.g., our attention
wanders when we read an uninteresting book. How do we get back?
Our method of control is by responding to the material in the book
over against the material in the other ideas. The control is through emphasis on response rather than on stimulation.

The feeling of self-consciousness, with its elements of self-control
and initiative, arises out of this consciousness of control over conduct
with reference to ourselves, through response to our own stimulations,
as opposed to control through selection and analysis of stimulations
from others. One that is relatively objective when following an argument is not, relatively speaking, self-conscious. But when the "ego"
element in the individual comes to the front, he realizes that he has a
different mind from others; he is conscious of his own responses, of his
likes and dislikes toward these ideas of his. It is the consciousness of
control over our social stimulations of ourselves through our responses
that distinguishes the "ego" from the "alteri." The distinction between
the "ego" and the "alteri" is that, in the case of the self, responses to
social acts (largely vocal gestures) control to a large degree the stimulations. In case of the "alteri," while the response gives meaning to the
stimulations, it does not control them, except indirectly.

Imitation and Imagination

We shall next consider the psychological mechanism by means of which
the conduct influences us and brings about imitation. There are other
contents which go to distinguish the ego from the alteri, organic sensations, cyclopean eye, feeling in the throat that accompanies articulation,
kinesthetic and visceral ideas that are identified with the physiological
self, and on the other hand are supposed to have the peculiar inner quality that attaches to the self.

Consciousness of response has much more importance in response to
one's self than in response to others. This gives that peculiar high degree

of subjectivity to self-consciousness. The words that I utter are as much outside as the words of another. They only become my words when I respond to them. They become mine because my response to them changes them and controls them. The same is true of the process of thought. We say an idea occurs to us. "It came into my mind." It is outside for the time being. What renders the idea mine is my response to it, my approval or disapproval. The idea is under control of my response.

My imagery is not mine because it is shut inside a particular skull. Coming to the process of social intercourse, we have a self which has arisen at the center of consciousness exercising control over its stimulations. In the memory of an idea that has taken place, we may of course reproduce what has taken place. If we do that, we are very apt to do more than bring back the memory. We are more or less aware of carrying ideas and instincts beyond that which took place. We carry the friends response further and wonder what he would have said, and we put words in his mouth. From that idea we can go over to construction of the imagination, as the novelists do. In such cases we speak of those individuals as creations. This is what we are doing all the time. In this process of imaginative creation or memory we have a mingling, so to speak, of the ego and the alteri. We refer to them as creations and yet the creations are made out of the alteri of our ideas. The artist simply analyzes, selects, and reconstructs. As a result of this combination by the individual, he is conscious of putting himself in the other person's place. He is playing the role of the other. This takes place in the child before his own ego is definitely formed, and in that situation he does not make the distinction between himself and others which the adult makes. The child's self is for the time being in the others. He has not isolated and organized the ego as the adults have. He has to live in the outside. The child carries over into his external world what, if he were an adult, he would recognize as himself. For he has no unique function in social conduct for which others hold him responsible.

Coming to the adult, we have the individual playing the role of the other, putting himself into another's place. This is the basis for the molding of individuals which communication exercises over those who enter into it. The situation in which the individual is not simply stimulating himself and responding, is one in which he is also presenting other persons to himself. Here he takes on the expression and the intonation of the other. He will come to present himself to himself as in the garb of another. The picture of himself conforming to some fashion may come suddenly. So far as this inner process of the idea involves taking the role of the others, and is not simply the presence of the others in memory, just so far the others must inevitably influence him; e.g., we find ourselves taking certain attitudes, accents, words, thinking of others. This embarrasses us. It is not because we have changed our principles, but we have been taking the part of another. An individual who could not play the role of another and put himself in another's place could not possibly imitate. If his conduct consisted simply in responding to them, nothing psychological could account for his taking on another's dress, words etc. But where he reconstructs them and talks through their mouths, he becomes as they are. This also makes the distinction between the two types of sympathy: (1) readiness to assist, (2) feeling with the person. Assistance may take place without one putting himself in the place of another. In the second, he does not merely respond to the other but is in the attitude that we call sympathy. Sympathy and imitation are both due to taking the role of another, reconstructing the individual—not simply accepting him as real, but actually constructing him, standing in his own shoes and speaking with his intonation. It is that sort of imitation which it is impossible for the lower animal to be subject to, because he has no self-consciousness or the mechanism for it. The parrot responding to another tends to bring out a response like the response of the other. That is the situation in which we have what is called imitation, but it is not a copying or putting oneself in the place of another. This is entirely distinct from the type of imitation to which we are now referring; the latter is at the bottom of most of those things with which sociologists have occupied their speculations. The dialogue is one of their forms of literary presentation of that process and it is a reflection of what goes on in the mind of people. The ego is more or less conscious, taking first one part and then the other. The individual constructs others and takes their roles over against himself, and in doing that and only then does he take on the fashion of others. If this process did not go on, an individual would not be influenced by the community in which he lived. It is the creative imagination that is responsible for the influence which others exercise over the self.

Frequently we are suddenly aware of ourselves in the attitude of using the words of another. Introspection shows that we are continually taking the roles of others. We can readily present to ourselves the situation in which our responses to another are made without taking on his role, as when a command brings out a response. The private soldier, for example, does not copy the officer; his response does not carry the tendency to take the other's place. The subordinate cannot put himself in the superior's place. So it is possible for groups in relatively close con-

tact to preserve separate manners and dialects. It is easier for a sophisticated person to put himself in an unsophisticated person's place than
vice versa. Mere intercommunication does not necessarily result in imitation. There must be a situation in which a person puts himself in
another's place. The imitation may or may not be conscious, e.g., you
may or may not be conscious of putting yourself in another person's
place. A person in one caste cannot imitate a person in another caste
because his caste-consciousness forbids it. Conscious attention is copying, and imitating properly is just this. An animal responding to another
tends to act similarly, but that is not imitation.

What is the situation in which imitation tends to take place? It is the
situation of imagination, in which reconstruction takes place; a social
problem in which there is a definite reconstruction of the social consciousness. This process moves just as self-consciousness does, from the
periphery toward the center. The individual reconstructs others before
he achieves the reconstruction of himself. He has to realize a new social
situation before he realizes himself as a new individual. We are aware of
this in profound spiritual changes. One gets a new view of obligations,
etc. before he reconstructs himself. This point has been quite overlooked
by many of our psychologists; Warner Fite assumes that the self must
remain the same. In social consciousness a social problem presents itself
which demands reconstruction. It is only here that one gets a reconstruction of himself. Where there is a fixed, stratified society, a person
does not present himself in the form of another, for there is no social
problem. Revolutions follow profound social changes which involve a
breakdown of castes. Hence revolutions do not occur at the point of
the greatest misery. The new economic situation raises a social problem.
For example, we have a social problem when an economic problem,
which can be put in economic form, is introduced into a society where
it has not existed before. You can put yourself in somebody else's place,
you can put your social situation in terms of other persons' places.
Nothing has been more effective than money in breaking down the
caste system. This abstract conception makes possible the putting of
one's self in the place of a larger range of persons.

It is not necessary that a person state a problem very definitely. The
child's idea is largely the meeting of problems in which he reconstructs
his environment and himself. The problem does not have to be in scientific form, but it must stimulate the individual to put himself in the
other's place, a situation in which one reconstructs others and after
them himself.

The means by which this is done is a conversation of gestures. It is
like the scientific hypothesis. The individual tries it and wonders how a

person would act in a given case. With every change comes an increase of subjectivity. There is more of the individual than there was before.

He states the new object in terms of a hypothesis which is his own. He has first of all his problems, facts in new forms, and, over against that, a new scientific consciousness which expresses itself in a hypothesis. This must be stated in terms of the data. You have the same process in the social problem. Conflict demands reconstruction; e.g., the adolescent passing beyond parental authority. Here there must be a social reconstruction. There is a new view of his parents and other members of the group. It appears first not as a conflict in himself but in these new individuals, parents infringing on him. Now in reconstructing himself he must present himself in terms of certain hypothetical conduct. He presents himself over against the others. In such a situation he becomes aware of his parents' attitude toward him. He may never before have been aware in the same way of his father's intonation. In becoming aware of these new individuals he has to put himself in their places. He must put himself in the role of father in order to find out how the father will act in the new situation.

This process of social intercourse is located, so to speak, in the mouth of the parent. Up to this time he has had an idea of what his father would do if he failed to obey and what his response would be. He does not mystically merge himself in another personality. The articulative self that has been in the self has to be in the father. There has to be this definite transfer of the individual from one role to another.

The manner by which an individual takes the role of another is not by merging his personality in the other but by speaking of one individual in place of the other. One is conscious of speaking and also of hearing himself speak. When another speaks we have no kinesthetic idea of speaking. When an individual puts himself in the place of another he is speaking as the other has spoken and is not simply hearing him. He has the kinesthetic idea. He is aware of the motor imagery, the process of speaking in addition to auditory imagery. Kinesthetic imagery and auditory imagery of how it will sound always appear when one takes the place of another in inner conversation and imaginative reconstruction.

When one speaks and hears himself reply he is able to control what he hears by kinesthetic imagery and by auditory imagery. We get a much higher degree of correlation between audition and speech than in other gestures. For instance, we cannot divide tennis playing into elements. It is the control in speech which gives the mechanism of self-consciousness. The difference between the speech of another and the playing of the role of another is the difference between an audition simply and the speaking for the other. Insofar as one takes the other's part there is a more or less definite tendency to speak as he speaks. That mutual control we transfer to the other person. We have a more or less definite image of the way we want to speak to a person, and when we find ourselves varying from it we tend to correct ourselves. There is a scheme in the mind which tends to control the articulatory process. When one is taking the part of another the scheme which takes place in our own manner of speaking is his manner as we know it. The control is a different one, another intonation. If you carry on a discussion with another person in your mind, you use the way you have heard him speak. The control is the intonation which you have picked from him. This seems to be the psychology of speaking as another speaks, of taking any attitude of his which we can appreciate. The image of his movement or words controls our speaking or movement just as our image of our own movement or articulation controls us when we are not putting ourselves in another's place. This is controlled not by the actual sound or gesture of the other person but by the effect of that sound or gesture on us.

The control of the spiritualist is nothing but an exaggeration of what is going on all the time in all of us. We are not listening to the other person but are talking for him. The same is true of other gestures. It is also true of the picture of ourselves which we are carrying about with us. If you suddenly see a person who looks like yourself, it gives you quite a start, it is quite uncanny. But one always carries with him a picture of himself which he has seen in the glass, and that is, in his consciousness, the individual to whom all these other individuals are responding. It is not the individual who speaks, but one's self as he sees and hears it when he takes the role of the second person. When he plays the part of a friend, he exists, in a certain sense, over against the friend. Just as soon as he takes the place of another, he will have to present himself over against the other, the looking-glass "I." There we get those selves to which James refers, ourselves as we see ourselves through another person's eyes. This is a percept of what we are saying and doing. We not only take on another's intonation and attitude but tend to take them into ourselves. If the second person is contemptuous, the self arises as one of the condemned, but one who resents the contempt. This effect of the imitation has not only the tendency of carrying over into our lives the attitude of others, but also the presenting of a certain self—the self or series of selves as presented from the point of view of others. We are aware of it when we find suddenly that a person is not what we had thought. He was a different individual from the person others had been observing. It is the possibility of putting ourselves in other's places that accounts for these different selves. We carry models indicating what we ought to be in different circumstances.

A dog could not do this, for he cannot put himself in another's place. We may not do this correctly, but we exist for ourselves as we believe we are regarded by others. In order to transfer his kinesthetic idea to other individuals and stand off from himself, one must present himself as the second person, and must regard himself as the other would regard him; this will vary in different groups. One may live in the company of the dead. They may constitute the most important selves. Or the other may be a supernatural being. When the situation is healthy, these may be merged into a single personality. When they are not merged, we have a disassociation of selves, and the cure involves bringing them together, becoming a self which can take the place of other selves. We are all persons of multiple selves, but all of these have their relation to the organic fundamental self. (Distinguish personality, a direct percept, hearing ourselves speak, etc.) Then we construct ourselves as personality B, in terms of that other person. There may be B1, B2, B3, according to the milieu to which we transfer ourselves.

In taking the part of other persons unconscious imitation takes place. This is much more powerful than the presentation of ourselves in their eyes; the latter may be quite different. We come to deal with ourselves as others deal with us and suddenly have a vision of ourselves as others see us. This accounts for the hold that fashion has. We do not like to be different from others. These secondary selves are continually molding us, sometimes consciously, sometimes unconsciously. It accounts also for sympathy, putting ourselves in another's place and controlling ourselves by the vision of their countenance, etc. We cannot imitate another's toothache, but we can have a general attitude of suffering which will control our activity. If we assume the outward aspect of kindness we tend to build up a kind of self. That gives us an inner consciousness which is a social consciousness. From the objective point of view it may be a true or false presentation. It does not exist simply by itself.

There are two kinds of selves. First, one has an immediate percept of oneself, as when hearing one's own voice one at the same time respond to these social stimulations. The self is relatively in the background and does not play a great part. The other self arises thus—we put ourselves in the place of others and in an imaginary conversion we have to direct ourselves as we would direct others. It is for this self that imitation plays a larger part in life. The image ghost goes back definitely to the first self, and we know that the part this plays in daily life is very small. It is assumed that such a self can be destroyed without the man being aware of it. The medicine man may destroy the soul and tell the owner pro tempore he is not affected, but after the information is communicated to him, he pines away. The soul is not a thing which comes into the foreground, but it is a presupposition of daily life, though it is not essential to it.

The social process goes on among the lower animals without consciousness for it. For the primitive consciousness is relatively unimportant. This is the self involved in the attitude of the other toward us. The first answers to the attitude of ourselves toward ourselves. The latter is unimportant insofar as we put ourselves in the place of others. We do not naturally and primarily turn ourselves upon how our voice sounds; it is not natural to give attention to that self. But when we put ourselves in the attitude of another, we direct our attention upon ourselves as a normal object. An unsophisticated person is relatively unconscious of self; his responses are rather immediate. The ability of a person to put himself in another's place, and to get his reflection of himself, constitutes sophistically the view of the self which answers to the other person's view of us, the self with which we work. The attitude which we take in introspection is simply an extension of this view. The individual self is referred to as secondary. The relation between the two is a good point of view from which to approach metaphysics and logic. We, however, are interested in the relation of others to the self.

Social Control

Whenever we come to the question of social control, we find that it is to be recognized in this conscious attitude of others toward the self, in criticism or approval. We are constantly carrying about with us this self which is seen through the eyes of others, and this is being criticized. This constitutes the process of social control. It is to be distinguished from imitation, which comes through the unconscious taking of another person's role. A person's ear may not make him aware of change in his speech; the child's speech is assimilated to the speech of the group as a result of taking another person's role. But his assimilation does not involve consciously putting himself over against the others. The matter is a direct conscious process and by means of it the community controls the individual. Of course, the individual may refuse to accept control and become an anarchist or an individualist.

It is interesting to note situations in which the individual does not put himself over against the group. They arise where there is no conflict in the process going on. This is the situation in mob consciousness. The individual is doing what every individual is doing. It is impossible for him to present himself to himself as differing from others. The situation of seeing himself as others see him disappears. This does not mean necessarily that his acts will be reprehensible. Chesterfield listened to White-

tive group. Over against the individual outside the group is the attitude of hostility, the instinct of injuring. Within the group the hostility has been organized so that these instincts lead to competition and rivalry. All other social institutions are so organized that such an impulse as this cannot come to expression except in the social process as a whole. Social organization arises through concrete interrelation in which individuals are brought into all sorts of relations to ourselves.

Over against this lies the attitude of the group, or of individuals within the group, to people outside. The normal thing is to harm the enemy. The bringing of these others into the group through slavery or capture, for a limited social function, is the mechanism by which society has enlarged itself. An individual from one caste meets one from another and there is mortal combat; one sees nothing in the other except an enemy. Through slavery there was developed the abstract conception of property. The one group is able through this to put itself in relation with persons outside the group; they are conceived of in abstract relations. This process leads to the founding of large cities. Out of that arises the process of rendering abstract social relations more concrete.

On the moral side, we have the same process in social integration and self-consciousness through the development of the individual by putting the self in the place of the other; thus the person comes to consider all the relations of the other, treating him as being a member of the group. Moral growth is the inner integration. We have to take these people completely into the group. This is not merely an act of parliament but actually of making the relations concrete. This is the means by which social integration takes place.

2 1927 Class Lectures in Social Psychology

The Act as a Basis for Understanding the
Life Process and Intelligence

The behavioristic approach to an understanding of the
self, the mind, and reflective intelligence is not a well worked out technique; it is more an attitude than a specific doctrine. It is an attempt to
deal with the phenomena of psychology from an objective viewpoint,
from observation of conduct and action. It grew out of comparative
psychology, and it has the advantage of being objective. Conduct and
action can be observed by many; in observing them you do not get
inside the subject but away from the subject. John B. Watson banished
consciousness as well as imagery of all kinds; he ignored an essential
part of the mental. The general approach of behaviorism is not based on
any doctrine or theory; it aims only to avoid introspection. Introspection is more or less individual, and divided by philosophical concepts
from the Renaissance on.

Introspective data have two characteristics: They are accessible only
to the individual, privately, and they can never be placed outside of a
spiritual protoplasm or mind. Introspection is solipsistic and has a
representative quality from which there is no final escape. Behaviorism
tries to solve this problem, which the Renaissance brought out with its
distinction between primary and secondary qualities. Science now has
driven the secondary qualities into the organism. It holds that reality
consists only of particles in motion or vibration and leaves the other
content of experience in the individual brain. We must now return these
so-called secondary qualities to the world; this is one of the tasks of the
psychology of behavior or of behavioristic psychology.

What we see in the external world is partly due to our filling in. A
memory image is not stuff; it is found in the world and the environment. Imagery is not a structure or conscious stuff different from the
physical world. It is not a stuff that enables us to tell the difference

between outside and inside, as the bifurcation of the world implies. We must consider inside and outside together, and the world cannot be divided into inside and outside. The bifurcation of the world comes from the Renaissance. It has back of it scientific and philosophical motives, an attempt to explain the nature of the world in terms of mass and motion. Whatever could not be included in these two concepts was put in "the mind." The physical and the psychical were regarded as antithetical. This belief has dominated modern thought; psychology is still on a program of parallelism.

In this course we are interested in the nature and genesis of self. We must be free from the assumption that the self is built from the physical world and conscious states. We must get rid of the bifurcation of the world and restore to nature or the objective order what belongs to it. The notion of consciousness always implies a reference to some self, but that self is not made up from psychical stuff. All things may be subjective at times. We start with an assumption of content, which implies a self or mind. We all have perspectives characterized by the self. We cannot separate consciousness as a stuff from the idea of the self. Consciousness is consciousness of belonging to something. We must identify consciousness as a stuff with ego or self. We always refer consciousness to a self when we conceive of it as a stuff. In this discussion we do not assume there is a self to begin with. Self is not presupposed as a stuff out of which the world arises. Rather the self arises in the world. Lower animals do not have selves. The self arises in this world and determines its perspectives. We want to leave out the category of states of consciousness as stuff; we shall use it only for convenience.

The social character of conduct is to be considered in this approach. Conduct is intercourse with other forms, and it is social in this respect. We use the social form only with the sense that the form is dependent in many ways on other forms. The self is not present in the early months of life. Psychology is a social science insofar as it deals with social stimuli and social dependence. When interested in this type of conduct psychology is social in this approach, and our particular interest is in the discovery of intelligence and the use of symbols in life forms. To account for the origin and use of symbols we must go back to the beginning of the life form. The human infant is born with no clear-cut instincts but only with some simple reactions—sucking, reaching, etc. Lower animals have many more and clearer responses than human infants.

The human animal is sensitive, with five channels for experience; but all of these reduce to distance experience and contact experience. All experience begins with contact, and distance experience develops afterward. Intelligence relates distance and contact experience. Intelligence is the use of signs in connecting the distance experience and the contact experience. The normal act, for instance, is a distance response; but contact experience alone makes intelligence possible. With the relation of the two, symbols emerge; one thing "stands for" another thing or experience, or evokes a response to another thing or experience.

Now let us approach the problem from the standpoint of the act. There is no essential difference between the physical constitution of a tree and that of an animal. Since the general surrounding environment is equally interrelated in both, there is no physical reason for marking off the animal from its environment more than the plant is marked off. This is not so, however, from the biological point of view, because to break down the individuality of the form or organism is to destroy its meaning. In living forms we deal with things that can be distinguished from their environment and from each other.

An act is not merely motion (although it can be analyzed into motions); it has a place and has meaning beyond mere motion. The act is a novelty, an emergent. It has behind it a life-preserving form. It leads to a certain result, it is purposive and teleological, and consequently it has survival powers. It may be called a motion that leads to definite results, but it has a unity of its own that cannot be analyzed.

We assume purposive acts in nature, plants, animals, etc., that are more than the energies constituting them, at least from the nonmechanical viewpoint. Such purposiveness is independent of any mind; organisms maintain themselves and in their action they proceed toward ends, and when the end is reached the act ceases. The vitalistic view sees in propagation something more than an act resting on physical force or energy; there is another kind of force involved. But what we observe is things maintaining themselves and working towards ends which are neither in the cause nor in any mind. The act, then, is a definitive entity leading up to an end. It may cease before the end is reached, if other acts supervene. It may be called a series of changes that lead up to a result that has some value to the organism but is not found inside it. Wherever we find living forms we find acts.

According to some, the universe is running down, but thermodynamic theory shows there is conservation of energy. The theory of entropy regards nature as being on a hill and running down, but living forms differ from this inasmuch as they are able to work uphill, to reinstate a lost situation. Life breaks down but arises again; a higher form emerges from a single cell; the life process pushes forward and upward.

The act is therefore more than a mere expenditure of energy. Science may assume that this reinstatement is merely an eddy, but the fact of reinstatement and building up remains.

The act reinstates a definite situation. We find that the reinstatement of the situation is a rhythmic affair; it goes on and off and thus imitates the situation that made the going off possible. From the psychological point of view it is only a borrowing process. The tendency to maintain a certain situation and to attain a higher situation is there as a part of life pushing it higher. We cannot interpret the act in terms of stimuli; if we do, we miss its significance. Rather, an impulse or a tendency to act is present, and it makes use of stimuli or selects stimuli to act, and this is characteristic of all life forms. Stimuli are means, but the tendency, the impulse, is essential for anything to be a stimulus. This tendency is what marks intelligence. We find it in all stages, perhaps even below life levels, in crystals. But intelligence is not the same as law. Intelligence is the selection by the organism of stimuli that will set free and maintain life and aid in rebuilding the form.

Mechanical explanation does not make room for this selecting process or act; there is no account of this tendency, process, or impulse. For this reason, there is no physical statement of a psychical process. Similarly, physiology gives no place to tendency or impulse; it is merely a statement of the nervous system in terms of stimuli and energy transfers. Life powers, however, set up energies that rebuild themselves. The process is thus a reversible one. All life systems have processes and impulses which must be recognized in the physiological activity of animal and plant life. Throughout all the wish-world we find the tendency or impulse to reinstate, to build up, to maintain and conserve.

Scientific psychology tends to divide the psychic situation into two parts, bifurcating states of consciousness and the causes of these states, thus setting up a sort of parallelism. This pushes all of consciousness into one field of observation and leads to the idea of the conscious world as opposed to the physical world, that of electrons and protons. This is the ground, the basis for experimental psychology, which, if carried out consistently, has no place for the act, since it can only distinguish between one state of consciousness and another, where each is merely a separate state of consciousness.

States of consciousness arise in connection with certain physiological conditions. Every psychosis has a neurosis; a certain nervous condition is paralleled by a certain physiological condition. This is a mechanical statement, where one response leads on to the next and the process is confined to the central nervous system and to the physical environment, with the assumption that there are corresponding states of consciousness. From this it would follow that states of consciousness are really passive. Under that claim there is no place for the act in the field of consciousness, if you carry out the parallelism. You cannot include the act in a statement of conscious states. The physical statement is a good working hypothesis, but it is a poor explanation or theory.

The act involves the expenditure of energy and replacing it by energy taken from some other source. This is what the living organism does; it takes the stored-up energy from what is known in psychology as the impulse. The impulse offers the occasion, and the stimulus pulls the trigger setting it off. The system sensitizes the organism to certain kinds of stimuli. Thus, the hungry animal responds in one way and the satisfied one in another; the system is not mechanical. The same stimuli do not always bring the same responses. There is a selective process dependent on the fact that the animal has an organization of responses essential for maintaining life or for reinstating the situation under which it thrives. This is the character of the act, which is calculated to maintain life under all conditions. The conscious states have no influence on the act; they only give an account of what is going on from the point of view of the parallelism.

Our psychology disregards conscious states and turns its attention to the act. It follows out the behavior of life forms. It must get into the nervous system, into the organism that makes the animal sensitive and relates the parts of the act. Behavior includes the neural organization as it functions, as well as the observed behavior of the animal. The nervous system is infinitely complex; there is an infinite number of possible acts or connections.

Science takes certain fields of experience and deals with them in an objective fashion, setting up working hypotheses. The assumption of a physiological organism in a physical environment has given rise to the concept of intelligence in biological forms. In the purely mechanistic statement there is something left over, and this is a necessary consequence of the method of physical science. Thus, if color were pigment in the object, instead of vibrations, there would be no bifurcation of nature. Science, however, demands what have traditionally been called primary and secondary qualities.

Physical science has no place for imagery or the meanings of things. Things have the meanings we find in them; the object is just there, and the experience of them is imagery. So far as physical science is concerned, all that is left over from its account of physical objects is disregarded. It interests itself in what can be controlled, stated in terms of mechanical control, which implies a direct causal relation throughout. Our scientific approach thus locates in the objects contents that the earlier philosophers put in consciousness. This is the approach of behavioristic psychology as opposed to introspective. But in the central nervous system we have to deal with introspection. Thus, if we are dealing with language, we must observe the nervous movements that accompany it, and we are driven into consciousness. Still psychology must reduce everything to behavior as far as possible.

We approach psychology in terms of attitudes, which are half psychical and half biological. You may have the same attitude in different situations. But in stating an attitude, we can refer to the position of the organism. This is what James calls the sensuous character, involving *if, but, though,* etc. It represents the ways in which we may act. We come back to a sense of differences that cannot be defined. This is stated in behaviorism; but in a situation where a man strikes another for insulting him, it is not so clear. There is a transformation in the organism, but this is just as much behavior as the blow struck. It is, however, a different type of behavior since it involves thinking. A. P. Weiss starts out with the central nervous system in electrons and protons and thence tries to reduce the entire central nervous system to a mechanical system.[1]

Behaviorism tries to get such a statement of the conditions of individuals that it can introduce controls. Thus, conduct is inside and outside, but all is behavior. We do not suggest that the organism is a physical entity without consciousness. But consciousness is only what we cannot find in overt behavior. We do not give up the significance of consciousness. When we say, "This is insulting to a man," we cannot neglect the attitude of the man, which lies in his social situation and its content. The parallelistic chain is crowded out of our statement of conduct.

The tendency of psychology is to get as complete a mechanical statement as possible and to leave in consciousness only that which cannot be gotten into behavior. Imagery is a good concept, but it is difficult to place it in a completely mechanical universe. The memory image is not located in the room where you are, and yet the image is in a certain sense there, with the spatial characteristic of extension. Its physical part has extension, but this cannot be put in the room where you are; and yet it belongs in the world in which you live. It is located out there, but it is not there. In a picture, you see more than is subtended on the retina. Consciousness does not represent a difference in entity and in

1. See Albert P. Weiss, "One Set of Postulates for a Behavioristic Psychology," *Psychological Review* 32 (1925), pp. 83–87.

stuff; it is not a case of spiritual and material. Imagery is at times an actual part of the house, depending on a functional distinction. (Thus we have the analogy between the mind acting and the crack of a whip; Where is it? It is not the whip but it is an activity of the whip.)

The distinction between color and vibration is an important one, just as are the different views of the penny, the perspectives of the realists, who try to put the content in the world, quite outside of us. So it is with color. The color of the wall is over there; or do we take a mental brush and put it on? But to speak of it as out there like a vibration is difficult and so far not possible. Therefore we use consciousness as a sort of scrap-basket for all difficulties which cannot be dealt with in terms of electrons and protons. We have, in other words, the problem of the bifurcation of nature. Behaviorism tries to get rid of this bifurcation.

We assume that there are impulses, the tendency of the organism to act in a certain way due to a sensitizing of the organism or the organization that will set free the tendency to act and to replace the energy expended in the act. Energy is expended in getting food, but the process includes or is based on a tendency aimed at replenishing energy which will keep the organism going. This is intelligence. Thus, if you wish to pick out a book, you sensitize yourself by the image of its color, size, etc., which may be a visual or motor attitude. We adjust ourselves to stimuli even if we are not aware of them, for instance, in crossing a street. This is a protective sensitization, with genetic origins. The adjustment of the organism expresses itself in impluses related to the environment. This is the character of the act; it is an impulse that maintains the life process by the selection of certain sorts of stimuli it needs. Thus, the organism creates its environment.

The Fallacy of Stimulus-Response Theory

The fallacy of the stimulus-response theory can be seen as follows. The stimulus is the occasion for the expression of the impulse. It does not hold the control mandate that psychology assumes. Rather, we start with impulses seeking expression, impulses manifested in feelings such as hunger. An impulse is an accumulation of energy that finds expression along determined lines; it is dependent for its expression upon stimuli of a definite character. The energy is there ready for expression, but this expression will be along lines determined by the structure of the organism, its sense organs, glands, muscles, etc. Impulses, therefore, require certain types of stimuli. The impulse is thus this tendency to act in the course of the life process, like the movement of moths toward a light, or of sap to the tree top. The impulses are there ready to be carried out, depending on a certain contact with nature. The stimulus is thus dependent on the structure of the organism itself.

Spencer dealt with protoplasm as transformed by physical influences from outside. This implies that protoplasm is homogeneous and is played upon by physical influences, so that the structure itself arises from the influence of forces around it. This is in keeping with the mechanical view of evolution, where the environment is like a civil service examination and the form best-adapted survives. Throughout, it is the organism that is played upon by outside influences.

But there is no indication of such a simple protoplasm. Rather it is highly complex, for it has in it all the life processes, expenditure of energy, digestion of food, circulation, reproduction. And below this there is the possibility of colloidal processes. All these processes may be regarded as explosions set off by certain types of stimuli. We do not need to call these conscious, or even vital, processes; they can be stated as mechanical impulses, conceived as processes arising from an organism with a structural relation to the environment. Some of the stimuli may be in the organism itself, but these are nonetheless part of the environment. Thus, respiration is due to salts in the blood, the presence of gland fluids, etc. Environment may be under the skin as well as outside it. For example, the body cells are still bathed in a fluid, and they still need iodine. In other words, the body still has within it a part of the ocean, and we need its salt constituents. In this inner ocean the cells continue to live and move and have their being, although the relation with the outside is indirect. Thus, the stimuli of the vital processes may be inside.

This is the basis for our consideration of the act. The act does not commence with the stimulus, although many acts seem to do so. In the instance of the firecracker exploded behind the chair, the stimulus is largely from the outside, but it depends on the organism itself as well. The more complex the structure of the organism, the more definite the stimulus must be.

The quarrel over instincts is unnecessary. It deals with behavior from the outside, and on this basis you can say there is an instinct for circulation, respiration, etc. The degree of external motion involved in instinctive behavior is determined in advance, and the degree of education is not the important point. We deal with external behavior, but there is a certain inheritance of structures in paths and synapses. The distinction between instinct and habit comes down to degrees of modification.

The way in which we move our legs is inherited, but it is subject to great change. You can teach a horse different gaits, but the movements involved are fundamentally instinctive.

The starting point of the act is the impulse and not the stimulus. Thus, in walking we are continually balancing ourselves and doing it by impulses of which we are not aware but which are nonetheless in constant operation. There are, however, some dangers for which we are not provided and to which we cannot respond, for instance, monoxide gas, whose odor we have no faculty for detecting. But the impulse is not a separate thing, like muscles and nerves. We can, it is true, stimulate the outside; and so we speak of the food impulse, as if each impulse existed by itself. But all impulses are parts of one living process. The parental impulse is on the same basis as the respiratory impulse.

The living process arose out of lower forms, from unicellular organisms that were plants or animals. From these arose complex forms and then social organizations of vertebrates and even of lower forms. Their structures are as definite as the cell-orders in animals or plants. Such is the attitude of behaviorism, and it proceeds on this as a postulate.

The role of impulse in the act can be expressed as impulse acting on the structure in the life process. We find we have been walking and did not know it (thus the story of William James back in Paris finding his way to his old college and suddenly finding himself before the door). There is no essential difference between the conscious and the unconscious process. There are only differences of degrees of consciousness. Error brings on consciousness: we use faulty grammar and then are conscious of it. Consciousness then represents a certain type of behavior.

Let us now consider the act from the standpoint of the impulse and the relation of the stimulus to the act. The act reduces to energy ready to express itself, but along lines determined by the character of the structure of the body. Intelligence lies in the selection of the stimuli that release this energy. The animal is hungry and seeks certain foods; here is intelligence, which belongs to the effort to maintain the life of the structure, or its continuance as a form. Intelligence is in the structure itself, and the process of expenditure of energy is part of the rhythmic process of maintenance. For behavior, intelligence lies in the selection of stimuli along lines determined in advance by the structure. The animal must have its food, but this food is already predetermined by the character of the organs of the animal. In other words, the organism sensitizes itself to particular sorts of stimuli. Consciousness is then the selection of those stimuli which will keep the process going. The eye responds to light, the digestive tract to proteins and hydrocarbons.

The form creates objects towards which it responds and within which it acts; it creates its environment. Food does not exist as an object till the there is an animal that can select and react to carbons and proteins. For something to be food, it must be in relationship with an organism.

Thus every form maps out its own environment, its line of influence, and so gives rise to other objects existing in relationship to the form itself. The environment emerges, and forms create environments, be they nests or homes.

A corresponding interrelationship is demanded for the form to continue to exist. Its environment may be suddenly altered, but if the form can eat something else, then the interruption of its usual diet will have no disastrous effects. Thus the ox has come to have his three stomachs, with the germs to digest away the cellulose that protects the plant from animals. Such an animal can survive a change in diet. The tiger has no such apparatus; it does not chew its food, and it feeds without the same bacteriological laboratory as the ox has. In each instance, the environment sets the conditions for the life process to continue. Organisms can create food that did not exist before as food. Thus humans have their stockyards to do the job for them.

Organisms Determine Their Environments–The Meaning of Intelligence

The selection of stimuli that occasion the expression of impulse is intelligence, and the impulse itself is a tendency to keep the process going. Behavior thus goes back to the life process. Environment is thus the creation of objects and, by this relationship, giving new content to things that did not have it before. If you assume that spatial dimensions are determined by the relative velocity of the observer and the object, you assume that the organism determines the distance of the object, and the world becomes what its frame of reference is. It can be in the nature of a grid, or in the nature of a chemical reaction, like the reactions of the digestive tract. Each organism puts its frame of reference on the world and gets its food. It creates an environment that is now there in nature. One must guard against setting up a uniform mechanism and putting everything in consciousness. The form has been there all the time, but the food is there only in the presence of the eye of the ox. Apart from this, it is only electrons and protons. But the electrons happen to be determined by the relationship between the intellect of the physicist and the proton; so the organism of the scientist also determines what the object out there is.

The biologist draws a line around the limits of an animal and the conditions necessary to its safety, but the line is not there in nature.

Intelligence is the selection of the stimuli that keep the life process going. The form is an organization of impulses, and it exercises intelligence in selecting the occasion for their expression. The process starts with dioxides and water, then passes into starches, sugars, etc., and finally ends with carbonic acid and N_2O.

The creation of the environment is more evident in the case of the human form than any other. We can determine what plants and animals shall exist, the organic content of our drinking water, the presence of smoke in our air, and, by our mechanical devices, the temperature at the poles or at the equator. We can even determine strains and traits in progeny. Throughout, this is a control of the environment. We use clothes and food to complete in external fashion what other forms do internally. Thus the bird picking up or selecting a grain is acting like a man determining his environment by external behavior.

The selective process is the process of constituting the object. We widen the field of intelligence, we show it in behavior, and we see in the display of intelligence a constitution of the environment. (When there are eyes color emerges.) The psychologist starts with life—this is the field of behavior and is properly the field of behaviorist psychology. The organic selection is in the form and the environment.

The selection of stimuli is the intelligence of the form. Intelligence is not consciousness as such, for the plant is expressing intelligence in getting its own protoplasm. The human animal is more elaborate but nonetheless an animal. It carries out its intelligence in a more refined manner; and what the animal takes millennia to accomplish, man may do in a few generations or years by selective breeding to improve particular stimuli that lead to the expression of impulses.

The life process is identical physically and chemically in all forms; it varies only in its situation. Respiration, digestion, mating and reproduction all belong to the life processes; and all are possible through selection of types of stimuli that set them free. By this selection the form constitutes its own environment, which it transforms and bounds, even to changing the physical matter in the human society. There is greater completeness in the expression of the life process here than among other forms, for the human form can determine its own plants, animals, temperature—things that might be reached through evolutionary process but only in the course of many years. The human can indeed go to the sea bottom, although it cannot become a fish.

The stimulus is thus an organized and selected occasion referred to as the environment, this being due to the activity of the form itself. The form has to live in a group of stimuli, which constitute the environment and also determine the form, because the form responds to the environment. The stimulus thus not only sets free the response, but it also forms and transforms the environment, which through the conduct of the form itself has a fundamental and characteristic relationship to the form as a distant object. Energy comes in from the sun and currents move the amoeba about, but in this instance the response is to the contact object and experience, not to the distant. The amoeba cannot get into relationship with objects at a distance. This is the case with the human ear and nose; there must be actual contact or its equivalent. But we do not live in an environment of the photochemical work of the retina. We live in a world of distant objects, of automobiles, of symbols. We do not need to identify color or taste with any object; sound may be in the head or in the room; stars may come from a blow on the head. In all these cases we act with reference to things not there, distant objects. This the amoeba cannot do; it is merely a jelly.

Distant Objects, Space and Time

Distant objects are distant, it is true, in terms of vision; and yet the blind live in terms of distant objects. In this instance, the relationship is of another character than that of color and light; sound and touch are refined. It is in fact possible to cut off one channel after another and still have intelligent responses. You cannot, in other words, shut off the experience of the distant object entirely. The blind will be sensitive to movements of air about objects which they cannot see and cannot reach; people in the dark will also feel this when they cannot see the furniture causing the air currents.

Distance implies spatial-temporal separation. Space-time is an abstraction from the relations of events to each other. Instead of being part of an absolute field, space and time merely belong to different relationship systems. For different series of events there are different organizations of space and time.

Thus, the character of the distant object, from the point of view of conduct, is in terms of movement of the form with reference to it. The completion of the act will either bring the form to the food or make good its escape from an enemy. Such movement, then, springs from a contact relationship with the environment which is spatially and temporally distant, but this rests on an earlier contact experience. Space and time are thus products of experience. In the railway coach we have a different order of space and time from the order we have when outside walking or lying in the sun of a summer's day. The passenger in the train finds the telegraph poles rushing past him; for the dozer nothing moves.

Furthermore, the world we live in has right and left, up and down. It has a bilateral symmetry. We do not use two right-hand gloves, and it makes considerable difference how far you are from the ground when you jump down. For mathematics there is none of this, neither right nor left, up nor down.

This bilateral symmetry arises from the sensitivity of the head; the whole organism is adjusted with reference to the head. This bilateral character, giving different reactions from the two sides of the form, is the basis of the process of locomotion; and the responses are functionally equal to each other as the animal approaches a distant object. The organism, in other words, must be balanced. Distance thus reduces to the equivalent of a walk of a certain number of steps, and the line of vision is thus made up of a set of responses broken up in our structure into a set of functions. Distance becomes, in functional terms, so many steps off, so that the wall may call out a stimulus of thirty steps or five. This, however, lies along the vision, which in turn is organized on a bilateral basis. That stimuli from the distant object affect both eyes is what assures the direct course. But here again, the muscular bilateralism makes for keeping true to the line; there must be equal pull on both sides. The erect position itself springs from a double lateral organization or responses, right and left, front and back. Thus the responses register an equal influence on both sides.

The nature of the act in its distance character is revealed in the changes in motion by which actual contact is attained or avoided. The stimulus is the occasion for the reaction that leads to contact and governs motion from the standpoint of the relation of contacts to each other. Reality reduces to possible contact experience, and distance and time are abstractions from contact experience.

The character of space and time derive from the nature of the organism in the environment. Distance is first of all the number of steps it takes to reach an object, and this is finally reduced to sets of equal elements that represent the total distance. This, as we have shown, depends in turn on the bilateral symmetry of the organism; from this arises the relationship among the physical things of experience. The physical thing is a something located through our tendency to approach it, or a something that arouses distance stimuli. There are no dimensions or boundaries, no static space—this occurs only in the space-time world, the conceptual world as distinguished from the perceptual. In the conceptual world we can have curved space, but not in the perceptual. (The former, however, is more convenient for scientific purposes.) The stimuli that help us to reach or avoid objects lie behind the space continuum.

In the world of physical things distance is a matter of responses, and it may be stated in terms of rhythmical responses that bring about contacts. When we say there is such a thing as something-or-other, we mean that if we move or get contact experience, it will be of such and such a character. Distance is a structure in behavior and should not be separated from other processes, nutritive, sexual, etc. Distance demands a fundamental equation: How many steps must we take to reach the object? It is possible to set up a conceptual space-time independent of such experience; mathematics does this in the form of fundamental postulates. But the extended world in which we live has its ups and downs, seasons and distances, all depending on our organism and its perspectives.

The structure of the act involves a relationship to a distant object, primarily through the eye. This visual experience is related to the process by which we reach for or avoid objects. Nativists assume that all experiences are spatial or extensive, and the development of the eye merely gives the visual data, other data being gotten from senstive skin-spots. But space is a correlation of elements gotten in vision with elements of manipulation, a correlation of vision and touch. Distant objects are stimuli calling out effort to move to or from them. Much here depends on the horizon. One looks over a wall, sees a birdbox and takes it for a distant cathedral; or one sees a gnat in his eye and takes it for a soaring eagle. In short, we build up our space-time on the basis of our responses.

In manipulation or contact the hand is of fundamental importance, and its high development is a mark of the intelligence of the human. The human is a tool-using animal who uses implements that can extend the length or power of the hand. The higher mentality of apes is their ability to use tools or means for physical ends. The mouth also has much of this power, being able to surround objects. Considered biologically, the act should be recognized as starting with the distant stimulus, for instance, with the food process. The act divides into mediation and consummation, getting and eating. Our world, as a physical world, is built up of contact experience through the hand. The dog's world is built up of odors. There is no world of physical experience between the stimuli for him, but we separate the mediate experience from the consummatory process. The atom, on this basis—tactile experience—is reached by a process of crumbling analysis carried to its extreme.

Objects are there for us only as occasions for feeling impulses in the organism. There are distant objects, but what they are in perception is contact-experience that we may have when we get hold of them. The wall is something one can get hold of, something that calls for so much resistance; but it consists of bricks, and one may follow this analysis further with the microscope and still further in the imagination by reducing oneself to the size of a Lilliputian. But the minimum visible object is like the distant object; reality reduces to contact-experience.

The Manipulatory Phase of the Act and Consummation

Manipulation lies between the beginning of the act and final consummation. The act from which the physical world arises stops before consummation. We can approach consummation in terms of the physical object, not vice versa. Successful digestion of food is a relation of physical particles. Consummation must be described in terms of the physical object that appears in the process of attainment or avoidance of the distant stimulus. Contact is what gives reality to the stimulus. Color, sound, etc., are perceptual when contact is realized by setting free the stimulus. Consummation in the case of eating is in terms of ultimate particles, fingerable. This is the nature of the perceptual object; it lies inside the act as a whole and is the field of intelligence. In the exercise of intelligence in perceptual experience we carry consummation as far as possible in the physical object. The perceptual incites to the physical experience; it is a reality that is short of consummation.

The materialist offers a technique which we use as far as possible, but we prefer the idealistic technique. We do not get successful control of life by simply following our impulses. We must state things scientifically, biochemically, before we can make up at the drugstore for the lack of pep.

The manipulatory phase of the act is concerned with the means of living, and we try to make the statement of means as complete as possible. We consider ends in terms of means. In building a house we must consider the desire for the house in financial terms and state it in dollars and cents before we can have any consummation. One must state the end in terms of means—this is intelligence. The intelligent man applies means to achieve results. Objects of perception are distant stimuli filled out in contact if the invitation to approach is carried out in contact.

The final stage is the result, or the consummatory phase of the act; what is real comes in between the means and the end. For control, the end must be translated into terms of means. The interest in biochemistry is found in health. For control, everything is stated in terms of contact-experience. Man uses intelligence as a tool just as much when he uses one act as a means toward another, as when he uses a material tool. In the dog there is no break between means and end; all is one, contact and eating and fighting. For the human, food is a perceptual object before being eaten; grain is prepared as flour and dough and then baked. From contact and crumbling analysis the physical world of particles arises. This is the fundamental equation. We divide the world with a line that passes from the cyclopean eye above the two eyes we use. This is a fundamental act, responsible for the sensuous world of our experience. Science can state space as order in coexistence or as an abstraction from the sensuous element of distance. But measured time and space arise from an abstraction from experience. (Bergsonian time and space is a sensuous postulate.)

The actual world is the world of our percepts. The problem of the relationship to sensuous qualities and the physical situation, the problem of mind and body, is not settled in psychology. We present it in terms of the act as such. The postulate of mind as the locus of a spiritual protoplasm is unwarranted. Our perceptual postulates are the tools or instruments used by the animal to reach its goal, and the perceptual object is filled in with contact experience that would be realized if the invitation to approach it were to be followed out. Distance experience acts as a stimulus, but there is no response unless there is something in the system ready to go off. It is like a Yale key and a Yale lock. You can take the distance experience as an abstraction, but it means a stimulus. If we do not approach the object, we fill it in with imagery. The wall is then something hard and cold and colored, but the experience is essentially what we get by handling it.

The involvement of pleasure in some acts is still a problem; thus the distinction between the content of a beefsteak and the pleasure we get from eating or consuming it is still problematic. The statement is thus one of perceptual means and is coincident with our human intelligence. It is a means for the attainment of ends. The hand is master of the human body and the basis of the central nervous system. It is thus the control means in conduct; it resolves things by its grasp and analyzes means and ends.

The act is differentiated from the perceptual and consummatory attitude. Beginning and consummation are not perceptual phases. Perception in the psychology was simple awareness, not visual experience. We start with the impulse that sensitizes the organism to the occasion that sets it free and we isolate the distance of the object appearing in the content of the stimulus. We include anticipation of the result that will follow the act. This may be imagery, for instance, the image of the responses that would occur should you go to the wall. (In thinking, there is a partial articulation of key words.) The result of the act may be in the beginning of the process; you may have in your attitude the perceptual goal out there. Or it may be in the attitude itself, the sort of adjustment you have to make to the objects about you. There are always attitudes answering to the things about you, adjustments of the individual to the object. For all of these objects there are organized attitudes capable of indefinite adjustment to immediate situations. The habit of sitting down and opening a book is modified by the size of the book, whether it be small or large. Physical things are then distant objects answering to the attitudes we have formed toward them.

No Physical Things for Lower Animals

There is a functional difference between contact and distance experience. Our intelligence consists in using contact experiences to reach the consummation implied by the act. Lower forms do not live in a world of physical things; their contacts are consummations, and there are no intermediate means. We can stretch out the act and shorten the consummation, and this implies the rational character of our intelligence, namely, the ability to relate means to ends.

Such a statement does not convey the experience of the animal being an object to himself. He is surrounded by objects, but he is a point in the center. He is not acting in reference to himself but in reference to other objects. The individual is not a percept in the perceptual world, but he is stimulated by any object he can see or feel. Hands, etc., are thus objects in the field, close to the center of the act, but they are not perceived as a body that is a physical self.

What the eye sees is an object one can scratch or reach. For man, objects get into the percept by means of images, even when it concerns his own self. This the animals cannot do. To be a physical object to yourself you must get outside yourself, but not only through contact with the surface of your body, for the dog can do this.

In setting up mind and awareness you set up an object outside the mind. In this sense the body may be an object to which we react. In responding to distant objects, the reaction goes out from a point in the body, some say the cyclopean eye, others the chest, others the throat; and from this point the body itself acts. Thus one may trip on his own foot, bite his own tongue.

We state these attitudes in terms of awareness and in terms of conduct, but awareness is the starting point of conduct. This does not give the animal body as content; this is a relationship beyond the physical object.

Intelligence which states ends in terms of means is a human development, superior to the animal's. Mind is the exploitation of human intelligence; it involves getting oneself into the field of one's action. Intelligence is already there in the relationship of the individual to the distant object. Mind is a definite use of means to ends.

Part of the act is the process by which the human makes use of tools. In the eating process, the object is a perceptual one related to the organism by its distance stimulation. As a result of reaching the distant object, the object comes into the manipulatory area, and consummation follows. The distant object may be thousands of miles or many years away, but we live in an environment of distant objects, each of which we tend to approach.

The manipulatory experience is the perceptual reality of the object. The object is real if we can finger it. Perception is thus constantly checked up on by tactile experience. The things we see at a distance or smell or hear all call for contact-experience as real objects of perception.

The act includes consummation, and the perceptual process is the means by which consummation is achieved. Insofar as the process occurs, the perceptual object is reached. Consummation may be described in terms of various physiological processes, but no one assumes that actual thought or good health is a movement of particles. Good health may be caused by such movements, but it is not itself the movements. In the same way, we may say that money makes it possible to build houses, but the house is not money. Only in one sense can we state the end in terms of the means.

In this phase of the act we identify reality with contact experience, for with contact experience the act is completed. Contact experience gives the reality of the thing sensed at a distance. The difference between sensing at a distance and contact experience corresponds to the distinction between primary and secondary qualities. We must avoid merging everything together as sensations; there is a functional difference between distance and contact experience. The former represents what appears, but reality comes only in the actual contact. A piece of chalk calls for analysis into a scientific object, so that from the scientific standpoint it is a distant object even when we hold it in our hand, for we are still far from our goal. Science tends to wipe out the difference between primary and secondary qualities; to feel an object is to be no closer to it than to see its color, so far as the final analysis of its reality is concerned. If the molecule is the ultimate element, then contact is still a long distance from the reality. We cannot state color in terms of color, but we state it in terms of the movement of particles that we can get hold of only conceptually. With tools and food the reality is in the final manipuulation, and sight, smell, and sound are occasions for getting hold of it. These are two sorts of experience that should not be merged in the general word "sensation."

The reality of the object is found in the consummation at the end of the act; resistance and distance experience may be simply the occasion for the act. If the process is not carried out, the distance experience stands for the contact experience; the sight of the tree stands for the contact we have with the tree when we run into it. In this case it may represent danger, but when we are pursued by a bull it represents safety. The notion of a goal is what leads to the second phase in the development of human intelligence, the use of tools. The beaver and the dog use their jaws as tools; so does the bird its bill in carrying material to its nest. But this use is not carried very far even in the ant, the bee, or the wasp. There is thus no real human intelligence in their use of these organs as tools.

The further phase in the development of human intelligence is the actual entering into contact with the implication of the distance stimulus, that it may be an object of contact experience. Most of our objects appear in experience; we are in actual contact with only a little part of our environment. But it does not follow that the objects we are not in contact with are any less real. The implication of the contact experience constitutes for us the reality of the world in which we live. One goes downtown and feels that one has come into contact with the reality of the Loop.[2]

But it does not follow that experience should include these implications. An absentminded person can undress and not know what he is doing; he may start out to prepare for dinner and find himself in pajamas in bed. A person has mind insofar as the consummatory phase of the act is controlling the manipulatory phase. What is peculiarly important is the recognition of the significance of the entry of the implications of action into our experience. How does meaning get into things? Some answer this in terms of imagery: we must see the wall and have images of what we see, its hardness, etc. These things fill in the act. There is thus perception that does not proceed into the act;

2. "The Loop" refers to the elevated railway transit system that circles downtown Chicago.

it is a collapsed act. In auditory experience we make use of speech in place of contact experience. We may have experience of the dog from the mere word "dog." If someone denies that we are having this experience, saying that our definition is wrong, we appeal to a dictionary, still having no contact experience with the dog. Here is the difference between word and image. In the case of the word there is a certain experience that answers to the musculature of the organ. There is a muscle image when a person says "dog." (Some people are wearied in their vocal cords by merely listening.)

It is difficult to state the implication of the distance experience. Manipulation does constitute the world in which we live; but without trying to resolve things into physical elements, we reject the collocation of states of consciousness as constituting the percept. The object is something that offers the occasion for the response and spells the difference between the stimulus and spiritual experience. Apart from the importance of the perceptual object, most objects are representative experience only by association plus something that gives the perceptual experience. Most of our world consists of objects of this nature, distance experience plus its implications. But one asks: To what is the implication of the perceptual object due? It is not an image, for in imagery there is no more than words spoken, heard, or seen. Speech stands for the content of the act itself; we can tell ourselves and others what a spade is. This content mediates what we ourselves feel in a spade, it describes the perceptual object, so that language is a medium for communication. It makes the content explicit so that we can tell others what the object is.

The language process sets free a set of other acts, a set of reactions that could take place if there were actual contact. In psychological terms, the language process represents a set of attitudes of the organism.

There are uses for objects, and these constitute the nature of the object for us. The meaning an object has for us is in our attitude or how we intend to react to it. They are attitudes in the individual that represent readiness to act. This is all that is present in experience if there is no actual contact; we are ready to sit on the chair if we get to it.

In the total body of reactions the contact experiences are almost negligible. There are only a few things in the environment which we actually get hold of. We may be subject to illusion in our experiences, but we retain them until actual contact disproves them; and for general purposes the percept has a contact content not different from actual contact experience. I need not have contact experience of a distant stimulus to be able to see it as hard, soft, cold, pleasurable, or painful.

The difference in contact experience given by percept or by imagery is only slight, that of motor or contact imagery only. We depend on language symbols and the attitude of response. It may be a pattern of coordination in the central nervous system, but we have a definite way of acting toward a dog, a horse, or a cat, our property and other people's property. These attitudes imply manipulation of objects and are part of the responses.

Getting this content into the percept is important. We may represent the world as a distance stimulus, the occasion, for example, of seizing food and eating it. This process lies within the field of intelligence, but the percept involved is not a percept of food as a human finds it in immediate experience. The perception of food is a distance experience in which the approach, the contour, the taste are given in the percept. But I see it as food, so the values are in the individual perceiving it.

We can speak of an attitude as a tendency to move towards an object, which changes as the approach is made—all of which enters into the object and makes it what it is. Our perception involves the attitude of going out, covering the distance from the organism to its content, and this is part of its meaning. The perceptual object has content as it appears in experience, subject to criticism and test, comparison with other things when we get to it. The orange may be sour or unripe; we may perceive one object and find ourselves eating another.

There is thus a consummatory element in the perceptual experience. In the world of the lower animals and of children, the stimulus does not call out all its implications. The question then becomes, How can we get the content into the object? How can we get the meaning of the object into the object? We can approach this from the standpoint of the anatomy of the central nervous system. There are certain responses mapped out in the brain, and thus content occurs in terms of attitudes. In this case, the stimulation of one tract arouses an attitude that puts a content into the object. In the afterglow there is no imagery; it may be merely a memory image due to the innervation of the retina. Faces seen on retiring or by eyelight are an instance of this phenomenon. These responses put a content into the object, but the content comes wholly from past experience. In reading, for instance, we go by jumps, all based on past experience of the looks of words. Science uses models, pictures of stones, to think out the nature of change in experience. But this is still of a perceptual character, since the object must be conceived although it does not reduce to a contact experience. This occurs in working out the history of the iron atom, its jumping from orbit to orbit. In this case, even if one were small enough to see, the particles could not be perceived because they do not subtend light on this small scale and the retina cannot respond. If this electron galaxy had an original content produced by rays of light caused by vibrations, it could not be perceived, although a Lilliputian could finger the particles.

Extended objects can be continuously subdivided, although we may get beyond the spot that can stimulate the human being. We retain the assumption of possible contact as a piece of imagery, however. When the scientists puts forward a model, he is talking of a conceptual object; but science advances by perceptual representations of, for instance, protons; this is the basis from which it works.

The Content of the Perceptual World and Meaning

Thus we live in a perceptual world when we speak of matter, but in introducing content into the object we introduce the problem of the content of consciousness. We speak of the central nervous system as there, and then we speak of the consciousness that goes with the nervous process. The object is there, however, and so is the organism, before there is any consciousness; consciousness comes only after the tract has been stirred up. This act or stimulus brings consciousness and puts content into the object. But this content is linked with past experience. We put old contents into the object; but when we ask what part the brain plays, we come back to a solipsism in which all is in consciousness. But we want to get rid of consciousness as an affection of the individual that arises with certain nervous processes. We wish to leave the content in the object. Science leaves some content in the object, but it confesses that not all content can be left there. It leaves the electrons there and explains them on the basis of certain experiences the object has had. But color is not part of the object, although the object must be there for us to have color stimulation.

There is thus a difference between the scientific object and the object one sees, and the problem is then to get content into the object and allow it to remain there. The penny, for instance, has many different perspectives. In one sense they are identical, but on the other hand they are different for each individual. Thus, while we do not wish to put the whole content of the object in the mind, some of it must be put there; and we put it in consciousness because it is the condition for the experience of other contents. In the case of color, for instance, we must consider the action of the molecule out there, the nature of the medium, and the reaction of the retina; and for these, past experience is the condition.

Our problem then becomes how to state the content of the percept in terms of behavior. To do this, you must set up distance experience and say the object is there anyway.

Universals

We wish now to describe the value the logician calls "universal," one that transcends the immediate experience of the stimulation and goes beyond the distance content.

Most of the objects in our environment are in the nature of perceptual experience; we touch or reach few of them. But if we see the object and do not touch it, we still get content into it, so that seeing becomes believing. In this study we confine ourselves to the perceptual world, where we tend to move to the object and get contact experience that makes implemental use possible.

We can get content into perception by means other than contact. There are fields of sensation; we can get contact experience by air currents, through skin sensation which together with past experience can be built into an image. But this is a dubious field, for we do not depend on contact experience for reality. We have no image of pressure when we look at a wall and say it is hard. The significant thing is the individual's attitude. We are ready to act in a certain way; our approach is governed by the attitude we would assume on getting to the thing.

There is the possibility of mapping out regions in the central nervous system which, on being innervated, bring forth attitudes. But the central nervous system is only a series of paths which may be opened or closed or may be differently organized through different connections in the synapses, different junctures of the dendrites. But to speak of retention in the central nervous system we must consider the maintaining of the paths. The passage through one dendrite is easier than through another. There are definite organizations in the central nervous system; it is not a jungle, but we do not know what goes on in it. There are many protoplasmic extensions from the cells; when a certain correlation is made and used it becomes a readier path. This is the only permanent element in it. There are no fixed images of red, blue, etc., but there are attitudes called forth by them as stimuli. In instances of poisoning, for instance, there is an increased excitement of the organism which eventually throws the whole out of order. It is characteristic of the higher forms that reactions are not limited to one path but can take many different paths. There is a certain set of paths readily used by the nervous excitement under certain conditions. There is thus selection in habit, and the stimulus will tend to flow on identical paths. These paths may be mapped out congenitally or they may be the result of earlier reactions.

These are not immediate responses; the immediate response is moving towards food. There are connections that come as the individual advances. When he approaches a tree, there are connections ready to go off in order; he sees the tree, when he is near it he is ready to jump up in it, put a leg over a limb, etc., depending on the social situation. All this is part of the organization of the stimuli. The organism is sensitive to odor when it is hungry and not when it is sated; it is sensitive to books when in search of a particular one. All this is a readiness to respond when the proper stimulus appears. It is a selective faculty of imagery. A successful march through a room requires that one be ready to avoid obstructions, but this future aspect is affecting the organism *now*. The tendency is thus to act in response to things that play back into the act and make possible the advance through the room. This is imagery, it is the attitude resting on later responses. In reading one must first become familiar with a man's style, and then all goes well. In the same way, we anticipate what a speaker is about to announce and finish his sentence for him (much to his annoyance). But there is no image of the sentence, merely readiness to respond in a certain way. It is like knowing a verse of poetry—you know it when you are prepared to recite it.

It is like a chain-response in insects, or commensalism among other forms, which may be responsible, for instance, for setting off the stimuli involved in building a nest. If any step is removed the act cannot proceed. Thus, in night moths there are complex responses which are closely connected and limited to short periods of time, all depending on stimuli being present.

In the human, however, we can seek out and select the stimulus and thus set up a selected sensitization. There is always an alternative process ready; if you cannot reach the fruit by knocking it down, you can climb. In this instance, the act may be completed in alternative ways. The attitude you will assume when you get in contact with the thing depends thus on its content. This is what makes the percept. Sight has meaning, therefore, insofar as it calls up readiness to act toward the object. The memory of driving a nail reinforces the ability to do it; the memory of a sonata is the readiness to execute it.

The attitude is perfected through the central nervous system, but the central nervous system itself is merely a series of objects, filaments, and nodes. Still the attitude gives us the content and the meaning of the object seen.

Things are spatiotemporally away from us because in perception they exist simultaneously with us. From this temporal standpoint the world is hypothetical, and its content is the way in which we will act when we get there. The mechanism of putting content into the object is symbolism. Things which stand for a later stage of the act play a part in the earlier stage; the ultimate act of driving a nail is for us the meaning of the hammer.

Behaviorism versus Introspective Psychology

Introspective psychology tries to discover the memory image and combine it with the distant stimulus. Behaviorism tries to be free from introspection and to deal with phenomena without it. For behaviorism the contact experience resulting from the act is the reality of the object. But the process of the act does not begin with the stimulus—there is already in the organism a tendency to make an adjustment. This accounts for the violent response in most protective acts, such as jumping out of the way of the speeding car. Our percepts are there in experience without the contact experience, for most of our actions do not involve actual contact with the physical object.

We return, then, to the fact that the fundamental content of the thing is the attitude called forth by contact responses which are constantly present in the process by which we approach the thing. But if "what we are going to do" is in the act determining it, it is something that influences the process by which we approach the object. The contact attitude is then in the act before there is contact experience. We approach the house from the point of view of how we are going to enter. But this is not the content of the percept. These attitudes may be in the act determining the response and yet not be present as reality or in isolable form. They do not appear in experience. You can note the cliff and see the places where you can climb up; but this does not reduce to contact experience, since you may never have climbed up or may not need to climb up now. The response merely sensitizes you to the stimuli that will help you carry out the act. This is not the reality of the object, however; to get this into the act this sort of element must be isolated.

Distant stimuli are representative of contact, and as such they stand for what the experience would be if we made contact. Everything has its date attached to it from the point of view of the individual. To get this reality into the percept itself we must be able to separate it, isolate it from other parts of experience.

Our perceptual experience presents the world at a moment, compresent with the individual. And our perception is of a world that is there now; we have stopped the process of passage that characterizes the specious present. Perception stops everything and presents a slab of the universe, the world at an instant, fixed in all relations. You have to deal with the reality of the wall now, immediately, not when you get there; so the question is, what is there in the experience that is a surrogate for the contact experience? Imagery is fleeting and uncertain, and yet the act contains the attitude of using the thing or manipulating it. This is a future contact given in the present, and it is in the attitude itself. In perception there is the halting of time and space as extensions.

The reality of the object is what is now and what will be experienced later by contact. This is the percept. Thus, we do not perceive color but the object that has the color. At a concert we perceive the music of the orchestra, but where is it, in the instrument or in the head? We perceive sense (Russell). So far as we perceive the object, we perceive no indefinite percepts. But apart from the experience in which we do perceive, there is the implication of something we could get into contact with if we got near enough.

Sound is a certain vibration that may be in the room, in the ear or in the instrument. Science considers the vibrating wave of air.

On the other hand, there may be perception without our being aware of it. We remove the hand from the hot radiator before we know what we perceive. So on the side of the cliff one becomes dizzy and must stop perceiving. (It is not always wise to perceive.)

Associational Psychology and Perception

Associational psychology holds that perception is an association of states of awareness. For this association to be a percept it must be permanently associated with other elements of experience. But associational psychologists say we see the object and this calls up images drawn from earlier contact experience of the object.

What we actually see has no immediate associations. We go back to past experience, and so sight is associated with other experiences. The association of immediate sight with former vision, with going toward and feeling the table—all this is involved in the perception. The ocular image is faint but it is there. Two optical illusions at least are involved.

This associationist view of perception is still given in many textbooks. Gestalt psychology protests against this, saying there is no simple sensation of the color itself. Sensation occurs only through a configuration. The separate sensation is not there; it is the result of abstraction and does not exist by itself. There is always some sort of configuration or whole given in perception.

The problem is thus to explain how perception is more than the stimulus that frees the response seeking expression.

Behaviorism helps us get rid of the old psychological talk of abstraction. There is, besides this, readiness to respond; and this is already there in the act, but not in the form of imagery, as was proposed by Locke, Berkeley, Hume, Mill, and Bain. We deal with the object in terms of attitudes, in motor terms. We see that the attitude can be there determining the process of the act, but this does not yield the percept. It is only a selected occasion, not a sense. We go no further. All that this gives is a selected group of stimuli by the organism that is ready to act. The selection of the occasion is determined by the structure of the organism. It is much like the chain-instincts of insects; but in the case of humans the later stage of the act is always there controlling the process that leads to the result. In the insect the next step is never present in the earlier stage.

The process is thus in constant change, such as appears in unconscious operations; and we act from the point of view of the immediate situation.

Gestalt theory says the configuration is there. What is there in behavior to show how the content gets into it? How do we perceive the hammer before we grasp it? This is our present problem.

The Social Element in Perception

The mechanism of this lies in the selection of the character that comes through symbolic experience. The process that controls the act from the standpoint of the attitude is isolated in the symbolic experience, for instance when in using the hammer we refer to the use of the hammer. The real meaning of the object is what you are going to do with it when you reach it. Thus all crude definitions always refer to an act; for a child, the spade is something to dig with.

The symbolism of imagery is often irrelevant. Thus, in sleep or in drowsiness we use irrelevant symbols to connect things. The bridge-player thinks of his friends as cards. The same character is seen in the old sciences of numerology and astrology, where an absolute relevance was tied to the name itself. But the important thing is that experience calls out the content. Without the ability to bring the attitude into relation with the object, there is no percept. The perception of a physical thing involves the presentation of the attitude we take when we get hold of the object.

There are two different phases of perception: (1) selection of the stimuli—we approach the hammer to grasp it, and thus the later part of the act is present in the earlier stage; (2) the response that brings this attitude into the experience to develop the control that we exercise. The latter is what social conduct has established. When we perceive, we not only control the approach, but our attitude to it stands out as an experience that can control the whole process.

An individual without a social structure has a different object from that of an individual in a social structure. A hammer is not a hammer to a gorilla. If all this is expressed in terms of images, everything is put on the same level; but this is not the nature of perception. At the same time, we have responses to a distant stimulus and to what it is. So there is no such thing as imageless thought. A man could pick up a hammer and drive a nail without there being any perception; but when the hammer is pointed out in isolation, then there is perception. The percept is thus a collapsed act which gets its full meaning only in the social structure of the group. This amounts to locating the meaning of the stimulus in the act.

In speaking of social conduct, we assume individuals with minds and feelings, in possession of social conduct. The individual cannot get ideas except through social conduct. We rouse the idea in the thing; it is only in the mythology of psychology that we take the hammer and put it into the head. We put it into the mind in a certain sense, but the character of the object lies in the object itself. The act is not to be located inside the brain; it belongs to the organism in its environment. Hammerness is in the hammer. This comes about through social mechanisms within a social structure.

The content of the percept is only secured by the organization of the organism's attitudes. Psychology called this the fixed association of psychical contents, but this overlooks the distant contact values of the perception of physical objects. The act of removing the hand from the hot radiator is not a matter of perceiving. We must know something before we can perceive it or see it from a distance. The resultant must be there in the first visual experience. We cannot express this by saying that the object seen is partly built up of previous images. Everything is in the attitude of the individual that will be expressed on approach. This attitude, as present in the experience, is the nature of the act. It may be present in experience as direction and organization, and not as perception. Our act can be directed by what we are going to do without any percept. In the percept we refer to the element of grasping; this is the perception of the object. What Gestalt psychology involves is a reference to the content of the organization of the whole organism. There may be stimuli in illustrations without there being any things.

The percept is problematical; we see it and put our hand on it, but it is not there. Still, the percept does enter into experience. Behavioristic psychology gives a mechanism that brings out this characteristic of the percept.

This whole matter is tied up with patterns of social conduct. For the child, stimuli are not objects in his experience. Conduct represents: (1) the occasion that sets free the response, (2) the conduct that becomes directive. Movement, in this instance, is directed and has meaning. The passage of the end of the act into the process of stimulation is an attribute of intelligence and is expressed later in the percept. Mere organization does not carry the idea of the percept; it only involves a chain of action, such as we have in the insect world. The object is a stimulus in relation to the response. The response seeking a stimulus picks it out from the environment. The passage of the saw along the line helps the eye as much as the line itself. These relationships are given in the case of reaction and in the conduct of animals that are secure in their own field of conduct, not needing percepts for their coordination. The development of the infant is in the line of being able to pick out stimuli. His conduct is directed largely by those around him. Parents take the attitude of children, but at the same time they give the child toys of their own construction, things that amuse them as well as the child. In fact, many things can be interesting to both, like *Alice in Wonderland*. The adult, in this process, is constantly indicating to the child the results of his own motions: the ball is something to get hold of and throw. Things done with the object are referred to the child, so that when the child plays he will see the end and learn to pick out the object's ultimate use. The child plays with all the things that the adult uses, although his objects may not be identical with the adult's, or they may be symbolic. A broken plate and a bit of wood will make a tea party for the child, whereas for us such a stimulus is inadequate. Through all this the child is busy getting the meaning of things. This is much the case in the play period of lower animals; they are learning things they will need later—meanings. For this end the ball will serve the kitten as a mouse.

Hume held that the fox has a congenital aversion to man's odor. This is false; in fact the behavior of the mother conditions the fox, and thus a certain set of stimuli are organized. The response here calls out the stimulus; what the individual will do tends to determine the selection of

his stimuli. In contrast with those of children, the play periods for the
insect are not necessary, for its responses are congenitally determined.

In the activity of the child, perception may not necessarily enter to
begin with. The child may move around the rooms of a house and not
perceive that it is a house; the perception is something that goes beyond
the visual experience. Thus, in selecting a group for his associates, the
newcomer first sees the entire group and later has the experience of the
individuals of the group. It is only when the child leaves home for the
first time that he perceives his house as a whole. This whole had been
there, but the child had never perceived its content in experience. The
whole end of the relation of the adult with the child is to bring out this
sort of response. The process is there, but there is no segregation or isolation of the content of the response.

The Ambiguous Character of the Percept

Psychology breaks up the percept into primary and secondary qualities,
putting the latter in consciousness. The *what* of the thing is the content
as perceived. A rebuff represents an attitude that reduces to a motor
experience. The distinction of tones in physical terms is merely a
phenomenon of vibrations, but this is not the thing that is experienced
in the discrimination of different tones. One tone is heard as higher
than another. Does this mean higher in the number of vibrations? For
the individual this relationship is something different from what it is in
science, where things are analyzed from the physical standpoint. H. L.
Hollingworth maintains that the relationship of tones is due to a relationship of sensuous experiences, not to a logical deduction. These
relations are representative relations and are no more fixed than representations in other fields. The perception of the tone in your throat is
of the same nature as your perception of one lady in the form of an ace
of spades or a two-spot.

There is thus a distinction between the world of things on the one
hand and the consciousness we have of the world on the other. The
problem is to discover the limits of each, the world in which we move
and live and have our being and the world with which the scientist
deals, assigning its characteristics to the experience or experiments of
individuals, as is more and more the case today. The line between them
is dependent on the self-consciousness of the individual, his ability to
refer certain characteristics to consciousness in terms of his own experience by the same mechanism with which he indicates his experience
to others.

This is the line dividing the perceptual world from the world in which the scientist carries on his experiments; in the perceptual world there is always a reference to the self. This reference, however, does not take place in the society of ants and bees; for there the whole is one interlocking chain. A nest of a million termites may depend for its very existence on a single individual, and this individual depends for its life on the entire community. It is a complex chain that involves a whole series of individual termites, resulting in a cumulative effect. The whole life is a common enterprise, each individual being important throughout. But this, like all communities, is subject to abuse; the larvae of the drones are cared for with the same attention as those of the workers. There is no mind here; it is simply a reaction with no regard to its benefit or harm to the community. There is interaction throughout, but in this relationship there is no assurance that the implications of the act are indicated to the actor in the same fashion in which they are indicated to the recipients. A herd of deer is stimulated to flee danger when one of them sniffs contaminated air, but there is no sign that the animal is indicating to himself the thing that he is indicating to others. He does not tell himself to run, for there is no significant symbol. No more is there reason to believe that the insect knows what it is doing.

Symbols Have Shared Meanings

In a human society, a language gesture is a stimulus that reverberates and calls out the same attitude in the individual who makes it as it does in others who respond to it; we hear what we say to others as well as what others say to us. Or the symbols may be transferred through hand signs, for instance among the deaf, the only condition being that they respond to the symbols in the same manner as do other individuals of the group. Such a gesture is reflexive. There is no absolute or peculiar efficacy in the spoken word (other than that it may be onomatopoetic) or in any other symbol. For the medievalists, however, the word had a specific and absolute content; and so for the ancients Adam had to give names to the animals, and the medievalists tried to discover the character of the leopard by a mixture of etymology and mythology, never troubling to study the animal itself.

To respond to one's gesture as others do is a phase of consciousness to be distinguished from the conception of consciousness according to which accessibility is the criterion. You close your eyes and you are no longer accessible to color; a local anaesthetic destroys pain. You can

thus shut the doors between the organism and the world. There is the further conception of consciousness according to which we speak of the privacy of our own thoughts, beginnings of activities that have not yet come to express themselves. By evoking in oneself by a gesture the same kind of response as that evoked in another, one is indicating to himself the response evoked in the other. Or, one is conscious of the response in its absence.

In indicating a thing to oneself, one carries out a different form of activity from that exhibited in the deer herd. This act of indicating the functional self-consciousness is not to be confused with accessibility. This type of conduct is characteristic of the human group and distinguishes the experience as analyzed by the psychologist from the subjective experience of perceiving. The distinction between sensation as *sensa* and as act of *sensing* involves a fine distinction between what goes on in the mind and the thing out there. But the distinction is not a dichotomy; it lies inside the world of experience between what you are thinking or feeling or willing and the object that is there. The latter may be hideous or beautiful to the individual, with no alteration in its physical character.

There remains, in short, a distinction between what is inside and the thing out there. You say "table," and this stirs up an attitude for using the table; there is something in the self, but the table is not in the self. The line between the two fields is a functional line. Within you there is the organization of responses, an attitude or readiness to act toward the thing; the rest of the thing remains out there.

The Percept from the Side of the Act

The percept is approached from the side of the act by control of the process of approach. Thus, no experience is fully defined by the act itself; there may be adjustments without perception of the nature of the adjustment. Thus the artist has a value in mind and works toward it by techniques which he cannot define or isolate. Similarly, the mountain climber and the swimmer attain results, but they cannot isolate the mechanism by which they attain them; or if they do, it is by regarding themselves as objects. All this lies outside the perception of the individual. The control is there, but it does not enter perception as such.

This is the character of the perception of the lower animals; they have control but they cannot isolate it. This content we get hold of, and it enters the character of the thing itself; we see it and sense it.

We link the content and the reality of the percept in tests, and at the same time differentiate between the percept and the stimulus.

Generally, we confine perception to physical objects we can handle, but much is perceived that goes beyond such content. We respond to beauty and artistic values, and we may be able to identify what is beautiful and respond to it without perceiving it. This may be the case, for instance, with a drama which leaves a sense of beauty which cannot be analyzed out. When one sees a hammer, a definite thing enters into the distance experience to make it a percept. Often the most acute element will call forth a response where the what of it cannot be isolated but is nonetheless the content of the perception, its reality. The mechanism that isolates this content is what constitutes human intelligence. You can teach a person to make a simple mechanism but not a statue or a painting; for if the artist cannot isolate the "reality" of the object, he cannot teach what it is or have others produce it. He can only teach the preliminary mechanism.

Perception thus lies in the field where we can isolate the content that controls the act, the mechanism of ultimate response, before we reach the object. We "see" the result before we begin; we indicate particular characters that represent results.

The response is in the organism; but if we are able to isolate the object that calls forth the response, we have the reality. In vision there are characters that make up the tree. It is more than color on a flat surface; it calls forth a three-dimensional response made possible by binocular vision. But the part of the response that constitutes "what the thing is" is in the object. Imagery may serve to represent it, but it is only symbolic and arbitrary. All manner of relations can exercise control under proper conditions; any relation may be devised to control sound or singing. Imagery is thus in relation with control centers.

This phase of the experience is connected with the social act, but without isolation there is no enduring object and no intelligent control. To present the reality, the enduring object, we must get back of the response to the field. But if we are only in the field there is response without perception. Control may be perfect, on the other hand, and yet not carry any experience of the object. There must be the outside attitude to get this experience of the what a thing is into the process of self-consciousness. In the process the individual surrenders to the inspiration; he cannot isolate the thing he is doing in terms of himself until the process has taken place. Becoming self-conscious is turning back on oneself and bringing oneself into the field of one's observations. It is the act of accompanying oneself. It is like a running footnote to all experience, and it is there except when we are swallowed up in the field, so absorbed that we no longer observe the process. This is what happens when we run along the edge of a cliff. Here there is little reaction to the self as self; if it does occur, it becomes dangerous.

The function of self-consciousness is to isolate important characters in the objects around us in the form of perceptions. We hold on to objects by means of the process of indicating them to ourselves. The possibility of bringing a thing out is the content of the percept. When we look at the thing and see what it is, the response is more than to a bright light—we are self-conscious of it then. The what of the thing is all-important in building up the percept. The content is not there except in the attitude that involves the indication of it; its significance is responsible for the percept. Thus, when one sees a thing for a second, for a moment, there is no picture; but on repetition the blur takes up strategic points, and these will form themselves into a picture. This is the discriminative element of attention. It is more than a response to the stimuli. Such indication is a process directed toward the self, not only toward the object.

Sensa are abstractions selected by the psychologist to build up a structure. He pulls down a structure in order to have material with which to build one up. We get sensations from perceptions, but we cannot get perceptions from sensations. What is implied in this statement is that when we have a sensation we are perceiving something and that we must start with a perception in order to get it. A sensation lies in some larger whole within which we identify it. The sensation of red that we get from a picture is abstracted from the picture. The abstraction of redness involves something more complex than what we start with. The sensa of psychology are thus presented in terms of a situation, for example, when one jumps from a loud noise. Sensations, on the other hand, must be taken from the perceptual field. The same phenomenon arises in the pulls and pushes that one experiences in entering a new group. The subject cannot identify them fully at first, but later he discovers these imponderables. This is the situation when he responds to stimuli that he cannot define. When he can define them he has a perceptual field. The perceptual situation contains more than the content of mere stimuli. You see the table in many different characteristics—it is round, you can sit on it, it is an antique to be handled carefully, it may serve for firewood—all of them are different values, each calling forth a definite attitude. To define an individual table you must take the whole situation into consideration. In other words, if you can define the situation, you can define the values involved in the attitudes it calls forth.

It is convenient to speak of the situation as a physical object or a chemical structure that answers to certain states, but this is outside experience. Within experience, the sensation is the occasion that sets free the response and it cannot be defined unless it has gotten into a perceptual situation. The "something" that creates the perceptual situation cannot be got hold of except as we come back to the situation from outside. This is the content in the percept that has to be termed self-consciousness.

Awareness, however, is something more than a response to a stimulus. In consciousness there may be something one can come back to even if one goes away; one finds oneself at home. But in this case the individual is acting a certain way toward himself. This implies reflexiveness. But the individual, like the outsider in a new social group, may pass the time of day and yet not belong in his situation. When he comes to belong he gets another self, so that, in looking back, he can judge his own conduct. He has acquired a self that did not previously exist. Learning a new language is an example of this; it gives one a new way of looking at oneself, a new self that did not exist before. If we remain in the situation of simply responding to stimuli and never have a perceptual experience, we remain on the animal level, with no consciousness.

The Child's World Is a Social World

Other instances of this appear in little children, whose responses are in the nature of social characters. If there are instincts in humans, as in animals, they lie in the social environment, for the stimuli to which the child responds are there. There are inherited coordinations, but they are few and simple. The random activities that become organized into complex acts are automatisms, but they will become much like the inherited instincts of insects. The coordinations are potentially infinite, but they are made by the child; thus walking is to a large extent a ripening of the coordinations. The organization of the random movements is the occupation of the child, and this occurs in the social structure. The child must act with reference to the structure that protects and supports him; he lives in a social medium, and through this he comes into relationship with his physical environment. He does not come into relationship with the physical world directly.

Primitive society still lives in a world that is friendly or hostile; Venus brings happiness and Jupiter gloom. It is much like the medium in which the child comes into the world. Nature poetry has the same attitude behind it. The social medium represents a certain type of activity; we are adjusting ourselves to the activities of other beings. Too much of our psychology is of the laboratory type that is as bad as arm-chair introspection. Conduct is not adjustment to static things; it is like catching the ball as it comes, meeting persons as they approach. The thing we react to is the thing that moves. The important stimuli are the moving ones, and responses to these constitute the important part of our intelligence. This is where the gesture enters.

The next step concerns how to make the object of experience intelligible, its character and our perception of it. To sense a thing is to set free the impulses that present the occasion, but this is not perception of the stimulus. For this we must turn back on the thing and perceive. We jerk the hand from the radiator, but whether we put the hotness in the mind or in the object depends on the philosophy we hold. We can have a relationship without perception.

Sophisticated attention picks out and isolates things, but beyond the spot of light we attend to, we work unconsciously. (Recall James before his Lycée in Paris.) Such unconscious conduct may be highly intelligent, but it is not in a perceptual world. In perception there is a content beyond what sets free the response or the consummation of the act. Thus one can take a meal without perception and still enjoy it.

In infancy essential processes are mediated by the group around the infant, which carries out the presence actually conditioning his life. In this process there are random acts in the course of organization, ripening of coordinations in the central nervous system, and the development of synapses. Conduct in infancy thus takes place in a social medium, so that the child actually uses his automatisms to secure his wants. He gets a response from those around him, and it is they who actually carry out or complete his act. In other words, he relies on others to complete his acts for him. We can carry out our own acts because we are in rapport with the medium.

The child's act is much like the infantilism of primitive groups. The child gets his food through being in rapport with his environment. So the savage must be in proper rapport with his world before he can set out to kill a bear. If he fails it is because the *mana* was not in the proper condition. In the same fashion the Greeks claimed that their gods won their battles for them. Thus they sent to Thebes a ship loaded with Greek gods. The Thebans lost and complained that they would rather have had a regiment of their soldiers. This is much like the attitude of Wordsworth: the work of nature complements the works of man, completing the act which otherwise would remain incomplete. Such is the early medium of the child's conduct and the medium in which it develops its own experience. A congenitally deaf child is no better off than a beast—it has no means of communication.

Language is an all-important medium of the social process that completes the act. The adjustment of the child to its environment is the basis of its intelligence. Those parts of the act to which the child responds are gestures. Darwin calls them the expression of the emotions of the individual. Gesture is part of the social act and serves as a stimulus to complete the process. Something becomes a gesture through certain types of social processes. Thus the snort of the sentinel deer is a stimulus to the herd to flee, though he is not consciously a sentinel and is not representing the same thing to himself.

Gestures, Attitudes, and Symbols

Gestures are an important form of stimulus in the child's life. He responds to smiles or frowns as expressions of emotion, but we can trace these expressions back to genetic situations and show that one is a part of the contortion of the face in rage and the other the attitude of seeking food, etc. All these represent attitudes by which forms adjust themselves to their environment. The dog takes attitudes that are gestures to other dogs; every dogfight has its preliminary snarls and barks, its advances and retreats. Like the Homeric struggles, it may end up with conversations among the heroes. Boxers and fencers exhibit the same type of gestures.

Attitudes represent indications, and so they are more than mere stimuli. This is what constitutes the meaning of the thing, but the meaning is not essential to activity. We can act without knowing that the object is hard, and indeed much activity is too rapid for perception.

The symbol must be isolated in order to isolate its content, that to which it refers. It must stand out in experience. This involves alternative responses but not necessarily perceptions. All deliberation requires that the meanings of different attitudes be present in the individual, and gestures are the answers to the different attitudes. It is not sufficient to recognize symbols; for there to be deliberation, contents must be held over against each other and indicated as contents over against some person.

The nature of the thing, its meaning, can only be gotten into the act when its character is referred to and isolated in the act itself. This does not take place when there is a mere relationship of stimulus and response; here there is only the setting free of appropriate reactions. If the responses are indicated, especially if there are alternatives, then we get the meaning into the percept. The stimulus becomes the immediate tendency to move toward the object and set up the beginning of the manipulatory process itself. When one sees an enemy one has something in mind, and when running at him with clenched fists one is reacting to this. But lions roar and spring all in the same process, and readiness to seize the prey and devour it is here as well, directing the act. If there were deliberation in the act of the lion, then the different movements would be meanings.

If we can get the pattern of the grain of sand by rolling it in the fingers, we can get this out, and then we have the meaning of the act in the perceptual form. So far as indications of character are present, they are present only as directions. The sentinel deer thus only directs other forms to other characters. One can point out something without indicating it to oneself; the hen does this in clucking. To get meaning into the object one must be able to indicate it to oneself; it will not get into the act before the something is held as a separate element.

If the individual can indicate the character and hold on to it as a something, then there must be a place for distinction and comparison. Thus perception involves some deliberation. The table becomes a thing with various uses indicated by the inhibitions of other uses. We do not act toward the table as toward a thing in itself, but in relation to many other possible things. If there were no such alternatives it could have no meaning. There must be alternatives to give perceptual value, and to get the content of the percept it must be possible that different values inhibit one another, and these characters the individual must be able to indicate to himself. The percept, in other words, contains more than bare stimulation, although a few objects contain only thereness; and these may be percepts if we can indicate certain of their characteristics.

The completions that need to occur before the act is completed are behavioristic meanings. (One perceives the meaning of the printed page, but our discussion here is limited to the meaning of physical things.) The stimulus is an occasion in the thing going on. All the characters that make up bigness, squareness, etc. (contact elements) are related to the stimuli and the occasion. One is the meaning of the other. The meaning of our running is the crash of the landslide. If you reach for an orange, what you get into the mouth is the meaning for you. When we indicate this pattern of final manipulation we indicate the meaning of the act. There are values that exceed the meaning in the sunset, but the bare perceptual things rest on earlier contact experiences.

Action, the Self, and the Group

The contact pattern of the thing is in one sense present in the structure of the individual. This is the meaning, if we can get it into a meaning. Getting such a content means getting a self. We are involved in the social just as much as the most helpless infant. The distance between the tendency to act and the "what" the thing is, is great. Our process is socially determined, and in infancy we can see the beginnings of the self arising. The child acts toward itself as an adult does; he arouses in himself the responses that belong to the activities of the adult. This is not imitation. It is impossible to present the organization of imitation. One cry can call out another cry, but there is no deliberate imitation of the sound; this is too complex an affair. The shaking of a man's fist may result in your imitation of him or in your flight. One cow wanders down a field, and this acts as a stimulus to other cows to wander down the field. When we hear ourselves in our rage, we are displeased or ashamed just the same as if it were another person. To be a significant symbol, something must affect oneself just as it affects others. This is the basis of the vocal gesture; we hear ourselves as others hear us who live in the same social medium. The group is essential for the completion of the normal act of the individual; all completion of acts occurs through this structure. Those parts of the act that call out responses are gestures. Such stimuli react on the form that makes the gesture just as they do on other forms.

If the faculty of speech continues after deafness, the muscular movements and set remain as the representatives of audition—thus, for instance, in a boiler factory. Symbols act upon the self as they act upon another. The parrot's talk, however, is not a significant gesture, since he does not understand what he says. So far as his speech is not intelligible, the human is the same as the parrot. On the other hand, a person can bring about the completion of the act by other symbols and order dinner in the same terms as the parrot.

Self-consciousness implies that one is the auditor of what he says in the same way as is another person. Symbolism is reflexive, and this is so only where there is self-consciousness. This means taking the role of another. When one is talking to oneself he is in the attitude of another to himself. In the same sense, one may make an exclamation without premeditation and then be surprised at the results just as much as if it had been some other person who made the exclamation. In the presence of a mouse a woman screams and then is surprised at herself. But when one is not in a social situation, there is no point in the scream, and it is not indulged in. This is the curious explanation of the woman who was silent even when a centipede fell on her while she was alone in the house. The secret is that there is no response and so no reason to scream. For much the same reason the bully will cower in the presence of another bully. One's attitude becomes the complement to the other's attitude; the attitude that answers to what we do, in other words, is present in our own attitude all the time. Insofar as the earlier attitude is one to which we respond, we have taken the attitude or role of another over against ourselves.

This gives us an idea of the abstractions of the universe of discourse of the logician. Play illustrates this: the child takes the role of the parent in playing with its doll. His own cry calls out the parental attitude in the child. In carrying out the social process by exciting in another the same attitude that is in himself, he is affecting himself in the same way as he affects the other. It is only as the child does this that he comes to have a full self. In dog-play there is a combination. The dog bites, but it is not a hard bite; since what is present is the organization of different impulses, he is not assuming a role as in the instance of the child. For the dog there is no beginning or end, no point at which a certain role is dropped and another assumed.

Role-Taking, Play, and Games

All mental activity consists in assuming roles, just as much as in the play or games of the child; all is an organization of roles. The difference between play and a game is that in a game the roles are so organized that all are there controlling the entire action. The player's gesture is aimed to call out different responses. If he throws the ball, he takes the attitude of the person who catches it. This is strikingly shown in the child's own active interest in the rules of the game; the game must be played according to rules.

In a certain sense the child takes the role of all the others, of the generalized other. In this instance, that is, where there is a generalized other involved in the activity, there is a great difference from mere play. When your act calls for something that does not come, when there is no response from the other, you are ready to respond to yourself, then there is morality.

The game, in other words, requires a whole self, whereas play requires only pieces of the self. The game has an organized set of others whose roles you can assume. Everyone in the game demands that the batter reach base or at least try to do so. Each speaks in the *vox populi*, which is, incidentally, the *vox Dei*. For this reason it is properly said that England's wars have been won on the playing fields of Eton. This mechanism is what makes reasoning possible. When the human can no longer stimulate himself as he stimulates others, he is on the level of the beast and has no personality. This does not restrict stimuli to any one series, for we may set up other symbols for sight; we may present reasons to ourselves by assuming other roles or attitudes toward situations just as another person would. Humanity is essentially social, and all its mechanisms are of this character.

We have a self when it has become an object to itself and has a relationship to itself in the same way as do other objects in the environment. In, this respect human behavior is distinguished from subhuman behavior; it can take the attitude of the environment as over against the form itself; its role embodies the environment. The field of activity for the human organism is the social field, where the organism is related to other similar organisms whose conduct is essential to their mutual life processes. Humans often act toward physical things as if they were social things. This is naively shown in primitive man, for he sees everything as directly active and participating in his own activities. The ax thus loves and hates, helps or hinders; the stars are favorable or malignant. Such infantilism finds in the motions of things the same type of gestures that it recognizes among humans in the social group. We are not so far from it when the collar button suddenly escapes, and this attitude lies at the basis of all nature poetry. Thales said the world was full of gods, alive. This is only the primitive attitude of the individual in the primitive community. But this is the attitude of the thinker, who moves and changes like others. The abstractions of physics seem to set up pictures with no social content; but the physical picture is reached step by step, and the fundamental principle is the same as that of human behavior, where the individual takes on the role of another. The scientist is merely taking on the role of the environment in relation to the object.

Responses to bodily reaction are not necessarily a matter of self-consciousness. Parts of the body are objects in the environment; legs are as much objects under the human as under the chair. One has a painful hand and acts toward it as toward a painful object.

We need not consider where the self as a whole acts. The individual is not composed into a self merely by uniting felt parts into a unity. The attitude of looking at the hand distinguishes it from the attitude of holding the hand. Whatever the situation of the aching hand, we cannot put all the rest of the body together and have it act toward the hand. The mere synthesis of the elements of the body does not make self-consciousness. The social process shows the means by which the individual comes back to himself and becomes an object to himself. The child answering to his own stimuli acts as others act toward him. The fact that the social group makes uniform demands upon the individual gives him self-consciousness. This is how individuals are controlled through mores. Where the group is closely organized, this power becomes overwhelming and there cannot even be difference of opinion. But when there is such complete adjustment and integration there is stagnation, and the only escape for the individual is to leave the community or group. The power of this is shown in the remorse experienced by criminals or those who have crossed social lines.

Where there is such an identity in response we have the rational situation. In the game everyone wants the pitcher to throw the ball; it is the attitude of the group that calls on the particular individual to do a particular thing. There is thus a universe of discourse, and this is the genius of the rational self and so of self-consciousness. The distinction of man as a rational animal is thus entirely legitimate; it is the difference between the corpse and the undertaker. When the child can take the attitude of the entire group, he can come back to himself the same way and thus come to have self-consciousness and a unitary self.

Mind, and the Self as Object to Itself

Symbols or language gestures imply organized activity with identical ends and processes. The setting off of responses is highly organized by symbolic expressions, but the symbol itself is not of the essence of the process. Where there is no such response there is disorganization, and the individual is *non compos mentis*. This does not mean that the attitude of the group is the one we always take, for the individual may be crazy or advanced beyond the level of the group in which he lives. But the essence of mind in the individual is the capacity for taking the attitudes of all those involved and picking out what is identical in the demands on the self and responding to that. This universal element is what makes the process rational—all respond in like fashion to money, land, bonds, or property. It is the basis of all social life.

The fact that distinguishes the human from the animal is that the self becomes an object to the organism itself. From the standpoint of biology the human is like the animal; the difference arises in the conduct of the two. The animal licking its paw is not reacting to itself; its behavior is like the interactions among the objects in its environment. Its hair, skin, etc., like the high heels or the hat of the human, are merely extensions of the organism itself. There is no distinction of the self in the experience. We do not feel the organism as a whole. The organism does not become an entity to itself except in a social context; as a whole it does not get into the environment except through the social process.

There is a fine distinction between color and tactile experience. Sound may be divided between the head and the bell, and pressure can be located in the hand and the table upon which you press;[3] but such is not the case in the matter of vision.

The organism as a whole becomes part of the environment only as it is involved in the social process. Where there is this process, the self can be distinguished from the organism. The self is a social entity that cannot be located, as the Greeks located the psyche, in the heart, head, or organs. It is a social entity that must be related to the entire body, and only insofar as the self is related to the body is it related to the environment.

It is difficult to construct the self as an organism in the same sense as other entities. The self involves a unity; it is there in the social process, but there is no self unless there is the possibility of regarding it as an object to itself. It is the center about which the individual is organized, and the body is an integral part of the self. Peter and Paul sleep in the same bed but wake up as the same Peter and Paul. In the old theory of metempsychosis, the self is a definite entity that can assume different forms. When we try to regard ourselves independently of our organisms, however, we may be put into an asylum. We may have our little illusions, but when they go beyond the ordinary limits they can no longer be permitted in the social organization. We are thus tied to the body insofar as we have a self.

Among primitive groups the gods acted as a sort of projection of the social experience of the community. This was sharply defined and limited to a particular region. When the community went beyond the region the gods could not at first be taken along; it was only the formulation of later theology that made this possible. Then the gods became identified with particular attributes.

The social process makes the individual an object to himself, and on this basis he can come back to himself as an organized whole. In this case he is taking the role of the other members of the group. When others call he can answer or fight, but it must be in keeping with the demands made by the social group, the demands of all the members of

3. This was Mead's "hobby." He often pressed his hand against a book or the table in order to illustrate that we have a direct experience of the resistance, the inertia of a physical thing. We experience the *inside* of physical objects through contact.—Ed.

the community. Against this he is helpless, he must obey. In the process, he gets his self. The child similarly gets his self through obedience to the group in which he is obliged to live by his own physical constitution. We are all, in short, constructs of the group in which we live.

Language is one of the most direct means of controlling and directing the social process, since it is through this medium that indications are most rapidly made. Thus the dog and the ape have the language tracts most highly developed; but the physical organization anticipates the social development, and the development of the function is caused by the social group.

Society can exist, however, without the emergence of selves, as with the bees and the ants. They have no selves because they cannot stimulate themselves in the same way in which they stimulate other ants or bees. They cannot stimulate themselves to do the things that the group demands.

The order of society depends upon the character of the self. In the economic process there is a social life that reaches the whole race. Men may trade even without meeting each other, but they are nonetheless tied together in the process. But this economic man is not a self in our sense of the word since he cannot or does not take the attitude of the group with which he deals.

There is a tendency to enrich the organization. Evolution is in a certain sense a catching up with what the community has as its consciousness. It is difficult to introduce the advances of a smaller group into the larger, but still this is the channel through which advance comes. The family originates the mores which later control the larger community. In other words. the values are higher in the smaller group. In the crowd there is an organization of individuals without the emergence of any self; this comes only when the individual meets others face to face as individuals. Then the self emerges, and we discover the thing that the other is trying to do and he learns what we are trying to do.

Self-consciousness in social behavior is the organization of the attitudes of the social group to which the individual belongs. He can address himself in the same terms with which he addresses others, bringing about the same responses in each instance. Addressing oneself requires having a delayed reaction; it deals with the earlier organization of the act, before it reaches expression or completion. As the individual takes this attitude or group of attitudes there is the emergence of the subconscious. The attitudes of others are the beginnings of their acts, a relationship which in turn marks the behavior of the individual in question. In self-consciousness there is the attitude as such, calling for a particular

response and stimulating the individual to this response. The conversation of gestures is like the dogfight, where each individual adjusts himself by the indication of the other's attitudes. In such a process of
adjustment there is a delayed response. It may be overt and not self-
conscious, only a mere passage of stimuli back and forth between A and
B. In this case, there is an importation of the gestures into the behavior
of the organism. We take over the attitudes of the other in his response
to us.

Rationality, Shared Attitudes, and Meanings

The process of social adjustment is important, but the condition that
gives it a rational character is that the attitude of the other is the attitude of the group; we see the attitude of the whole group there. Another type of interaction involves cooperative reaction. The individual
can take the attitude of the group because of the identity of the organization of the act. In the social act each fits into the other; there is a
unity of stimuli because the individual can take the attitude of others.
When he does this he comes back to himself with the single demand
that is made by all the members of the group in a particular situation.
Thus he must be honorable and respect property, because this is the
voice of the entire community and he must obey in order to live in it.
This, in fact, is the entire thought process. If, on the contrary, people
take attitudes contrary to the demand of the group, they are adjudged
insane or criminal.

The child makes use of abstract universals, and it is because the
word-symbol can be in the mouth of all that he can speak with the
voice of the community. Among primitives there is a greater range
of universals; all manner of movements in nature have their definite
meanings and make certain demands on all members of the community.
The entrails of birds have definite meanings which all must accept
without criticism. When fundamental concepts are brought under
criticism there are curious effects; thus, even for us, when there is
serious doubt thrown on our notion of space and time the community
is deeply stirred.

Self-Consciousness and Universals, Rights and Obligations

The universal is involved in self-consciousness, and all rationality turns
on it in one shape or another. In the child the self is not so organized
that he can keep up conduct; this depends on nature and organized activity stretching over long periods of time, with foresight and hind-
sight. This brings responsibility with it. One can stand on his rights,

but he can do this only to the extent that he has the sanctions of the group behind him, unless he resorts to the animal level of fighting. Rights and obligations go together, however. This is the imperative character of conduct, which springs ultimately from the social situation. It is only a Diogenes content to live in a tub who can afford to disregard rights and obligations, and even he appeals to rights that are rooted in social life.

On the other hand, however, this latter type of life is more universal, because it deliberately disregards the conventions of the smaller group in which the critic finds himself. The only escape from the small society is to join the larger, unless the self is surrendered. The larger society includes broader categories. It may even take in fowls, as did the Jewish picture of the son of man. Eastern religions get at the same thing by suppressing the self, getting rid of all desire. When the self disappears, so does the world, and it becomes a mere illusion. But this gives a pessimistic color to Eastern society. We, on the contrary, attack society and try to produce a better society instead of suppressing the self, which is literally putting the ax to the root of the tree.

We can express this in psychological formulas. We start with organized activity, where each is related in some way to the life of the organization as such. We assume a process where the attitude of one member of the group stimulates others to respond, much like the chemical process in the body where the expenditure of carbonic acid gas stimulates breathing and circulation. We have the same form as other humans, furthermore, and can take identical attitudes to theirs.

The playwright can live a separate life and assume different roles; but this is not so in direct relations with the group, for we can be Janes or Helens only insofar as all make the same demands upon us. This universality arises in the use of vocal gestures, but it rests on the universal character of the society in which it is current. The alley gang has its vocabulary, and so does the club. When the individual is beside himself he still keeps his own self as the accuser.

The self, as such, is a rational entity and always involves talking to oneself in terms of the group, the generalized other. Reverie is a flow of responses and images outside the organized self, but it contains innerlocution that says what everyone would say under the same circumstances. This is the basis of all rational thinking and thought.

The self is that structure in experience which arises when the social act becomes part of the conduct of the individual in the sense that the individual can take the attitude of the group and address himself in the same terms as he addresses the group. It calls out in the individual the responses of another. Insofar as the gesture can give the attitude of the group as a whole, this constitutes the self; it is in a certain sense a logical structure. The entire group makes the same demand on the individual.

In cooperative activity the organization implies that each function makes the same demand on the individual. Just as the organ, when stimulated, responds in terms of its particular function but as an element in an organized whole (the eye sees, but it sees what will protect or *warn* the rest of the entire organism), so each individual is under obligation to the whole organized activity. When he replies, he does so in terms of his self. The self has, then, a logical structure, that is, the psychology of the group. We speak in terms of the whole group and are what our interests are. What makes the self is the capacity to put the self in the place of the group and speak to oneself with the voice of the group. The self is thus a reflexive entity, as is reflected in grammar. When you have it in the objective case—"myself," "yourself"—the same self is the agent. These reactions represent traits of character, which are egocentric or altruistic. It does not necessarily imply the self, for the beast of prey is no more selfish than man, nor are animals altruistic when they protect their young (as is illustrated in the tale of the cow that licked its young, which had been stuffed in order to encourage her to give milk, and after she had licked through the skin ate the stuffing!). When the self is in some manner an object to itself, then you have consciousness of the self. Back of this is the social mechanism that operates similarly to the parrotlike babbling of the child; there is a social stimulus that calls out the social response. When one bird follows another's song it is not imitating but calling up in itself its own song. If the sound it hears from the other bird calls out a different response but one nearly like the original, there is an assimilation of repertoires. There is thus something of the canary's song in the sparrow, and the sparrow responding to the canary has in its response some of the notes of the canary. There is stimulus and response in the organism, but there is no experience of self. The parrot can be trained in this fashion, but the parrot does not know what it is saying; for it cannot stimulate itself in the same manner in which it stimulates others, and it has therefore no self-consciousness. The mechanism of the attainment of the self is social, but the content of the self is its capacity for taking the attitudes of others of the group.

The object *chair* may suggest a whole series of responses; it may suggest to sell, buy, sit, burn, etc., each of which is represented by an organization of paths in the central nervous system. There are unlimited connections possible in the central nervous system, more numerous than the members of our galaxy. All reactions to the *chair* are so organized that they are represented by a certain group of paths. These are connected temporally and spatially. The chair may be regarded as a piece of furniture, or as a curio, each of which implies different attitudes toward it and excites special paths, which may lead off into further paths that seem to have no connection with the original article for sale. There is the whole field of trade, money, value, etc. Thus while reacting to a single character we are in effect preparing ourselves to act in an unlimited variety of ways. But the thing exists as an organized whole because these processes have some sort of relationship throughout.

The various social objects to which we refer have a social organization the individual may put himself into. In the instance of the chair, the social organization involves individuals from the master carpenter to the final buyer. The nature of the organization is such that the price of the article is largely determined by the activities of the organization's intermediate members. But insofar as we put ourselves into any one of the various stages of the process, we have the attitudes of all the intermediate members or we can assume them on demand. In so doing we manifest a rationality that includes in it a relationship with the entire group; for we may, for instance, insist that the chair is too costly, that it is not worth the price, because we can put ourselves in the various stages of its production and see it as the producer and the buyer at the same time. In a word, we take the attitude of the entire group.

Self-consciousness arises in reply to such a situation. The group organization is in some sense present in the individual, as it is possible to have a representative sense of the group as a whole in the central nervous system of each individual. When one offers a price for a chair, for instance, one is taking all the roles from producer to banker. In this way one responds to the entire group; it is a sort of universal.

The self is not responsible for the social organization; it is there long before the self. Neither is the mind there in advance, for it is merely the indication of attitudes and contents to others and to oneself. But the appearance of mind presupposes social organization. There is social life in invertebrates and other forms that group themselves in families or herds. In man there is a society that depends upon the social organization that makes for his own development. And development depends directly upon social organization, on the ability to communicate with different members of the group. We can, however, have communication without mind; thus the herd-sentinel communicates with the remainder of the group by his action when he senses the taint in the air. But this is a matter of conduct.

Thinking is communication with oneself when one speaks in the voice of the entire group to which one belongs. But if we assume that thought is something implied in thinking, then we assume that thinking is something done inside the head; but this raises the problem of how people communicate such thinking. Some assume that thinking is done inside the head and broadcast, and happens to hit someone.

But conduct is social prior to thinking; although thinking cannot be carried on outside individuals, it involves the entire social organization, much as circulation involves the entire man. When we reach the point where mind calls out in the self the attitudes of the other, then we have an individual who speaks to himself in terms of the whole group. We have a group process in the individual. This is what we mean by mind and thinking; it is the getting hold of universals by individuals. This implies a relationship of one form to another. When, for example, you tell a person something, you tell him something that is already in yourself. Thinking is communicating with yourself, and this is the basis, the essence, of mind.

Secondary Qualities Are Returned to the World

The philosophical value of this position is that it restores stolen goods to the world. Philosophy had stolen qualities and meaning from the world and placed them in a mind that is entirely supposititious, and then abandoned the task of getting from this mind to other minds and to the world. But if we continue to describe the world in terms of physical particles, we must put some things in mind.

Thinking. Communication is the statement of the symbols by which individuals think. Constructive thinking occurs when the individual does more than carry out his own act. Where an adjustment takes place, there is an organization of the synapses that allows for an infinite number of combinations and connections. Unguided evolution involves a terrible waste, as shown in the ancient fossils, all of which have been part of the adjustment necessary for the form to fit itself to the environment. We can now breed humans like pigs and determine our physical life (for example in business) without this expensive trial and error, which involves the loss of 90 percent of all effort.

A medium of communication means that one takes the attitude of the results of the act; the arrangement is there in the central nervous system by habit and adjustment or with conscious thinking. Taking the attitude of the results of the act may lead to representing different possible results—this will harmonize, that will bring such and such a result. By taking all these attitudes, one can organize conflicting tendencies. One does this on the basis of a social process, relations with other persons. The individual is in the social process, and its organization makes such an act possible for him. Thinking is the same as talking to other people. A thing has universal significance when everyone understands it. There is always a social process where there is, as it were, a republic of letters to appeal to. But thinking is a process that involves the social whole in the expression of all its parts. (See Dewey, *How We Think.*)

There is no fundamental difference between thinking and the process of trial and error, only the social process is more economical. We select our methods of thought, although we cannot always use them. Thought is the internalizing of the method of trial and error in the inner forum of the individual. What is referred to is anticipation; when we see the hammer, we are ready to use it. If we can assume this attitude, we get the future into the present and are in a position to control the present act, to take losses and gains. Evolution lies in the ability to go on with the act, a physiological test. Thus, one can test his ability to jump the ditch only by jumping. If we look around to find something that will take the place of a hammer, to pound a nail in a shoe for instance, we isolate something in the act; but the ability to pick this thing out is made possible by the process of communication. Thus ideas are not uncanny things; the idea is the character that is there in the hammer. The idea is the ability to use that part of the hammer you can isolate.

The Social Character of Experience from the Standpoint of Perception

The social character of experience from the standpoint of perception is very important for its psychological implications. Personality is social. The work of writers influenced by Gabriel Tarde shows that the self exists only in relationship with other selves and cannot be reached except through other selves. If we approach the self from this standpoint, we see that the individual can enter into the experience of the group only as he develops his self among others. This recognition carries the assumption that we must get others into the field of the self. The old view held that the self could be directly consciousness of itself.

Thus, presumably the child had within him a primary recognition of the self, and he advanced to other selves by projecting this recognition into other selves. This consciousness was supposed to be consciousness of itself as suffering or as happy. The attribution of such consciousness to a clock would imply that the clock knew that its wheels were in a certain relation to its hands. Implied in this scheme of Lloyd Morgan's is the assumption that the clock becomes an object to itself before other objects come into its experience. The assumption that the child has self-consciousness and relates it to himself and primarily builds up such an object and then goes over to other objects and assumes they have the same character as his own—this is the common assumption, but it is not true. The self cannot arise in experience except as there are others there. The other is essential to the appearance of the self. We do not approach the organism from within. There are pains and pleasures within the organism, but the child does not delimit its organism from inside its own skin. It does not start from inside and go outside to its own skin. The actual process begins at the periphery and goes to the center. The child experiences sounds, etc., before it has experience of its own body; there is nothing in the child that arises as his own experience and then is referred to the outside thing. There are hurt fingers, but they are not referred to the self until the child enters into relationship with other selves.

Psychoanalysis provides an interesting demonstration of what actually takes place within us by showing that the self, as an object, stands on a level with other things. We are liable to be mistaken about ourselves just as we are about other things; in fact, other people know more of us than we ourselves know. Only a superficial philosophy demands the old view that we start with ourselves. In Hume you may go back to certain impressions but you cannot come back to a self, and this is the primary order. There is no self before there is a world, and no world before the self. The process of the formation of the self is social. The reference to a self takes place through individuals taking the attitude of the other. This is so in the case of the child taking the attitude of the other even in play. Upon putting a hand on the table, you have the experience of the hand and the table at the same time. The table resists the hand just as much as the hand resists the table. You could not get the sense of resistance if there were not a table to resist your effort. You can push your hand hard enough to make it hurt, but the resistance of the table is of the same character as the resistance your hand offers to the table. The experience is divided between the two.

Thus, to get the experience of pressure on the table, you must put yourself in the attitude of the table.[4]

Real things are those we can handle, actually or figuratively. This makes experiences, such as our experience of tables, peculiarly important; the object becomes an object to us only as we have the attitude of the object.

For primitive folk all objects are social; primitive societies recognize that objects are vague and uncertain. Their reaction to them is admittedly social, with a vague self acting toward the individual. We show the same attitude when we kick a chair.

Taking the Role of the Physical Thing

In abstracting characters we put ourselves into the role of the physical thing, just as, in the social field, we do with persons. So there is as much abstraction in dealing with oneself as in dealing with others. We are identified with the body, which makes it seem that there has been an abstraction. This is not so among primitives; for them everything is social, even sticks and stones, but not personified. We abstract these things and say that there are sticks and stones, in the same way we make the abstraction between the body as bone and the soul, etc. The physical object as an object depends on our putting ourselves in the role of the other. This implies that the individual assumes an attitude of resistance that answers to the table, which makes it possible to treat the table as an object. It is the social mechanism that makes the physical object an object.

Perception has a social character, especially insofar as it involves meaning. The world has meaning to us, for there are no perceptions without meanings. Meaning has been treated by logicians as if it belonged to a separate order of things, a subsistent world of meaning. The associational school tries to deal with meanings through the associa-

---

4. By taking the role of a physical thing (say a table) or by being in the attitude of the table, Mead means one must be in readiness (anticipate) the resistance or the inertia of the table prior to touching it or pressing on it. Since the table can press on or act on one's own body (hand, in this case) only and precisely to the extent that the hand presses on it, action and reaction are equal and numerically identical. Thus one can, in one's effort, experience the inertia of the physical thing, which is of the essence of the thing and *inside* the thing. Hence, one can take the role of the physical thing. See Mead's *The Philosophy of the Present*, pp. 199-39. Thus, through contact experience, touch, as Locke suggested, we have a direct experience of the physical thing. We experience the resistance, the inertia, the "pushiness" of the physical thing simultaneously with its reaction to our pushing on it. —Ed.

tion of other meanings. The situation where the meaning arises is a social situation. Infancy is the period in which the family gathers. It is not due to the urges of sex alone that it is kept together; it is due to the presence of the child and its needs. This is the beginning of society in the vertebrate form. The organization is more developed in the herd, but in the herd there is little adhesion. The family is not divided among the different members; all do the same things together. When cattle organize themselves against attack, there is the first stage in such common organization, for the young are all put in the center. But a distinction must be made between doing things together and each performing a definite part in an action.

The basis for the development of the complex human society lies in the central nervous system and cerebrum. Instead of physiological plasticity we have an organism in which it is possible for the various stages of complexities to be aroused, and this makes it possible to set up an act in the central nervous system in a time scheme. The different stages of an act can be aroused before the act is accomplished. If the person must pass through a landscape to reach a distant goal, the various objects in the landscape can be seen in relation to the goal, but they are then spatially and temporally analyzed. One tree is so many steps away, another is more; but both are expressed in steps and in time. In this manner temporal distance can be organized in the central nervous system. The steps the person takes now are determined by what he will do afterwards. If he is to turn to the right or left, the central nervous system can affect the organism at present with this future act. It all comes back to a world in a now. It is the ability of later responses to play back into immediate responses that gives us our flexibility and power of choice. The central nervous system makes possible this temporal organization of the act.

The meanings of the act are the things we can do, how one will move in reference to different objects, right or left, etc. So far as obstacles are present influencing our act they are the meanings of the act. A prod of one sort means moving in a certain direction, a prod of another means moving in another. The meaning of what the person starts out to do is what he accomplishes. It is only insofar as the results of an act play into each other that we can get the meaning of the act. Ordinarily the meaning is not separated from the act. I walk this way now because I am going to turn to the right, but this is not abstracted; it is part of the present act. In experience the meaning of the act appears as a certain way in which we act; it is not isolated. Contact and distance experience illustrate this. The readiness to utilize the object at a distance affects our approach to it; all this is fused into the percept. We perceive things that can be manipulated. The meanings of things are resultants that control the present act, ends of the act present in the ongoing process. This is thought of as a well-worn path in the central nervous system, but there are a variety of paths, fixed paths and alternative paths, or ways of acting. To get these resultants into the present act is to get the meaning into the percept. It is present at the moment as something that will take place later. But this does not isolate the character so that we can distinguish it. It is the social process that gives the mechanism for isolating the meanings. The table has a certain character for us if we are to use it, and thus its value goes into the percept.

Mechanisms of communication provide a means of indicating what the resultants will be. One may point out a resultant without its being significant. The sentinel of the herd indicates certain particulars that answer to a certain terminus. But, in language, what is significant is arousing in the individual speaker the reaction of the other form. When the individual points out the object to others, he also indicates it to himself. If the hen could point out the worm, she would be taking the attitude of the chick. In the behavior of the hen there is a connection between the food and the parental attitude; and if the hen could mean this, then her act would be a significant gesture; the chick's eating the worm may be present in her conduct in some way, but she is unable to isolate it from the entire social act. Now while she takes the attitude of the chick she does not isolate it, and therefore it is not a perception. Similarly, when a man points out another man's act and not his own, it does not pass into his perception. In dealing with a log he does not take the meaning out; it is simply something to be moved from this spot, and he approaches it from the spot where it will most fully respond; but this act is controlled by the conception of a later result. If you point to a person and say that is the spot to hold it, you have picked out the later part, but it is not in the percept itself.

Significant Symbols, Indication, and the Function of Language

Insofar as the individual isolates the temini of the acts that others carry out and does so in terms of his own conduct, to this extent we have the significant symbol. If one rat-dog is in one corner, others will come and dig there. With us the individual does not carry out the act, he only indicates it to himself and others. It is, then, this mechanism of indication, showing the final result of the act in the present activity, that gives importance to language and communication. We emphasize this meaning of the symbol, the later part of the act insofar as it determines the present situation.

Our central nervous system makes this temporal relationship possible. The attitude of the terminus of the act acts to determine the present. This may pass over into immediate perception, and then it gives something more than mere excitement of the tracts. But it can pass into experience without taking the form of perception. In a social process where persons work together and one gives a symbol or sign to the others, he gives a rational signal if he can indicate it to himself. If he can do this, he can analyze it and get the meaning out. Language refers to this.

The symbol is important, but to have full meaning it must affect the one who uses it as it affects those to whom it is given. Herein lies the importance of the vocal gesture.

Self-consciousness is a mechanism for social organization as distinguished from the physiological mechanism of lower vertebrate society and from situations where we are not self-conscious. Self-consciousness gives meaning; the characters are uniform to all members of the group in which the self belongs. One can point out the same things to others that he points out to himself. The self is thus an expression of the organization of the group, like the child who can take the roles of all the individuals of his group in his play. This organization is the interlocutor that calls on us to do this or that; it brings out the meanings of things. This is the function of language; it indicates what is uniform in situations where all are concerned. Thus, in a ball game, all expect the catcher to do one certain thing. This is an expression of what he is saying to himself. It means that the symbols used are universal, that all say the same thing to him as to others. Language isolates the something that is demanded by the social organization of each individual. It expresses identity in diversity. Each has a different attitude, and yet each calls for the same thing. A note must be paid whether one wants to pay it or not—the sheriff provides for this, and it is the social organization that makes the obligation binding. It is the imperative mood, the primitive mood of all language that starts with groans or grunts accompanied by a directive symbol. At first the sound is not even functional; it is merely a disturbance of rhythmical breathing called forth by a change in the social situation. The indication is here in the medical sense, so to speak, of a wound indicating a certain treatment.

In the beehive there are individuals acting as stimuli, but the individual does not indicate to himself. There is indicating to oneself only where there is telling. If there is a response of revolt, it is because there has been understanding of the thing indicated.

There may be stimuli in the sense of suggestion through hypnosis, and one may read without consciousness; but suggestibility means that the individual is acting without knowing why. In the posthypnotic stage the person takes off his coat at eleven o'clock but does not know why.

If a person is not forced to carry out a response to a social suggestion, he can suggest alternatives to himself. From this come deliberation and decision, passing from imperatives to subjunctives and optatives. If the symbol is merely a stimulus, it either achieves its results or fails; but if there is deliberation there is consciousness.

With reference to the distant object, if we feel that it is hard, this means that we indicate a response that tries to avoid collision. The central nervous system stands for the ability to present alternatives by introducing a temporal dimension into action. To get the different possibilities into the present situation, one can suggest the other alternatives. Here, then, is deliberation, conversation, an inner forum or council. The rational process is the indication of alternatives, different possible conclusions of the act which the particular social situation calls for. The essential thing is that the alternatives shall be indicated in the immediate act. Reaction becomes mental when an alternative course is present (it may be that inhibition supervenes) and definitely indicated. This call for decision is an indicative mood, but not in the medical sense above referred to; it comes after the process of deliberation. Following the imperative, optative, or subjunctive moods there is a showdown, an indicated situation which demands a response. The act cannot be carried on unless there is an intention. The individual must take the attitude of the group; one is always speaking to audiences or communities, expressing universals that are significant to others.

There is organization among a set of individuals who are rational and who put this rationality into universal demands. Thus, to make an analogy, the eye must see in order that the legs may move efficiently, and the whole body makes a demand on each member to function in a way related to the entire body. There is an element of universality in the social object where there is a single meaning that is identical for all. Hypnosis is a short-circuiting of deliberation such as also occurs in conventional acts, except that in the latter case one can recover the act, go back over it and explain it, without having been conscious of it at the time of the act.

Language and the Vocal Gesture, Perception

The function and importance of the vocal gesture is that it is an indication that one gives to oneself, and it calls out the same response in others as in oneself. Imitation is not a sufficient explanation of the vocal gesture, for imitation does not arise in the social mechanism of conduct prior to significant symbols. It remains in the vocal gesture; as we listen to others we tend to repeat what they say, but it is because we take the attitude of the group that we do so.

In perception the meaning of the object, as the character of the object in our attitude, is there in advance of the completion of the act. Perceptions may be hypothetical perceivings based on completed acts and indicating the character that belongs to the completion. If the object is not there, it is a hallucination, a case of false perception. Even if we attribute the hallucinatory experience to the self, it is dependent on social experience for its coming into existence. So we distinguish between the organism and the self. The organism is there before the self. In this stage the individual can indicate to himself what he indicates to others, and this is dependent on the group. So the self is a later development. There must be organized activity for the development of the self. There must be situations where the individual can get the attitude of members of the group. There is then a self in a situation which involves society in relation to the individual. A self can exist only under these conditions, but a mind cannot be located in the organism.

Solipsism and Multiple Personality

Mind is coterminous with the group. The self comes into existence only over against the group. There cannot be a solipsistic situation; there must be other selves. They may, however, be different in character from the attitude of the organism. Impulses are not coterminous with the self, as psychoanalysis shows. What we are indicating may be different from what we think we are indicating; we may forget the name of the street where the enemy lives, but it is not really a forgetting but something that lies outside in the social mechanism, a matter of relationships with another individual of the group. This avoidance, however, does not become a conscious activity. The self is continually coming into existence, like the rest of experience; it shifts and changes with the social situation. Part of this occurs in the organism and its fundamental impulses, but these impulses are not present in the self, for we can analyze its experiences but not the impulse. The self comes into experience as other *things* do. We are inclined to retain a metaphysical attitude to the self as a final entity *(cogito ergo sum)* even though we cannot substantiate it because the emergence of the self results from the same mechanism that accounts for the emergence of other objects. Experiences are there. Whether they are hallucinations or will prove to be what the self takes them to be depends on the circumstances. When a person comes out of an anesthetic he may have experiences that do not involve the full self; they may not be organized into the full self but only into a part of it. The reality of an experience is what it implies. If a man falls down he is not what he sets himself up to be. We set up a self and try to maintain it, but it may not prove to be what we think it is; it may not be there in reality. Reality lies in the completion of the act and not in the process immediately going on.

Multiple personality is the breakup of the personality or self; there is no background for the organization of memory. In this case, the person may wake up in a western mining town. He is responsible for his conduct, but not for the community in which he finds himself. When the organism becomes a self it can act by using the mind.

Insofar as the organization does not exceed the individual, he can criticize it. Mere numbers in a community, however, do not promise quality. Persia gave rise only to loose aggregates, whereas Athens produced a Socrates who had a universal self. For a highly developed self there must be a highly developed community. Socrates and Jesus transcended the traditional, because each had the highest possible experience of the community. Neighborliness only appears where it is denied; thus the Samaritan and the Jew.

The Unity of the Self

The unity of the self requires the organization of attitudes that are shared by members of the group to which the individual belongs. A social process involving a number of persons provides the basis for the unity of the self. There is also the unity of the organism. The individual in his group attitude talks to his organism, and such conversation creates the self and self-consciousness. We always try to look at ourselves as others see us, although we may not see ourselves precisely in this way. The individual is always dependent on the group for his self. Thus, in the matter of property, we regard it from the point of view of the community; it is a rational affair, expressed in terms of rules. In the same fashion the child gets into the game by following a set of rules. Some people cannot react to abstractions but must put them in terms of "What would X say about it?"; they must see the world through other eyes. This is the case in politics and business; they are organized in terms of parties. To get selves, people must come back to the logical situations that have arisen in society. We depend on parties to keep our political machine going. We cannot get a response to an issue directly; there is a psychological necessity to work in parties. This unity is that of the group, and we depend upon it without placing it before ourselves. We enter business without knowing the exact structure of the business world. Here we have a certain organization and unity without the whole being there. In a game of bridge there is a simple organization, but foreign investment presents a complex situation. But all rational action is based on the feeling that one belongs to a definite group. There is a feeling of balance. In such processes one has a heightened sense of the self. Failure to remain in a particular group may mean the breakdown of the self. If one is taking advantage of the group, he does not fully belong to the group. But one cannot exist as a self without the universal, the group, that makes the self possible.

The unity that makes up the self is the unity of a social organization that makes one feel part of the social process, where one is ready to put oneself in the position of others. The unity of the self involves an organization of all the other selves. We do not deliberately create higher organizations; we do not gather in families and then set up nations. The nation is there before the individual family is fully organized or developed as a logical economic relationship. A natural catastrophe quickly shows us how closely we are all related; we all belong. Conditions hold people to one stage or group although they may not realize it at the time. Thus in self-consciousness we react more truly to organizations that are there than we do when we create new ones. So in dialects the people of one group develop a certain characteristic speech without being aware of it. In this case the purist who emerges is one who is merely aware of it. But many, on the other hand, find such unity with a group indispensable to their full life; they are born joiners. The unity of the self is the unity of the social process in terms of which we can come back to the organism itself. There are other processes, but they do not come directly into the self.

The Physical Organism and the Psychological Organism

There are two different integrations of the self; the physical organism and the psychical organism. The difference between them is recognized in the terms *soul* and *body*. The theories of Plato and Aristotle recognize the principle of reason as something not to be identified with the body, although Aristotle held that the soul was the entelechy of the body. Man had a principle of reason that was not to be identified with the body as such. The soul dealt with universals on a different level from that of the body. The body's character was different from that of the rational process. Thus reason dealt with universals beyond particulars or particles such as compose the body. Its new and different character is that of experience. Experience could act intelligently, but it required no universal law or rule. The concept of the soul which appeared later in European thought was different from that of Aristotle or Plato in terms of reason. This soul was akin to a double such as we find among primitives. The primitive soul can be killed; it has its own life and has to be placated with foods and offerings. There is largely present in the European idea of the soul an affective element not present in Aristotle or Plato. For Plato and Aristotle reason could not suffer either pleasure or pain; it had no sensuous experience. It had an integration of logic, of a universe of discourse. The unity of the soul, however, was like that of the body and demanded a sort of body, subject to sensuous experience. We trace the emergence of the self to the social process, but for Aristotle it occurs in terms of a logical process leading to conclusions. If three terms are involved, they are related in a logical conclusion containing all. The essential character of reason was that it is a medium for correlating meanings.

In experience we have cooperative conduct and behavior. We have an act that transcends the individual act, and its unity leads back to the organism involved. In this process, where there is an indication by the individual, the action transcends the life process of the separate form. He is there living and acting in a larger process. It is like the organization of different protoplasms in animals and plants; the protoplasm as part of the plant is living in a world wider than that of mere protoplasm. So also in muscular situations there is a balance of acid stimuli on all the muscle cells that take part in a wider process. This could not occur except as the cell is in relation with all the other groups of cells, and yet it is living its own life together with the life of the whole group. The muscle cell does not indicate to others what it shall do; but each tissue provides stimulations that are effective in carrying out the work of the other tissues, and so they carry out the whole life of the organism. In this respect the life of the organism resembles the life of bees and ants. The unity that transcends the organism does not enter into the life of the separate cells of the organism. There is a unity of the organism, but it does not get into the separate units.

With humans, who have significant symbols, the whole process enters into the life of the separate organism. Where one individual working with another provides the stimulus and the stimulus enters into the total act, you have the unity of the organism working in the individual. This is the situation in the ball game. We call it consciousness, but it is merely a carrying of the larger social act into the individual's activity. This changes the individual's attitude itself. Such consciousness is not merely awareness but an indication of stimuli that others can point out as well. The individual is thus able to change with the situation; he is conscious of it and can get it into himself. Consciousness is the introduction of the larger activity into the activity of the individual. This distinguishes the social individual from the organic. We cannot say this of the cell, although the passage of dioxides is registered in the individual cell. The fact that the more inclusive social process is registered in the individual self constitutes the difference between mind and body.

If we go back to Aristotle's psychology, we do not find this functional relationship between reason and the organism. Reason for Aristotle is an extraneous force that comes in and determines the form as an individual. In this respect, the problem becomes serious; there is a metaphysical point of great difficulty in separating the affections of the soul from those of the body. We distinguish mind as an organization of the activities of the individual that belongs to the whole as over against the body itself. There are two types of acting, that of the individual as an individual and that of the individual as incorporating a social organization. Where one person provides food, it is a process not to be stated in terms of each organism; it is part of the larger social organism. We cannot give a satisfactory account of the act of each muscle cell independently of the activity of the whole body. When the individual takes a role in which he brings in the whole as a part of his activity, there is consciousness. The person eating food not only satisfies his hunger but is engaged in a social affair as well; he takes account of what food is presented, how and why all of this enters into the process of elimination. In this he shows the difference between men on the one hand and ants and bees on the other.

Consciousness is the entrance into the life activity of the individual of the organization of the larger whole to which he belongs. The relationship of these two types of behavior, that of the individual as an individual and that of the individual as incorporating a part of the larger organization, constitutes the difference between mind and body. The self may be involved in a social process, but the process determines one's behavior only insofar as one takes the attitude of others. It is possible to say that the life of the whole does not enter into the organism, for if we assume that we can take the attitudes of others, we assume that this is in terms of the central nervous system. If the social process does enter into the life of the individual but without direct control, there would be a physiological process without any consciousness. What happens in the central nervous system is referred to the physiological process that is taking place there. We can follow the paths of excitement, they remain within the organism; but there is a parallel relating them with mind. But the larger act which enters into the activity of the self does not enter into the brain in physical terms. There is an abstraction of the self from the mass of activity of the social group.

The relationship of mind with the attitude of the other and of the organized group of others is put in relation with what goes on in the organism. They may be parallel, but they are not indicated. The behavior of the organism is different from the behavior of the self; the relationship between the two behaviors is like that between mind and body. The world in which we live cannot be identified with the central nervous system. Consciousness cannot be identified with neural reactions in physical or chemical terms. For Descartes there was a physical and a psychical realm, but this does not meet the problem. The statement for physical science cannot be extracted from the central nervous system. Meanings are involved in the physical, extended world. The distinction between the sensum and the process does not answer the problem of spirit and body. Mind and body are not to be separated on the basis of our present physical science.

There is, however, the separation in terms of behavior. The organism behaves in terms of its environment; it has the environmental pattern and its own individual pattern. Such patterns are found in acts where there is a process requiring time to take place. It behaves in relationship to its environment (so too do the electron and proton). The living object has a like pattern and structure and preserves it in transfer. An iron atom has identical electrons and protons, and it may lose or regain electrons. Still, we say it is not alive. It preserves the same stuff, and its process is the kind that does this. The change of the stuff does not belong to the process. In life, the process involves continued exchange of material. There is good reason for holding that the entire human body is changed within the course of some seven years. In the instance of the sock and mending, it is not the sock that mends itself; there is no life and this cannot be done, as a replacing of the self by means of the process that underlies the self. This, then, is a criterion of life.

There is a definite behavior in the systems of electrons and protons and in the galaxies, but they keep the same stuff, although there is an interchange of electrons through loss and replacement. But here there is a maintenance of the stuff as it is. From this emerges the animate form that introduces relationship into the stuff. There is a progress of stuff in the organism, but the pattern remains the same; there is a similar passage of energy to and from the environment and the organism. Iron, on the other hand, keeps up a definite quantum of energy in the revolutions of electrons.

In the corpuscular theory of light, the luminous structure takes on energy and then shoots it out on the saturation point. There is the filling up of a cup, but this is not the character of the physical cup. In the nonliving world there is a relation between the iron atom and the environment, but it is of a different type from that of living forms. The living form has a certain pattern of acting that means a continual taking in of materials and changing them. Thus we have dioxides, water, gas, and starches and a process that makes a cycle in the forms of plant and animal life. And if this is the case, the form is making a new environment.

The form, then, has a social environment in relation to other forms with which it carries out the life process on a larger scale. All living forms start from one cell, which by subdivision takes over the heredity of the original. There is further differentiation, and there is behavior of different tissues, but through the function of the independent tissue there is a unified life, and this preserves the organism. Each element acts in reference to the others, so that the whole body constitutes an envrionment, apart from the immediate environment of the fluids in which the tissue happens to live. In the social process of animals, there is a relationship between forms and the environment which is generally similar to that between the human form and its environment. Human society not only includes groups, as in the case of ants and bees, but it is a society in which each individual is activated by the life process of the whole to determine its own behavior. The individual thinks in terms of the group as a whole.

Morality

Morality is constituted where the person has in his own conduct the universals that govern the whole community. The community thus becomes moral, as it can recognize itself in one of its citizens. This is characteristic of human society; the behavior of the group as a whole enters into the separate individual. This morality may become universal when each can act as a member of a universal group. The individual has a community pattern if he lives in society. It is a process of education, though not of determination of facts. Our conduct is governed by highly complex relations of which we are largely unaware. With the development of communities, economic exchanges, and communication, these relations increase and morality grows. Thus morality may arise, but it is not a cognitive process; it arises through the recognition in one's society of those elements which are universal.

The question of mind and body from the standpoint of social relations concerns certain patterns of social response that involve individuals identified with a social group. This response constitutes the making of mind as it appears in the individual and distinguishes mind from the unity of the organism, with which it is not identical. If all are involved in the social process, the patterns belong to all the individuals and give universality to experience. The group is not limited to its members, but there is a differentiation in the functions which go together to make up the complete pattern. The same life process goes on in all the members and exceeds those of the individual organs, which may, however, assume other functions when necessity arises.

In invertebrate societies there are physiological differences; thus, fighting ants and working ants are fundamentally different in physical structure, and they depend on the society for their life and functions. The fighting ant and the queen bee must be fed by the workers, who in turn are protected by the fighters and given birth by the queen. Human society does not pattern itself on this basis, since the only physiological difference among humans is that of sex. In infancy humans are almost completely identical, but they are entirely dependent on the group for their livelihood. This, incidentally, works for the preservation of the society and for its progress. By putting off maturity, room is given for adaptation and alteration in the patterns, which works for the evolution and progress of the patterns. If the child had full language facilities at birth, there could not be the possibility of carrying over the essentials of the group into the next generation. The language process involves an interpretation of the world; the child finds itself in a world organized by society and can thus carry on its values to the next generation. We do not sufficiently emphasize the period of infancy in determining the child's world. This use of the period of immaturity is often too much neglected in the development of the community.

Freedom

The social process leaves the individual free. He has no physiological process fastened upon him, but stands on the basis of all other citizens of the community. There may be only slight advance, but it is advance nonetheless. The child gets the mind of the group, that pattern of social reactions which determines his own environment. The child takes over this common heritage of mind that goes over to the individual and so constitutes the unity of the self. It is a selective process, and its selections do not answer physiological needs of the organism. What the child hears and smells is a selection that answers the demands of his organism. The selection is made by the community to which he belongs. The child looks at a different heaven, food, etc., from what the children of other generations did. Mind and body is a relationship different from that of the organized stimulations existing in the subhuman animal. What the animal sees and hears calls forth a direct motor response. Bergson says we cut out the world to which we respond.

Early psychology held that all was a rain of stimuli, but now we recognize that the organism picks out responses and effects; the energy for and the impulse of seeking lie in the form itself. In cognitive selection this is mind in the individual form. The mind in the human form represents responses going on beyond the psychological reactions of the specific organism. The sun and moon of the child are a sun and moon revealed to him by the social process, through the telescope and then through language. His response, therefore, is not a response to light but to the moon or the sun as objects that endure. The sun and moon thus enter into his world from an early period, and they may therefore be registered in his central nervous system. There is a lack of individual coordination of mind and responses of the individuals. If you could lengthen the life period, each response could be carried out. These implications are there only in emotional responses that function. The child may thus enter the world of Galileo, but his own reactions are indirect—there is no idea that answers to the response. There is no direct stimulus–response situation. This is the world of the animal. The child lives in the world of the community with all its past experience. There is a great difference between the world the child looks out upon and the world involved in his immediate responses—eating, etc. The child sees and hears only the things to which he can respond, but as adults we see and hear a world much greater than we can possibly respond to. These two must be interrelated. The child cannot select his food on the basis of his sweet tooth. The old fallacy in education of trying to instill knowledge by repetition is now found to be a fallacy; there must be some occasion for calling out a response in the child.

The sun is only so much light for primitives, but for us it is the center of the solar system. In the economic and social life of the family there is a set of responses which the individual takes over as he puts himself in the position of other individuals of the group. These are ideas. The relationship of these ideas to the organism is one aspect of the body–mind problem. It involves a whole series of reactions. The human animal, by social endowment, can take over the whole train of social responses. The meaning of what one does may lie far beyond the actual act or the physical responses of the animal. Between this and the immediate world there is a great gap. The organism has few overt physical responses, but these responses may refer in their purely physical character to a very wide and complex field.

Mind and Body

The doctrine of the mind-body relation found in most texts is parallelism or interactionism. Our statement so far has distinguished between mind and body as organizations of behavior, but the unity of behavior in the human lies outside the organism itself. Its biological conditions may be overlooked for the purpose of social inspection. We must deal, as far as possible, in abstract terms that approach the mathematical and universal. If we follow human development back to the Heidelberg man, meaning disappears in terms of life; we cannot carry life all through the universe, for the world as a whole is not a living affair. The advantage of a mathematical statement is that it is applicable everywhere and at all times.

In the living form we consider the condensation of the hydrogen ion, not respiration. Sometimes, like the vitalists, we abuse science because it ignores life. But there is only a short distance we can go on the teleological program. It is possible to take values and try to make an intelligible universe, with a statement of energies and motion. This makes an intelligible statement of the world. It is a world one can manipulate and control. You can make things which you could not have made if you had all the values in the old forms. Form persists through all ages. But the human body cannot be treated in terms of life beyond a certain point unless we introduce the idea of entelechy. There are life values, but we cannot read our whole life in relationship with the world. There is a universal value in the approach of these two points of view. By this we can criticize the old values, and this is possible in terms of abstractions.

In consciousness alone does the individual become an object to himself, and thus the whole social process gets into the conduct of the individual. So mind and body is a relationship between the conduct of individuals and what goes on in the organism. There is a great disparity between conscious action and physiological conduct, the action of the organism. A person's leaving the room cannot be fully stated in physiological terms, for the physiological statement offers nothing more than a statement of the functions of his muscles, etc. The mechanical and teleological situations together constitute the situation of body and mind; this alone can give a full explanation of conduct. In the abstract mechanical laws of electrons and protons the human experience of the world can be carried back thousands of years to a period prior to the emergence of life. The world thus becomes intelligible—but the abstract account takes most values and puts them into footnotes.

The other plan of explanation is based on the type of conduct of the organism, reaction to stimuli. The human can be understood only in relation to the whole group. The action of the group must be present in his own activity; he does not only fit in like the ant and the bee. His conduct must be related with the conduct of the group.

Experiments with light, red and yellow for instance, transcend the mere animal reaction, for the subject is indicating to himself what his conduct will be in relation to them. The self then transcends the reaction. There are connections, but they are not facts of the same process; the parallelism does not extend to the whole. How are these to be brought into relationship? Each statement must be made in its own terms, but we must not sacrifice intelligibility by stating it in terms of vitalism or simple interaction. James's idea of "holding on to the skirts of an idea" implies that the mind controls the body. To say mind controls the action of the body is to make an account of the body incongruous. The proof is a statement in mechanical terms. When you describe a man acting as a social being you do not state this description in mechanical terms. The two accounts or descriptions must be brought together, but without sacrifice of intelligibility. In the same way the individual acts as a self to other individuals, and from this standpoint his organism is a self with characters of emotional experience—pleasure, pain, etc. If we resolve the organism into a mechanism, we act logically, for we learn how to bring up moral beings. But this mechanical arrangement of selections is not human. Emotions are not to be stated in terms of a mechanical relationship between the self and the organism. Philosophy and theology have tried to state the relationship between mind and body, but their statements are dogmatic and have not succeeded, not even when it was said that God used a mechanism in relating mind and body.

We still employ one form or another of parallelism of body and mind for working purposes, and we resolve the phenomena of the body into events that may be made to answer to consciousness. The problem of what is to be done with the two series has been sidestepped by psychologists. The basis of all science lies in the general supposition that the world can be conceived of as physical particles in certain strata that constitute the whole of nature. Physical science deals with situations on a hypothetical basis. This comes from the conservation of matter and energy. Into such a series you cannot get the object. The states of consciousness is described in terms of physical particles temporally and spatially located, and the postulate is that the universe at one moment is like it is at another. This postulate cannot be abandoned. But consciousness cannot be introduced, as science does, as a causal factor. So while it is a condition, it is not a direct causal element. There is a parallelism between the glory of the sunset and the process of change, but the glory does not enter into the process itself. Whether the sunset is out there or in consciousness is a problem; that there is a parallelism is all we can say. There are, however, interactionists who introduce consciousness as a causal factor.

We have a different demarcation between mind and body—things in relation to others insofar as they indicate to themselves and to others. The mind is there insofar as there is consummation in the indication. This gives a field of behavior not identical with the unity of the organism, but in relation to the group. The process does appear in a certain sense in the central nervous system, as we take the role of others; still, the unity or pattern does not belong to the organism but to the group. Any person who uses property is taking the attitude of the community; he does not simply seize anything that he wants. This organization of the process lies in the group, just as much as when he registers and votes. An organization of the body is a physiological organization, not to be identified with that of the group. The individual may indeed sacrifice the physiological organism for the benefit of the group; man as an organism may go down and give his life for the group which persists. Body and mind thus have different unities. There is much that goes on that does not appear in consciousness. We get tired and want to read and go to bed; the whole series is essential to the body but does not appear in self-direction. The organism of the body is not the organism of the self. We may have as little relation to our bodies as to the bodies of others. We can anatomize ourselves. There are excitements going on, and these answer to thoughts about them; but they are not part of the thought. To state the excitement in terms of the organism is not the same as our thinking about it. We could not identify what is going on in the organism by reference to the mind process.

The account of the scientist in physical and biological terms is different from what we are thinking of. There is an organic union between mind and body, they could not exist without each other, but we can think of them separately. To the savage, the self leaves the body in sleep. This separability indicates the relationship of mind and body. The self is an organization of mind through the group and communication and representation.

The Physical Thing as a Means to Ends

The physical thing is experienced in contact that answers to distance experience. It can be used in an implemental way in various activities. The physical thing lies in between the act and its consummation. Before we taste food it is something that we get hold of and take to the mouth; it is created by the hand and can be controlled and utilized by the hand; we get it between the thumb and finger. The human body is resolved into such physical things insofar as it has an atomic structure. These physical characters, however, stop short of the consummation of the act; it is a mediating conception. Science describes the world in terms of energy or particles, and by this we get the greatest control possible. But this is not the completion of the act, although it presents that form of reality that defeats illusion. If we say we have illusions of touch, we test the thing by other experiences. These physical things, however, are only mediatory; it is the philosopher's work to show values in the mechanical series. In the psychological statement we stop with the means. We are interested in food only as we get satisfaction out of it; as it gives an outlet and satisfaction, though, we do not stop with the physical statement alone. Mind has a consummatory value in its experience. We identify things as real physically, but we enjoy and suffer them apart from their physical character. The statement of the central nervous system, however, stops short of these values. So the parallelism between mind and body is not between series on the same level; they are on different levels. The self is an organization that is not like the physical organs of the body. The self transcends all these. We can burn the candle at both ends, neglect the body for the sake of the self, according as it fits into the larger social pattern. This is not so with the lower animals.

We state ends in terms of means; we make ends fit our means. This is the business of mind. But the body to be controlled is stated in terms of contact processes that are not to be the end of the act but only preliminary phases. So the parallelism of the mental state and the physiological process are on different levels. The two realms are exclusive.

It is important to discover the demarcation between mind and body, between the realms of the self and the physiological organism. Among the lower animals there is agreement here and no division. But for humans the physical statement falls short of values. The two realms are separate and different.

In perception as distance experience there is an attitude of contact experience. The self cannot be analyzed into its component elements, as psychology does with its apparatus for the interactions. There is a self there; back of this are the conditions in which it arises. What it is depends on analysis of experience. The distinction between the whole social situation and its patterns displayed in the conduct of the individual makes the difference between mind and body. The legitimate basis of distinction between the two is the distinction between the social patterns and the patterns confined to the organism itself. In the lower animals there is no such line; all go together. The lower animal's intelligent adjustment is to immediate stimuli. There is no sacrificing of the organism for the ideal, no basis for the distinction between mind and body. Where we have an organized other and the possibility of coming back to the self, there is a difference from the patterns of the physiological organism. The two patterns can be distinguished and separated. Anything that can be vocalized is a part of the self. The self is confined to fields of consciousness where there is communication. The impulses in the organism which break into the self may become part of the self and must be considered in this light. There are, for instance, many such characters that come into the self from this field. The child is carried off by passion and so the man; both are beside themselves.

The bringing of the two, mind and body, into close relation is the major problem of education and of life after the period of education. The past includes physiological changes that break into the self; they become part of the self. But there is much that cannot enter into the self.

There is another distinction between the organism as a physical thing and the mental process. The perceptual object must be considered in its character of matter and significance, or meaning and character. The table is thus an affair of electrons or of social usage; the distinction between the two is that between the self or mind and the aggregate of electrons that make up the brain. The brain, like the table, is something more than an aggregate of electrons. This distinction has a different line of demarcation from other things. The mind of the human as a pattern of universal conduct is far wider than the organism as a physiological entity affected by parents, etc. The two cannot be merged and included in one category, for we have so far no comprehensive category for the two. This does not mean that there is anything against it logically; it is merely a lack of our apparatus or knowledge.

Nor does this mean that the physiologist should abandon his effort to get back to chemical reactions; for in terms of such reactions he includes in the scope of his study realms that exceed the character of the individual and become universals that carry through all processes. Neither does it mean that the psychologist should restrict his study to such terms. The two are necessary in an adequate statement of behavior. The task of behavior-psychology is thus to present a statement of the two. They may not be included in one category and for the present remain in two; but as we have suggested, there is no reason for holding that they cannot be included in one. This is the aim of our future investigations.

3   Consciousness, Mind, the Self, and Scientific Objects

What is the meaning of the expression "loss of consciousness"? The event which it describes follows upon the effect of a blow, of a poison, or of some physiological abnormality, or of profound sleep.

It is a ceasing of experience in respect of the individual concerned, while experience continues in respect of others not affected by the conditions inimical to the organism. When the effects have worn off, experience resumes in the case of the individual, and he recognizes that events have transpired during the period of his so-called unconsciousness which would otherwise have been registered in memory, but which absolutely do not exist for him as matters of experience.

It is an extension of the losses of experience which follow upon the closing of the eyes or the other sense organs, the local anaesthesias, due to the local effects of temperatures or drugs, as well as of the shifting of attention so completely from certain parts of experience that they disappear.

It is evident that it is but logical to assume a zero point in experience in which all disappears, if its diameter can be diminished, or different parts of it be withdrawn.

The term "loss of consciousness" is the statement of this defection of experience as a whole, when it is dependent on conditions of the organism which preclude experience.

When an expected event does not transpire, experience is diminished. If some external shutter bars vision, experience is again curtailed. But these sublations of experience are due to conditions outside the organism. Loss of consciousness represents the defection of the organism or some of its mechanisms in that interplay of world and organism which is essential to experience. When consciousness returns experience is again resumed because the organism again enters into functional relationship with the environment.

Has the event of loss of consciousness any bearing upon that phase of experience which we term mind, or upon the socalled body-mind problem? In the light of the above statement it is evident that consciousness only has existence and meaning in the statement of experience from the standpoint of the organism, it being recognized that both organism and environment must interact for the existence of experience. Loss of consciousness does not then imply something that is separable from the experience in which both organism and its environment appear. It is meaningless in view of such a description to speak of the consciousness as leaving the body and existing in some other dimension of experience. It cannot therefore indicate the nature of mind.

Mind is that part of experience in which the individual becomes an object to himself in the presentation of possible lines of conduct. This presentation takes place by means of the imagery of past experience whose presence is conditioned by the past experience of the individual and the attitudes which it has left. This imagery is therefore as dependent upon the structure and functioning of the organism as is the sense experience. And as the self appears as an object only through the individual addressing himself by vocal and other gestures, this phase of experience also is dependent on the structure and functioning of the organism.

The relation of the body and mind is then the relation between the functioning of the individual organism and that part of experience in which the individual does address himself, presenting possible conduct through the use of imagery.

The only characteristic difference between this relation and that lying between the objects in the environment and sense experience is that it lies between the individual as an object and the individual answering to this object, for imagery is also present in sense experience of objects in the environment. Consciousness has no other meaning here than that the organism is functioning normally. The characteristic difference appears in the expression "self-consciousness."

What is the relation of the reality in experience and that existing under conditions in which there could be no experience? By experience is implied reality in which living organisms are essential parts, not in the sense that the objects in the environment appear as presentations of the organisms, or that the relation between the objects and the organisms is that of awareness, but that what constitutes the object in the experience is dependent on the selection of content and imagery which the sensitivities of the organisms involve. In other words the environment and the form are objectively real. This is clearly evident in the interweaving of plant and insect life, or in the creations of human industry.

One could pass from one experience to another or to others only insofar as the individual could become an object—as an individual— instead of the organism that answers to an environment. This would involve also the presence in his organism of sufficient affinities to other forms so that he could take the role of the other form into whose environment he wished to enter. Insofar as there are common attitudes in all these roles assumed, and insofar therefore as there are common objects answering to these attitudes, there appears what may be called a generalized environment and a generalized organism. Such experience as this must of course have its own function in the concrete experience of the society within which it arises. The objects of the objective sciences are evidently, from this standpoint, the objects of this general- ized experience, and their relation to the concrete organism on the one side and to the concrete environment on the other have provided the two great speculative problems, the one the relation of mind and body, the other the relation of metaphysical entities to the objects of imme- diate experience.

The effect of taking the role of anyone is to eliminate the peculiarity of the environment of any one individual and to substitute for any con- crete individual an abstraction—a generalized individual, the thinker. The result of the analysis which the thinker makes is to set up an ob- server with a field which underlies both the environment and the indi- vidual of immediate experience. In the immediate experience there is a sensitive organism and a world of color and other qualities. It is not necessary that objects in immediate experience should be colored. Those born blind live in a world of immediate experience. What is essential is that objects should have some quality or groups of qualities which affect the organism from a distance. In scientific imagination or otherwise we may replace the characters that affect us by other con- tents. We may replace in immediate experience the color with a con- geries of atoms and electrons if need be, so long as these simply take the place of the character we are analyzing, and we sense them in imagination as surrogates of the original characters; but if the process of analysis is carried so far that we also substitute for the individual orga- nism a congeries of atoms and then, for those, galaxies of electrons, and put them into relationship with the objects by way of the interplay of forces between the one congeries and the other, then immediate experi- ence is gone unless it is salvaged as a consciousness that is separable from the organism: for such an explanation of characters of things wipes out the characters explained. There is no color in a world without things covered with surfaces which reflect some rays of light while they absorb other rays and send on the reflected rays by way of vibrations of ether to affect the rods and cones of a retina.

There are, in my judgment, two logically different tendencies in the thinking of scientists when dealing with such problems: either they tend to replace the object with imagery of minuter particles and uncritically to imply a microscopic eye that takes the place of the sensing organism, thus substituting a suppositious direct experience for that of the eye and hand; or else they undertake to reject all imagery of a physical object in thinking things, and rigorously to confine their thought to the statement of inferred relations between posited metaphysical objects which are by definition beyond any conceivable experience.

This latter attitude, which has the appearance of being the correct attitude, has generally led to placing in a field of consciousness all the characters of the world of immediate experience except the abstract relations with which mathematics and a mathematical logic are occupied. It leaves thought with the epistemological problem of getting from an immediate experience within which knowledge lies over into a metaphysical field that seems to be entirely beyond reach. There is a more modern philosophic movement which finds its origin in the scientific tendency under consideration—neo-realism with its symbolic logic. This doctrine, proceeding by a ruthless analysis, leaves all of reality in the form of ultimate elements—such as points and moments, and sensations, and concepts, and external relations. Such a doctrine conceives its task not to be that of relating objects in immediate experience with metaphysical objects, but that of taking everything to pieces. The epistemological problem here seems to evaporate, though it condenses again, refusing to be thus conjured out of existence.

What is of striking interest is that the differences of attitude represented by these different tendencies seems to have no bearing on the work of the research scientist. Neither the question of the existence of a consciousness, or of a metaphysical object, though both seem to be implied in scientific findings, have provoked any interest in the scientist. This may be due to the fact that the problems of the physical sciences take the form of an analysis of a distant object in terms of possible contacts. It is the relation of elements of the retina to those of the surface of the epidermis. How many of the latter will answer to a given quantity of the former is a question solely of the distance of the object. The same object expressed in terms of excitement of rods and cones may answer to any number of square centimeters identified by actual placing of the rule by the hand, depending entirely upon the distance to which we project the object. The increased diameter of the moon or sun at the horizon is a familiar illustration. This may be called the process of telescopic analysis.

On the other hand, an object within the field of immediate experience, the relationship of whose distance and contact values has been determined, i.e., an object which we both see and handle and which has therefore been measured, such an object under a refracting medium affects a larger number of retinal elements. It is said to be magnified. In terms of immediate experience this may be interpreted either as the actual increase in dimensions of the object, or as such an increase in the fineness of the vision as the apparatus of distance perception might attain through the approach to the object at closer and closer intervals. This latter interpretation in terms of immediate experience implies a continually proportionate reduction in the size of the observer. If the size of the observer is reduced with respect to that of the objects observed the relative size of the objects will be increased. This may be called microscopic analysis.

Out of the formulation and refinement of the relations between the distance and contact experience of the object has arisen the apparatus of the exact sciences, the mathematical sciences. The form of their problems therefore always involves simply the relation of the distant environment to the organism as shown above. It is not possible to translate a problem of the exact sciences into the form of the relation of organism to immediate experience, for they undertake to gain the conditions of any experience. This is what is implied in the problem of the relation of the organism to consciousness. It is the problem of the pseudo-science of psycho-physics. Fechner's unsuccessful attempt to establish a logarithmic relation between the quantity of the stimulus and the number of conscious elements that went to make up a sensation, proceeded on the false assumption that there is a consciousness separable from things, and that it is made up of elements which are found in just perceptible differences of sensation. These are entirely unjustifiable metaphysical assumptions. These assumptions are due to the form which the analysis of the exact sciences gives to the problem.

As indicated above, the objects are subdivided until they lie beyond the realm of a possible immediate experience, and this analysis is inevitably carried into the structure of the organism itself. The whole process of experience is then stated in terms of the changes of minute particles which lie beyond a possible experience. The immediate experience of which this is a formulation remains thus outside the process which science presents, and is relegated to another field, that of a so-called consciousness. The metaphysical interpretation of this situation seems to be unjustified, for consciousness represents simply the normal response of the organism in its interplay with its environment. Further-more there is apparently no serious difficulty involved in the assump-tion that a world constituted of the elements posited by the physical sciences should give rise to objects and organisms within which this immediate experience arises. We are, however, bound to consider the character of the experience within which these subexponential objects of the physical sciences are posited on this assumption. This is also an experience and implies objects over against individuals. There is here the same relation of environment and individual which exists in imme-diate experience. The two determine each other in terms of selection. A supposititious individual is implied that can experience electrons revolv-ing around positive electrical charges that together constitute atoms. Distance experience and possible contact experience are implied, other-wise the elements would not be physical objects.

We cannot minimize the parts of physical things without at the same time implying a conceivable corresponding reduction of the powers of perception by which they would enter into a conceivable physical experience. Science rigorously abstracts from all the implications of such a perception except for the determinations of relative velocities and changes in velocity and the inertias of the physical particles; but does such an abstraction free these objects from the implications of lying within a field of experience? The realist asserts that it does. He assumes that the object can enter the mind as thought without any implications of perception. He assumes that ultimate elements and relations can be recognized as such because they simply happen in upon the mind.

The effect of this analytical method of the realist is to break up the objects of immediate experience and the objects with which science is occupied into elements of quite varied and logically different characters, such as points and moments, that are not the points and moments of experience and can be only negatively defined. These characters are said to have relations which are external to the relata and separable in know-ledge of ordinary objects. Such an analysis makes possible very com-prehensive formulae which have enormously wide application, rigorous demonstration within the realms of mathematics and symbolic logic. But it is a method that never has been used on the actual frontiers of science; for science has always proceeded by the hypothetical positing of objects which are logically of the same character as the objects of immediate experience.

Science has always analyzed its objects into other objects, never into the logical elements out of which objects may be conceived of as put together. So far as it is possible, the scientist conceives his object as occupying the field of immediate experience, as being simply a minimal object differing from the object of direct experience only in being beyond the vision and tactile limit of direct experience, as for example microscopic and submicroscopic disease organisms. Even molecules, atoms, and electrons are presented as far as possible in terms of reduced dimensions of objects of direct experience. It is only when science undertakes to explain the process of immediate experience itself that its objects pass logically out of the field of possible immediate experience.

The problem is therefore the import of the undertaking to explain immediate experience in terms of objects whose existence must lie outside of immediate experience. I have already suggested that the problem may not carry with it the difficulties which exist on the face of it. It may be that there is in existence a world of subexperiential objects within which organisms and their environments arise together with immediate experience. The legitimacy of this assumption becomes questionable when we recognize that in the world of subexperiential objects it leaves the characters of objects which they explain without objects to which they belong. Inevitably they are associated with the mind that carries on the analysis and they seem to imply some nature of which they can be regarded as states. Whatever else may be said of these characters they must be regarded as belonging to objects. Either to make them over into states of consciousness or to leave them as bare universals existing in a Platonic world runs counter to the nature of experience within which we find and identify reality. One or the other of these alternatives are necessary unless we assume that the characters in question come into existence with the immediate experience, i.e., that color and sound, odor and taste arise not as states of consciousness but as qualities of objects together with the sensibilities of animal forms. Otherwise stated, the surfaces are colored the vibrations visible to the eyes and audible to the ears; without eyes and ears they are merely surfaces and vibrations. This would imply that in an experience there is not only the selection of objects in an environment for which the attention and interests of organisms are responsible, but also that increased sensitivities of organisms actually add contents to the objects within the environments; in other words that the eye creates color in the object and the ear creates sound.

Stated in this form, the assumption is not an attractive one. But it may be claimed that with the higher organization of things such characters as these may come to objects though they are by definition lacking to their constituent parts. The results of combinations may be qualitatively unlike those of what goes to make them up. From this point of view the eye and the ear would not create the characters. The characters would be there, and the eye and the ear would respond to them. If we return to the immediate experience within which objects have these characters, we find that the organism that perceives them is not the organism that physiology, physics, and chemistry analyze. On the contrary, this organism so studied is itself perceived. We place ourselves outside it and analyze it into the same elements as those out of which the objects that affect it are made up. The sensuous characters exist in the world of immediate experience, but in that experience the analysis does not take place. For that analysis inevitably includes the perceiving organism. In the analyzed world color and sound, etc. do not exist. They do exist in the world of immediate experience. The problem is then the relation of these two worlds to each other.

The first point to be noticed is that the individual remains in the world of immediate experience in regard to all that lies outside the field of thought. The field of immediate experience is the support for getting his lever under the world of reflective thought. Insofar he can present the objects that result from his analysis as parts of this world he does so. It is only when his explanations of the characters of the world lead him to objects which cannot themselves have these characters and states the organism in the same terms that these objects pass out of a possible world of immediate experience. He could and is apt uncritically to assume that when atomic and molecular objects reach a certain size and organization they become colored and sounding, but he runs upon a difficulty when he identifies the molecular and atomic organism, that is, an object over against the perceiving individual, with this perceiving individual. This makes it necessary to find in the perceiving individual contents answering to the physiological processes caused by the molecular and atomic world, while in immediate experience perception is simply the relation to the object that is there.

The only content that can be found in immediate experience answering to the effect on the organism of surfaces, which through reflection of ether waves stimulate the retina, is the color which for immediate experience is the colored object. Thus this identification carries over into the perceiving individual of immediate experience the objects of his perception. It is evident that, logically, the physiological system must be kept as a part of the objective world and cannot be identified with the perceiving individual.

This brings us to the question of the situation in which the individual can be an object to himself, and the relation of that self to the physiological organism as presented by scientific analysis. The criterion already given of the appearance in experience of the individual as an object is that action directed toward an object should also be directed toward the individual. Such action, in case the individual responds to it, identifies him as an object. This action also places the individual in the attitude of an other—an object reacting to himself. It is only when such conduct leads to assuming the role of another that it can be logically completed. In this case an entire social act lies within the conduct of the individual. He hears his voice as an expression of an object—a social object—and he responds to this stimulation as he would respond to the vocal gesture of another. When he has taken the other phases of the act, which is the attitude of the other, so that his response will be in character, that is, so that the reply has all the essential implications of reaction to another, the individual will have appeared as an object in experience. In this complication of social conduct the individual does become an object insofar as the individual also becomes another.

It is true that in the contacts of the different parts of the body with each other, especially with the hands, the organism becomes in a sense an object to itself. However, the body as an object—a purely physical object—enters hardly at all into the field of adjustment to the other objects. It appears as an object almost entirely in the application of the hands to its surfaces and their appendages, in rubbing, scratching, etc. The adjustments of the body as an object to other physical objects take place quite automatically. It is not the body that we feel and partially see that makes its adjustments to distances and anticipated contacts. While these experiences of sight, touch, odor, taste coming from the body do fuse with the experiences of movement and adjustment to the objects in the environment, the former do not serve purposes of control in the conduct of the body. We do not see ourselves making a leap by this experience.

In the immediate experience of purely physical objects the body of the individual as an object does not enter the field of adjustment. As an object it is of interest practically only in its own care. In social conduct of the deliberative type, the self as a social object enters the field of adjustment on the same basis as other objects. Where this takes place there appears what is called mind. This sort of experience involves not only the immediate presence of objects, but also the conversation of the persons and things with the individual, the persons and things whose roles the individual assumes in so-called thinking, and the imagery, some of it organized as memory and some simply there but dependent for its appearance and continued presence upon the interests of the individual, especially the interests of thought. The thinking in its simplest form is the presentation of possible conduct under conditions of reflection, i.e., in inhibitions which are involved in the adjustment through gesture of complex social conduct. In thinking the individual replies to the gesture, while both gesture and reply become the symbols of the anticipated experiences which the conduct implied in the attitude would bring with it. The effect of this thinking is to put into the objects of immediate experience values which did not exist there before and to lead to conduct which overcomes difficulties otherwise insurmountable.

The world which answers to the composite thinking individual includes the hypothetical structures of things which these different alternative lines of conduct imply. We will assume that a man rehearses a conversation with an acquaintance in persuading him to undertake some piece of work together with the individual in question. The acquaintance objects and the man replies with common advantage and later gains. Out of the imagery conversation arises a plan of approach and attack which promises success. This hypothetical world of imagery and vocal gestures developed into symbols implying things and occurrences grows out of the objects of immediate experiences and must eventually fit into the world of experience within which the conduct must take place. For the time being, however, it has not this immediacy or its sort of reality. However secure it may be in the intelligence which inspires it and the past experience it reflects, it has not the security of accomplished fact. Its reality depends on the outcome of the projected conversation on the morrow. In this world is a self of the individual which is an object over against the self in whose mind the whole thinking goes on. It stands for the individual as he will conduct the discussion tomorrow. In other words it is the self that is not in immediate experience, that is not only continuous in memory from the past, but in anticipation into the future, that stretches over the vacuities and interstices of sleep, and the so-called losses of consciousness, that includes the springs of action which lie beyond the range of reflective control, but especially that has such an organization for future conduct that present conduct becomes possible and intelligent. It is that hypothesis of the self which enables the individual to act with reference to the future.

Insofar as this hypothetical self includes elements which by definition cannot be in immediate experience, to this degree it is metaphysical, and it is the precipitation of these metaphysical elements that have in the past crystallized into a soul. These elements include: the continuity of interrupted experience, of past and future experience, the springs of social conduct that do not themselves appear in experience, those contents of selves and other social objects which belong to them in immediate experience but which the accepted hypothesis of the self does not admit of, e.g., the so-called altruistic expressions which a hedonistic doctrine explains psychologically, or the unsophisticated impulsive goodness which a Calvinistic theology explains as self-deception, or the characters which mistaken judgments of others have ascribed to them. In general the self as an object, that is, the self which the individual presents to himself, takes into itself contents which belong to the objects of the perceiving individual in immediate experience. This is also true of the relation of the immediate experience of physical objects to the physical organism over against its physical environment.

In immediate experience the perceiving individual, apart from the self that arises in social conduct, is merely a point over against the object, that is, perception is only the presence of objects. The contents in the objects which psychological analysis places in the individual, the imagery from past experience, the imagery from motor responses, the meaning and ideas, are all in the object. Its distance, its solidity, its roughness or smoothness, its attractiveness or repulsion, its aesthetic values, are all in the object. This is not the relationship that exists between the physical organism and the physical objects that affect it in the process of perception. The whole content of imagery can be stated only in terms of the central nervous system, the re-excitement of tracts which have been affected in the past. The same is true of meaning. It can be stated in terms of the physical organism only in the excitement of the motor responses, which are held in check. A very considerable part of the object of immediate experience must be located not in the physical object but in the physical organism. If now we identify, in any sense, the perceiving individual with the physical organism, these contents which are placed in the central nervous system of the organism can only be put into the perceiving individual of immediate experience by taking them out of the object and calling them states of consciousness of the self or, metaphysically conceived, of the soul. We must also include in this list of contents of the self, which the identification of the physical organism with the perceiving individual forces upon the self, the secondary qualities insofar as they cannot by definition exist either in the physical organism or the physical objects of its environment, since the elements out of which physical science conceives the stimulating surfaces and chemical structures of the objects and the end organs and nervous apparatus of the organism are made up could not have the characters of the experience which they are supposed to condition. These then have been also regarded as states of consciousness. However this identification of the perceiving individual and the organism in perception is subject to the most serious question.

The identification takes place in the social process out of which mind arises. It is the process in which the individual addresses himself and thus becomes an object to himself. The individual who addresses himself is the perceiving individual, responding directly to the stimulation which his own gesture and attitude have called out. To this extent the self thus addressed exists for him as an object, while the addressing individual is without content except that of the gesture involved in addressing himself, and this appears as an object only in the response it arouses and the memory image of the act. The self addressed, on the other hand, stands out as a social object viewed from the standpoint of social conduct, and as physical object over against physical conduct. As the individual takes the part of the other or the generalized other he is object to himself. Insofar as he takes the part of the individual in reply to this address, the other or others are objects to him, and he is in the attitude of immediate experience. It is important to note that the relation of the social self to the physical organism lies between these two in the objective field and never includes the self of immediate experience. The relation between mind and body is an analysis of an object. This object is mental insofar as the contents are the interplay of the inner conversation with the imagery and meanings which the so-called thought isolates from the objects. It is the body insofar as the organism as an object is distinguishable from the interplay of inner conversation consisting of its imagery, meanings, and the affective characters that attach themselves to them. This body in primitive communities is still a social object, as are all other physical objects in which vivid interest centers, even after death.

Our unreflective attitude toward the self as a social object includes the physical organism insofar as this is involved in social stimulation and response. The man is his facial expression, his tone of voice, his threatening or friendly pose, and his conversation. Insofar as the physical organism does not play a part in this social stimulation and response, insofar even as it is or can be ignored without the disappearance of the self as an essential social object, insofar as parts of the organism can be actually lost without this disappearance, it may be and comes to be regarded as purely physical. Insofar as the inner interplay of inner conversation can go on without evident bodily expression, it comes to be regarded as separable from the body and capable of existence apart from the body, though the immediate attitude of those who have entertained this belief has given the self disembodied from this body another tenuous body which is capable of conveying those social stimulations and making those social responses which have been the essence of the self as a social object. While the original distinction was between a self that could leave the body and a body which after the double had left it was also a social object, the development of the physical object has led to an entirely logical situation. The soul or self that belonged to the object that was becoming impersonal, i.e., was ceasing to arouse or answer to social stimulations, became the nature of things, its tendency to react in a definite manner, a force which inhabited the object as the spirit had inhabited the body. Such a change in the character of the object could not take place with a corresponding change in the attitude of the individual toward the object. This change is the evolution of the process of thought out of the conversation between selves.

The evolution of things and thought has been and must have been parallel. In this evolution, because the individual addresses himself and replies to himself, the interest and attention shift from the social object and its gestures and turn to that which the gestures indicate, and to the attitude of the individual toward the thing indicated. In actual cooperative action with others in a group not only do the different individuals indicate to each other the objects of mutual interest, both to themselves in their attitudes [in] preparations for later conduct, but also they indicate objects about them that are involved in the cooperative conduct. In this conversation of gestures, as a rule, the other individuals remain of outstanding interest. Attention centers *on* them as social objects rather than on the gestures as such and their implications. In conversation with one's self the interest turns to the implications of the gesture rather than to the self as an object, though daydreaming with the self as the central figure on the scene may seriously interfere with attention given to a train of thought. Still, in general, the self that speaks in thinking and the self that replies are tenuous figures, and in

highly developed thought they disappear entirely and reveal their
implicit presence only by their implication of an audience which is
essential to their own existence. The effect of this fading away of the
self behind its conversations is inevitably to reduce the social character
of the objects. Even other selves and one's own self become things,
as distinguished from persons, for purposes of thought, though this
abstraction is resented whenever the values that attach to persons,
as distinguished from things, are considered. Another important result
of the deflection of interest from the selves that enter into the inner
conversation we call thought to what I have called the implications of
these gestures, is the mechanism they provide for the analysis of the
object and the reference of the parts of the objects as stimuli to the
tendencies to respond which are aroused but inhibited in a situation
that involves conflict. This relation of the stimulus to the tendency to
respond does not in itself constitute significance. For this there must be
indication of the relation, and this can appear in the experience of the
individual through the indication to himself of the value of the stimulus.

The analysis of the object thus conceived must involve a corresponding analysis of the group of reactions by which the individual responds
to the organized group of stimuli which constitute the object. This
analysis of the individual's reactions at first goes no further than the
analysis of the object into parts which are or can be parts of the immediate experience. This would bound the field of the contrivances and
mechanisms which up to the seventeenth century provided the physical
basis of civilization. The relation of mind and body up to this time
presented no serious difficulties, insofar as the implications of immediate
experience are concerned. The identification of the body as the organ
of perception in reflective experience did not transfer to the self the
characters and qualities of objects; for these characters and qualities
were found in all the elements into which analysis divided the objects.
There was a realm of sensuous things and of bodies endowed with
sensitivity, and there was a realm of ideas, or forms or meanings, and
of a mind which perceived them. It was only this rational soul that
Platonism and Aristotelianism regarded as existing after the death of
the body. The motives that led to the conception of the immortality of
a soul capable of sensuous experience were found in the religious cults
of the old world and the social problems which Christianity undertook
to meet. It was the successful analysis of motion and matter by the
physical dynamics introduced as a science by Galileo which brought
into the world the modern problem of mind and body as a problem
involved in the account which science gives of the physical world and

hence of the physical body as well. With this appears the doctrine of a consciousness which is not only the realm of thought but of all the qualities of immediate experience, which disappear under the scientific analysis of matter.

As I have indicated above, the body as an organ of perception is the field of a much larger part of the experience of objects than is the perceiving individual of immediate experience, if we undertake to state the experience of perception both in terms of immediate experience and in terms of a science that deals both with the organism and its environment; from the standpoint of the world of social objects, part of the object which is there for the perceiving individual of immediate experience is included in the self, physical or social. This part of the object which reflective experience includes in the experiencing individual but which is not there in immediate experience is, in each case, that of physical and social reflection, put into the self through the passage of the perceiving individual into the object, from which point of view the perceiving individual regards the self. It is the content of the experience which is then identified with the perceiving individual of immediate experience. I have described the process of social experience as that of taking the role of the other. The mental rehearsal of a conversation to take place at a later date is an example of this including a part of the object for immediate experience in the perceiving individual through reflection. For the perceiving individual in presenting himself, as he will respond to the man whose role he is taking in thought, identifies with himself the attitudes and responses which will be his when the conversationist addresses him. Such a self is dependent upon the hypothetical social environment within which it arises in so-called imagination. Its relationship to the perceiving individual is stated in terms of motives, faculties, powers, or impulses and instincts.

The hoary problem of the freedom of the individual is a problem of the relation of this self to the individual of immediate experience, and is logically of the same type as that of the relation of mind and body. For into this self is taken up all the objective social values, aesthetic, moral, economic, and logical. What an introspective psychological analysis does is to present the hypothetical conditions under which social conduct can go forward. As it states these conditions both in terms of the individual and of those involved with him in the same problematic situation, and as the elements into which the acts and their values are analyzed could not by definition have the imports and meanings which they possess in objective social conduct, these imports and values are carried over in the form of culture, subjective morality, subjective economic valuations, and subjective judgments of truth and error. For example, an economics or an anthropogeography which undertakes to show that certain results necessarily follow from certain conditions found in human nature inevitably refers to the consciousness of individuals and the voluntary acts by which men thought that they brought these events about. It follows that the mind with its reflective experience is taken up into the individual of immediate experience. The object of this experience is not simply that of immediate experience but includes also a reconstruction of part of the world of immediate experience. The reconstruction is hypothetical and depends for its validity upon later immediate experience. Insofar as it is identified with the self, it involves a reconstruction of the individual as well, for there has been a selective process going on in the mind. What is picked out of the analyzed object is dependent upon the interest and attention of the individual and upon the imagery which lies for the time being in his mind.

A successful result of the experimental experience means therefore not only a different objective world but a different self. The hypothetical structure both of object and of the individual is a schema which is universal in its implication, inevitably applicable in theory to the whole structure of the world of experience. If thought assumes atoms as the elements of the object, it must assume that they are the structure of all material objects, not merely of those about which the problem of thought gathers. Thus thought projects a world of atoms which it substitutes for the objects of immediate experience. To this degree it presents a world of knowledge which seems to take the place of the world of immediate experience—things that are known or thought, for things that are. An idealistic system argues that the success of the experiment in the world of immediate experience transfers the existence of immediate experience to that of thought, even when these thought objects lie beyond the realm of possible experience. In order that such an inference be drawn it is necessary to state the individual as a perceiving individual, that this play of atoms or electrons may affect him, even if the effect cannot be in terms of immediate experience. Such a world of atoms including both the objects and the individual actually eliminates immediate experience, as it sets up atomic structures for every part of immediate experience, including the relation of perception or existence. In other words it eliminates the experience from which it gets its assurance of existence. Nor is it possible to maintain that out of such a congeries of ultimate elements of things there has arisen such a world and such an individual that immediate experience appears, for there are certain contents of the objects which have by definition been transferred to the individual. These elements are the structure of the thing as determined by the interest and organized habits of conduct, the imagery which has been detached from the object and is significant of meanings which are denied and of meanings which may exist. Furthermore the biological organism conceived as the physical self, which can enter into complete relation with its atomic environment, is presented in contact terms, terms of a possible immediate experience for an individual with an organism fine enough to feel the resistances which even an electron possesses and in some way to sense its spatial relations. Its color, sound, etc., cannot be so sensed even by such an individual, for color, sound, etc., arise through the operation of electrons.

So far as we identify the individual of immediate experience with this biologic body so conceived, the secondary qualities must be placed in a consciousness. If we undertake to make use of the conception presented above, that the increased complexity of the structure of objects and of the biologic organism can give rise to new characters in the objects, we are forced to recognize that, while the conception of the world and the organism as made up of physical elements which in their elementary form could not by definition possess the so-called secondary qualities, dovetails well enough with the doctrine of a consciousness in which these characters as well as the contents of mind are placed, this conception of the ultimate reality of things does not readily conform to the assumption of radical empiricism that perceptions are things which are there without awareness. If these secondary qualities appear in the things as the result of their complex organization and are, as radical empiricism affirms, there in the objects, then the color, etc., of things which have arisen through their complex organization do not affect us directly. The effect is through the corpuscular structure of things and of the body. If color is in the object, the theory of color perception will not account for its being perceived. From the standpoint of such a theory there is no place for the color except in a consciousness. If we put the apparatus of color perception in the physical body, there is no way of getting the color from the object to the individual. From the standpoint of immediate experience there is no need of getting the color over. It is simply there in the object and its being there for the individual is what is called perception—but not a perception that is stated in terms of physical theory. We seem to keep up an immediate experience in imagination of body as tactual and as resisting effort to occupy its own space or movement or change in direction of movement. The corpuscles are after all but smaller bits of matter of immediate experience though it is only by imaginary presentation they are as corpuscles brought into the range of immediate experience, but to account for our perception of their color and other so-called secondary qualities by this corpuscular structure in things and in the body leaves these qualities out of any relation with the perceiving individual of immediate experience. We must return to a consideration of what this theory of structure of things and the body and its attendant theory of sense perception mean for our immediate experience.

The self comes into existence as soon as the individual becomes an object to itself. This takes place insofar as the individual by its own response to physical or social objects finds itself stimulating itself to such a response as the object makes and besides this tendency to respond indicates to itself by gesture this response as the attitude of the object toward itself. In this fashion the individual takes the place of the object toward itself and thus becomes an object to itself in its own experience. The field within which the individual can take the place of the physical object toward itself is only that of contact experiences, including the reaction of motor response to these. When we have placed ourselves in the place of the physical thing over against ourselves, we do not see, hear, smell, or taste ourselves, but we do feel ourselves in contact with the object and with our effort expended in resistance. The other characters of things we are bound to state in terms of contact experience as it is only in the field of contact experience that we can become objects to ourselves directly.

The theory of perception undertakes to place the physical body of the individual in the field common to it and other objects which are perceived and to state the process by which the relations between objects and the individual arise and are determined. It is only the thing, in the place of which we can place ourselves, that can have an inside—an interior—and it is only in terms of contact experience that we can put ourselves in the place of the physical thing, since it is only the pressure that we exert upon physical things that calls out in us a pressure corresponding to that which things exert in us. A man pushing against a massive object arouses in himself such a tendency to heave against his own pressure that he puts himself in the thing. It is an other to him whose role he can take. Inevitably reality will be in terms of pressures and contacts, and other experiences of physical things will be stated as far as possible in terms of objects that occupy space and have inertia. It is true that the exact measurements of objects and their motions is through the application of visible spatial discriminations to those of contact, and that the imagery of objects even lying beyond the range of possible vision is in visual form, but our judgments of reality places contact contents as the real elements behind the visual forms.

The function of the visual determination is found in the coincidence of the minute discriminations of a distance sense with the coarser experience of contact. That this distance sense should be visual is immaterial. Color differences are not of the nature of matter as is its extension, movability, and its inertia. The vast importance of the dynamic doctrine of nature lies in the fact that an exact statement of inertia can be made in terms of velocity and its acceleration. It is this method which has enabled us to state in terms of mass and motion the other characters of body except those of contact experience. If we abstract from the epistemological problems that have occupied philosophy since Descartes, the function of a theory of perception has been such a statement of the physical organism and the physical world that it will be possible to give an explanation of all the characters of experience in terms of mass and motion, that is, in terms of the qualities which arise in contact experience. Stated in the terms used earlier, this comes back to using that experience in which the individual arouses in himself the response which he calls out in the other thing—physical or social—as the fundamental reality in terms of which other phases of experience are to be stated. The importance of this is found in the fact that in this experience the individual becomes an object, over against other objects; or, better stated, other things become objects with such a content that the individual becomes also an object. This content we have traced to the individual himself taking the attitude of the other, whether physical or social. Insofar as the individual takes the attitude of the other, he is playing the role of the other, and in this attitude can regard himself. This attitude becomes effective in conduct only insofar as the gestures of the individual indicate to himself as to others the relation of this essential content to other phases of experience which it is to explain. Thus in social experience, the tendency to respond as the other in answer to one's own stimulation—e.g., the play of the child, in which he stimulates himself as a child to respond as a mother—gives him the reality of the other as well as that of himself. But it is the language in which he indicates himself as a child or himself as a parent, to himself, which enables him to present both social objects in their relationship to each other, and thus gradually to explain the one in terms of the other. The child comes back to the essential character of selfhood in each—of personality—in the family group, as the basis of explanation. The indication of the dependence of all conduct and attitude upon this selfhood is the explanation. In the same fashion one indicates to himself the dependence of all qualities upon those of contact.

The other important phase of the theory of perception is found in the relation of the contents found in perception to the perceiving individual. These contents are the qualities of things regarded in their relation to the organs of perception and the things themselves considered as made up of the finer elements—the corpuscles—which do not themselves appear in immediate experience; this attitude toward the qualities of things obtains not only for the so-called secondary qualities but also for the primary qualities so far as these appear in the immediate experience. Immediate experience cannot be of the finer elements of things by definition. The distinction between the secondary and primary qualities lies in the fact that our assumptions present physical objects made up of corpuscles which occupy space and have inertia—that is, the characters which we find in objects of immediate experience, though the elements are so minute that they cannot affect the organs of sense, while the secondary qualities of things cannot belong to the corpuscles since they are assumed to be the resultants of changes that are due to the corpuscular structure of things. Secondly, in the perception are found the images which are assumed to be dependent upon past experience, and to arise in some sense because of the excitation of those parts of the nervous system which have been affected when these past experiences took place. These images are identified with contents which go into the perception of things in immediate experience, and as such are in the things in immediate experience. The theory of perception dislodges them from things insofar as things are stated in terms of corpuscular structure which are not found in immediate experience. Thirdly, characters of things are found which are of an affective nature, that in immediate experience may be in things and may be placed in the self. A thing may be pleasant or the pleasure may be in the individual self. The object may be hateful or lovely, or the emotions may be located in the self. The theory of perception places all these characters in the self, finding in the things only structures which directly or indirectly arouse in the individual the affective states.

Fourthly, it must include those meanings of things which do not attach themselves to objects insofar as they are regarded as belonging

only to a world with a corpuscular structure. These would include all
the meanings of things except those which could be stated in the
mechanics of the interrelations of the organism considered as a molecular structure among other molecular structures. This would take us
from the percept to the concept, but no hard-and-fast line can be drawn
between the percept and the concept. It is evident that the theory of
perception arises to account for the contents which a corpuscular doctrine of the physical world and organism take out of the immediate
experience. It is a necessary outgrowth of the dynamic theory applied
to the structure of matter. The second point of general interest from
which this theory of perception should be considered is its relation to
the perceiving individual. This physical theory of existences recognizes
certain elements and their combinations that are there. It assumes to
start from the problems of immediate experience and to infer from
what takes place there to the truth of the hypotheses of the corpuscular
structure of matter. It is, indeed, possible to state the spatial and
temporal characters of the elements of matter, as well as those involved
in their inertia, in terms which abstract from immediate experience,
using definitions which refer to the elements and their changes, without
involving any of the contents of an actual or imaginary immediate
experience. In this case, these elements would be in some sense thought
but would not be presented. As I have indicated above, this is not
necessary for the hypotheses of science, which are dealing with objects
which are but finer divisions of the matter of our contact experience.
They are reductions of the physical objects of our immediate experience, but so far as they occupy space and move and have inertia they
do not differ in nature from objects about us. The scientist who is
actively engaged on the frontiers of science uses them as simple smaller
particles of the matter of immediate experience, minus the characters
of which his definition deprives them. Over against these particles of
matter stands the imaginative scientist as an immediately perceiving
individual.

Appendix

Functional Identity of Response

1. We have said communicative or significant behavior is possible only if there is a functional identity of response in the activity of two or more organisms sensitive to the gesture of one of these organisms. This means that the identical response in question must be present in the behavior of the form making the gesture and present in the behavior of all the other forms sensitive to that gesture. The question now arises as to just what, precisely, is meant by the functional identity of response. In fact, this question forces us to cut still deeper and ask what is meant by the principle of functional identity, for the identity of response is but a special case in which this general principle is applied to the subject matter of psychology.

2. First, of what is it that we can certainly say that functional identity is not? Functional identity is not equivalent to existential or substantial identity. The reason is that existential identity would mean that two or more things are substantially similar in *all* those respects essential to the things in question. For example, effective occupation of a given spatial volume, to the exclusion of other things from that spatial volume, is essential to the existence of a given physical thing, be it an electron or Mount Everest. If, now, two or more physical entities were existentially identical, then these entities would have to occupy the same spatial volume. But this is impossible since it annihilates the very condition upon which the existence of a thing is possible. Substantial identity between existent entities is self-contradictory.

Take another example. We say this yard is the same as that yard. Scissor off a fixed amount of space anywhere and you will always get an identical yard. But any given yard *is* a given stretch of space to the exclusion of any other given yard. Existentially all yards are different. Existentially things are just absolutely different, and this irreducible difference is expressed by the proposition that one thing is not another thing. Existential identity is not the identity involved in measurement. Existential identity is a non-entity; and the only mystery involved in this is how the notion of existential identity could have ever got started traveling through our neurons. Existential identity, upon analysis, turns out to be the sheerest sort of nonsense.

3. It is not nonsense, however, but the highest-caliber horse sense to assert that two physical things are the same, that two feet are the same, or that two or more men are the same. And when we say they are the same, we mean they are identical. But it is high time the meaning of such identity is made explicit.

4. When two or more entities are truly said to be identical, then they are the same *with respect to some function* possessed in common by these two or more *existentially different* entities. The principle of identity is the sameness of function between things which existentially are different. *Real functions are functions of existent entities.* But existent entities are different by the very necessity of their nature. It therefore follows as night the day that *functional identities presuppose the unique and absolute differences between existent individual things.* We hope this makes clear what we mean when we say that *there is no identity without difference.*

5. We shall now exemplify the principle of functional identity. Two or more physical things are existentially different because each effectively occupies its own individual volume of space. No power in heaven or earth can muscle in on the space of this particular thing. Matter, so to speak, has individualized this volume so that it is different from any other portion of space. But these different physical things are the same with respect to a certain function that each existentially different thing exercises when they stand in a contact relation with each other. For when in this relation, each different body tends to resist the other body's effort to occupy the same spatial volume. With respect to each other, they are all functionally identical. It is just because each is existentially different that each can have the same function as another, and it is just because each is functionally identical with another that both remain existentially different. Their identities preserve their differences, and their differences make possible their functional identity. Take the example of our yards. Two or more yards are each different yards. There is *this* yard and *that* yard. Yet they are all identical in being a yard. How? Because in a relation of superimposition corresponding parts of each different yard will coincide with each other. A portion

of one will spread over a similar portion of another. It should be apparent now that functional identity is *sameness of the way* in which two or more existentially things *react* to each other when they stand in common relation to common conditions. It should also be a little clearer that functional identity of things is found in a certain relational structure of existentially different entities. It is clear, too, that functional identities always presuppose things which *as existing* are irreducibly different.

6. We are now ready to apply this principle of functional identity to the subject matter of psychology. Here it is recognized as the functional identity of response. By the principle of functional identity it is hoped to make a little clearer the proposition that in order for the behavior of an individual to be significant, X's gesture must tend to stimulate in X a response k which is functionally identical to the response which X's gesture tends to stimulate in all other individuals sensitive to this gesture of X.

7. Just how does the principle of functional identity clarify this identity of response between two or more individuals, which is a necessary fact, if a gesture of any given one of these is to be a symbol, i.e., a significant gesture?

8. This question can be answered better by first raising questions about the conceivability of the identity of response. It was with profound insight that Socrates, in constructing his theory of an ideal state, said that, before raising questions as to the actual possibility of there ever being in practical reality such a state, we must determine whether the *conceivability* of such a state is rationally possible. In all constructions of theory, the problem of conceivability is *prior* to the question of factual existence of the object to be conceived. Our present problem is of exactly the same kind. We have stated that identity of response to a gesture of X, where X is also one of those making such a response is necessary if X's behavior is to have meaning or be symbolic. Three types of questions immediately arise: (1) How is it possible to conceive of such identity of response? (2) Does such response actually exist? (3) What are the material factors necessary if such identity actually exists? The second must be determined by experimental discovery. The third involves a statement of the mechanism of such a response. The first is a logical question of how the conceptualization of such identity of social response is intellectually possible. Mead, with rare insight solved, we believe, the questions of fact and mechanism of the identity of response. But so far as we can determine, he did not so well

raise the first question. We abundantly grant that the second and third questions are far more important, but nevertheless his omission of the first has subjected us to years of muddling.

9. What kind of questions raise the problem of the conceivability of an identity of response among two or more organisms? Well, it could be said that the identity of response is inconceivable because in spite of all you say, X and Y can both strike the piano in reply to X's gesture which stimulates this response of both X and Y; yet X striking is X's striking, and Y striking is Y's striking, and they are irreducibly different because to the end of time X's is X's and Y's is Y's. In order to have identity of response, X would have to be inside of Y's skin. X would have to be Y's bones, muscles, and nervous system for it is through and only through these that the act of Y travels. Identity of response is inconceivable for it implies that X would literally have to be inside of Y, and then there would be no X. Not only are responses of X and Y to X's gesture materially different but they may be quantitatively different. One occurs in one place, one in another; one occurs faster than the other; one has more force than the other; one may last longer or pass over more space than the other. No two responses are ever the same. To be the same, one would have to be inside the other and they would be no longer two responses. We often wish we could be inside the other's skin so we could know just what he is thinking, feeling, and acting. But we never get there, and no mechanism will ever make this possible. I once raised these questions in a conversation with Mead. A smile sparkled through his whiskers as he said, "Well, I guess there isn't any identity of response." He was dead right so far as existential identity is concerned.

10. But these difficulties are dissipated as soon as we recognize that existential identity is a nonexistent spook and recognize that actual identities are functional identities among existentially different entities. All science is after functional identities among existentially different facts, events, things. The sciences of measurement keep an eye peeled for quantitative though functional identities. The science of symbolic conduct must be on the lookout for identities of responses (i.e., behavioral identities) among existentially different organisms with respect to a given gesture and then search far and wide for the mechanisms of such identities of responses. *We must be different in order to act the same.* The physics and chemistry of an act are quite important but they will never give the meaning of an act; not even the meaning of "physics" and "chemistry."

11. But just how does the principle of functional identity state the above difficulties and make conceivable, therefore, the identity of response?

12. Functional identity of response, to begin with, implies that the responses in question must be responses of existentially different individuals, and hence the responses themselves are existentially different. Thus functional identity of response implies the very existential differences which before were employed to make identity of response inconceivable.

13. Functional identity of response (involved in all significant behavior) means that with respect to a gesture of X, X and all others make a response k which is *behaviorally* the same. Thus when X says "strike the key," and this gesture is followed by the act of striking the key, then certainly these different organisms have done the same thing. Whether one does it faster, or more forcefully, or from a different angle does not alter the fact that these acts with all their differences are still functionally identical with respect to X's gesture. X has called in himself a response functionally the same as the response he has stimulated in Y.

14. But there is another angle to the difficulty which has not been cleared up. The matter is not so easy as this. Our opponent replies that we know the meaning of our gestures (symbols) before we carry out the overt response which they signify. In fact X may not carry out the response which his gesture signifies and yet he knows the meaning of his gesture. Most frequently it is the other fellow who responds to our gesture. If we tell a lost country boy the way to the Empire State Building, we make the gestures and know the meaning of them. But the boy makes the response to the gestures, and it may be doubtful if he got completely the meaning of what we said. In fact no one to whom our gesture is addressed (and this includes ourselves) may actually carry out the response which our gesture signifies. He may simply reply with another gesture. Thus you have significant conversation where responses are not carried out by either yourself or another.

15. How then is it conceivable that the meaning of a gesture can be stated in terms of functionally identical responses, if it is a fact that (1) X, who makes the gesture, does not have to carry out the signified response, and if (2) not even any other has to actually respond in order that X may know what his gesture means? More precisely, we know the meaning of our significant gestures prior to any response that may follow them. *Our gestures do not symbolize something that is already*

there. Meaning is ideal. It is not given to the senses. The meaning is not *there*, it is symbolized. But if the meaning is not a bare stimulus (i.e., given to sensitivity) and is prior to the response, then how is it conceivable that such meaning can be stated in terms of functional identity of response between two or more organisms? For the response, in order to be a response, must be a given act. We must remember that it is properly the job of psychology to explain meanings and not to relegate them to the limbo of spooks on the ground that they are irrevelant to the subject matter of psychology.

16. These are crucial questions. It is certainly true that the meaning of our significant gestures is prior to the overt responses that may follow them. It truly follows that such symbols do not symbolize something which is already there. Hence merely to show that the gestures of X may be followed by a response of X, Y, Z–X^n does not make an adequate behavioral statement of the meaning of significant gestures. It is true that the *content of meaning is ideally accessible only to a thinker, whereas the actual response signified is an overt event and as much accessible to the observation of others as a bumblebee.* How then can the content of a response be stated as an ideal content? That is the problem, is it not?

17. The nature of this objection forces us to (1) ask and state in part at least the function of an idea (which the gesture or sign symbolizes) and then (2) show how such an ideal content is conceivable in terms of response.

18. An ideal content is one which a thinker may substitute for an *actual instance of the idea*. A meaning is an ideal content (accessible to the thinker) which may be substituted for what is meant. For example, my idea of putting on my shoe is a mental content which stands for the act of reaching for them, slipping my feet in, and lacing up the strings. The idea of a response is a content which is prior to the response but which can be substituted for the later act. The act may not occur, but it remains a fact that if it is a true idea, and not an illusion, it is a content which can be so substituted. And the only way that we know of to determine whether the idea is true, or an error or illusion, is actually to endeavor to carry out the response for which it stands. If we cannot carry out the signified act, then the idea is erroneous, but the attempted response is the only ground upon which the idea *becomes* an error. It was not an error before the experimental response.

19. The act for which the idea stands is one specific existential fact. There is possible an indefinite number of such specific acts. Each of such acts is existentially different (e.g., separate acts of putting on my

shoes are different). But they are all functionally identical (cf. above). Each act is an identical putting on of shoes.

20. These existentially separate, but functionally identical, acts constitute the class of acts to which the idea refers, and each act (i.e., each member of the class) is an instance of the idea. Instances, therefore, are only functionally identical. Existentially, these instances may comprise a host of differences, but are irrelevant to what is signified by the idea of an instance.

21. The relation, then, between an idea and an actual instance is the same as the relation of the idea to a class of instances, for the class is gotten by multiplying the instances. This is the relation of being *substituted for*.

22. In behavior, the actualization of this relation of substituting an idea for an instance is the very behavioral process of carrying out the response for which the idea stands. The ideal content literally grows into the actual content for which it stands. The idea is the end, the goal, the form of the latter, actual response prior to the beginning of the act and controls the development or growth of the act for which it stands. If the idea becomes the response, behaviorists would study Aristotle instead of lambasting him, they would at least find him suggestive on fundamental principles of behavior, though not on the matter of mechanisms of behavior. Modern psychology is interested in mechanisms, but neither psychology nor any other science does little more than stumble in the tall grass until it is able to state the nature of the process for which a discovery of its mechanisms is then desired. Knowledge of mechanisms gives control. Knowledge of principles gives understanding of what is to be controlled but no great degree of control. But to search for mechanisms of a process without first understanding is usually to bark up the wrong tree.

23. It has been said that the meaning of one phase of a process is some other phase of the same process. For example, in uniform motion, distance refers to the rate of motion per unit of time. Potential energy refers to the spatial position of a given mass as fixed by other masses at an instant. In psychology, the process is an act, and the meaning of one phase of an act is some other, different, phase of that act. The act under analysis here is a social act, whose phases are the functionally dependent actions and reactions of the various forms involved in the complex social act. Hence, behaviorally, the meaning of the act of one form is the reaction of another form.

24. Thus the idea of a symbolic gesture would be the presence, in the form making the gesture, of a response k functionally identical with

the reaction which this gesture tends to stimulate in another form. And the capacity of being substitutable for an actual instance of the complete signified act. We have explained the meaning of substitution.

25. But here is the problem which has not been solved. The idea or meaning of a gesture is simultaneous with the significant gesture. If the meaning is therefore prior to the response, then how can the content of the response be identical with the content of the response to which it refers? Further, the idea belongs to the individual who makes the gesture, whereas the response belongs to another. How, then, can an individual X in having an idea, which is his own, be said to have a content in that idea which is functionally identical with the response of another to his gesture?

26. We shall answer the last question first. What particular organism makes the reaction to X's gesture is irrelevant to the essential nature of that reaction. For example, if X says, "Cut the cake," then it matters not whether $X, Y, Z-X^n$ cuts the cake, the response is *cutting the cake*, and this is unaltered by the fact that either Tom, Dick, or Harry does the job.

27. The essential nature of the reaction, which is meant by a gesture, is functionally the act of another. Let us be clear on this point. The property of a response being the response of another is entirely independent of the actual given organism making the response. Another simply has no sense in terms of a single organism. The nature of both a gesture and another is determined by the form of a social act in the following manner. A gesture is that phase of a social act as exhibited in the action of a given organism X which in relation to another form Y stimulates a reaction of Y to the gesture of X. That phase of a social act, which is exhibited by any organism Y with respect to the gesture of organism X, is said to be the response of another with respect to that gesture. It is not X's body, but X's gesture, which defines the reaction of Y as the response of another. It therefore follows that the meaning of X's gesture is the reaction of another with respect to his gesture. If X in making a gesture gets the meaning of his gesture, then the content of this idea is functionally the reaction of another to his gesture. The mere fact that this reaction of another happens in X's organism does not alter in the least the fact that this reaction, with respect to his gesture, is functionally the response of another. All it means is that X has reacted as another to his own gesture. It follows that if the nature of a response with respect to a gesture is a response of another regardless of whether this response is found in X, Y, or Z, who makes the gesture, then the essential nature of such a response

allows that an organism X, in having the meaning of his gesture, may have in his idea a content functionally identical with the actual response of another.

28. The fact that an organism reacts as another to his gesture adds to the reaction of another a very important property, namely, the property of being an idea, a meaning. So long as the response of another to X's gesture is the reaction of another organism Y, then such a response is not an idea. The mere fact that a response to a gesture is a response of another certainly does not imply that such a response is an idea. Ideas, meanings belong to the individual making the significant symbols. The reaction of another (the phase of a social act, cf. 27) with respect to the gesture of X, is an idea or meaning when, and only when, X in making the gesture responds as another Y with respect to his gesture.

29. Does the response of another, considered as an idea, have new behavioral functions which the mere reaction of an organism other than the organism making the gesture does not have? Only if the idea has new behavioral functions can it be said that the above definition really defines something. Otherwise the definition of an idea as the reaction of X with respect to his own gesture is merely verbal.

30. We shall discuss more fully in this section the behavioral value of symbols. Here we mention two new types of function which a reaction of another attains when such reaction is found in the organism X who makes the gesture stimulating this reaction of another (i.e., idea) instead of remaining the reaction of another organism Y (i.e., not an idea).

The reaction of another as an idea of X has the new functions of enabling Y to have a content which he can substitute for an indefinite number of responses, instances of his idea as exhibited by both himself and other organisms. Secondly, the behavioral function of the response of another organism Y to a gesture of X is that of stimulating another reaction of X with respect to this gesture of Y. Hence if X's gesture arouses in X the reaction of another Y, this reaction is an idea and its function will be to stimulate another response to Y, whose ideal role X took in getting the meaning of his first gesture. That is, when the responses of another become ideas of an individual then that individual may control his reactions to another, as this other organism's actual reactions would tend to control his behavior.

31. But this immediately raises again the first question. The behavioral meaning of a gesture is the reaction of another thereto. But the meaning is simultaneous with the gesture of X, while the actual response occurs later in time. The meaning already is, whereas the response is

not. How then can an event (idea) at one date be even functionally identical with an event (response of another) at a later date? We believe that the facts are that, in behavior at least, functional identities imply exactly such differences in dates between meaning and what is meant.

32. How, then, can the response of another be present in the behavior of organism X with respect to the gesture of X? This is equivalent to asking how the early phase of a part of the social act as exhibited in the behavior of X becomes a gesture to X instead of a gesture to Y (cf. 27).

33. It is to be noted in the first place that how much of a given activity (how long it has lasted, how much space it has stretched over, how great or small may be any of its dimensions) is entirely irrelevant to its essential nature. The nature of an act is not identified by the quantity thereof. This is easily seen by our identification of mechanical activity as expressed in inertia. The activity of any material body is recognized as a *tendency* to maintain its present state throughout an infinite duration. The amount of inertia is completely irrelevant to the nature of inertial activity.

34. The essential nature of an action is found in its function or tendency, and this tendency at any given time is identified by that toward which it tends at any subsequent time in the history of that action. In the case of mechanical action, the inertial tendency of a given mass is identified as a tendency to maintain at any and all subsequent times its present spatial position or rate and direction of change of spatial and temporal position. There must of course be some quantity of inertia, but the amount is irrelevant to the nature of inertia. Whatever the amount, the inertial tendency is always functionally the same. Throughout all differences in amount of inertia, one functional identity obtains, namely, the inertial tendency.

35. This same principle holds in our identification of teleological actions of organic matter. How much of an act has been expressed has nothing to do with its nature. Take, for example, an act of eating. Its early stages are very small, a flow of gastric juices and saliva, contraction of the walls of the stomach. At a later stage it finds expression in a sensitized nervous system, extends into the skeletal muscles, and then extends over time and distance in overt quest of the food object, thence to preparation and mastication and swallowing. We do not identify an act by the amount thereof. Nor can we, because any amount we might assign would have to be an amount of a certain kind of an act, and this presupposes we already know what sort of an act it is.

36. For all different stages of a given act, be it eating or driving a nail or greeting a guest, there is a feature which is functionally identical throughout these stages, namely, the tendency of the given act to effect a terminal result at a subsequent time. Whether the act of driving a nail now is a tension of the muscles or delivering the last blow, it is at both stages an act of driving a nail. Any given phase of an act is identified as a tendency to develop into the terminal phase of that act. Each part is existentially or qualitatively different from every other part but every part expresses the same functionally identical tendencies.

37. It is appropriate here to bring out another point which rests on the essential differences between inorganic activity and organic activity. Organic activities are characterized as actions whose tendencies are to bring about in a limited time some terminal result which is qualitatively different from any prior phase of the act. Mechanical activites are homogeneous with respect to time. Living, or teleological, activities are heterogeneous with respect to time. Masticating the food is a qualitatively different phase of eating than the phase of searching for the food object. Any phase of an act prior to its termination might be called a terminal attitude.

38. The action of a physical thing, on the other hand, is a tendency to maintain at all future times the same present spatiotemporal condition of the body. Thus the inertial tendency is one which tends to repeat at all times a qualitatively homogeneous condition. Hence in a mechanical process the distinction between attitude and terminal goal, want and purposed end, is entirely impossible since these are distinguished as qualitatively different phases of organic action.

39. For an organic body, even a unicellular one, is capable of carrying out functionally different kinds of activities such as securing and ingestion of foods, respiration, excretion of waste materials, reproduction of its species.

40. A physical body on the other hand, is limited to only one kind of activity, namely inertia. A mass is homogeneous with respect to its functions, whereas an organic body is functionally heterogeneous.

41. This difference of function is expressed in difference in kind of structure. Kind of structure can be known only in terms of kind of function or activity it performs.

42. An activity which is completely homogeneous would be one which tends to maintain or repeat a qualitatively identical condition with respect to all instances of time. Such is inertia. And, as we would expect, the structure of inertial action is a bare, homogeneous mass.

43. Every living activity tends to effect a qualitatively different condition of the organism at successive times. For example, the tendency to secure food, shelter, companionship.

44. Again, every living organism—clear down to the unicellular bodies—performs functionally different activities such as securing and ingesting food, digestion, excretion of waste, and reproduction.

45. And in like manner we find no homogeneous protoplasm. It is structurally heterogeneous, and these different structures perform different functions. And as we ascend the animal scale, the complexity of functions of a given organism is expressed in a corresponding complexity of living tissues.

46. The problem of the functional identity of response now resolves itself into two questions. (1) if the idea is simultaneous with a given gesture, how can the content of the idea be functionally identical with the responses for which it stands? The answer to this will be based on paragraphs 33–36. (2) The kind of a given act is identified by the terminal limit (or result toward which it tends). All instances of such a given tendency would constitute a given behavioral class. There are as many behavioral classes as there are functionally different kinds of acts. Now a given gesture of X is an arbitrary phase of a given tendency of X's behavior. Very frequently the appropriate response of another organism Y is a different kind of act from that of X. There is no ground for supposing that the social function of a gesture of X is to stimulate Y to do the same thing that X is doing. This sometimes happens but it is not the usual thing in our social conduct. We would not get far in a conversation if X's gestures always stimulated Y to repeat what X has said. This would be mocking X, and the continuation of it would likely lead to a fight. Usually the gesture of X is a stimulus for a functionally different kind of response on the part of Y. For example the salesman's talk is a phase of his tendency to sell his goods. But tendency to purchase, which he tries to stimulate by his talk, is functionally a different kind of act than selling, though they are interdependent parts of a common social act of exchanging commodities. The constituents of a social act are usually functionally different kinds. Now the meanings of our gestures are often a whole raft of different kinds of acts. Hence if the content of the idea of a given gesture is functionally identical with the response for which it stands, then X in getting the meaning of his gesture would have to have present in his behavior, in addition to his own gesture, also the content of the different kind of response that belongs to another. And when we reflect on the number of significant symbols that are at even a moron's command, each iden-

tical with the corresponding response of another, this implies that the number of attitudes present in any X identical with responses of others Y, Z–X^n is perfectly enormous. How is it conceivable then that ideas of all our social gestures are in content functionally identical with the reaction of others thereto when a great number of such reactions are functionally different from our gestures which tend to call them out? The answer to this question is based on paragraphs 37–45.

47. How, then, is it conceivable that the content of ideas be behavioral states instead of the conscious states of the older psychology? How, in other words, can the content of the idea of a gesture of X be a reaction k which is functionally identical with the response which X's gesture would stimulate in another organism Y, when it is true that the meaning or idea exists prior to the response which it signifies and is existentially different from the meaning?

48. The answer is as follows. It was seen above that the amount of an act as well as the qualitative differences are irrelevant to its essential nature. By the essential character of an act we understand its tendency to effect a terminal result (cf. above for illustrations). This terminal tendency is identical throughout every stage of the quantitative and qualitative differences of an act. The terminal tendency of any given act is functionally identical in every phase however minute it may be. The act of X throwing the ball to Y, in its very early stage might be conceived as consisting of an almost infinitesimal activity of some cortical dendrite. But it would still be a tendency of X to throw the ball to Y. X's act of throwing may travel through the muscles and bones, becoming so gross a size that the whole grandstand may see it, but it will still be a tendency to throw the ball to Y.

49. Here is another important fact. An act, we have said, is identified by its tendency toward a terminal condition. What particular organism is enacting a given act (e.g., eating) is entirely irrelevant to the nature of the act, namely, that toward which the act tends. We do not identify a type of response by the particular organism that happens to be responding. Rather the organism is behaviorally identified at a given time by the type of act it is performing, as for example, X is singing, dressing, dancing etc.

50. It is quite true that no act exists except as the behavior of some particular organism, just as inertial action exists only in some particular physical thing. It is true that organisms are existentially, i.e., qualitatively, different, just as it is true that physical things are existentially, i.e., qualitatively, different, and without this difference they could not be actively (inertially) identical. We often suffer from the strange

quirk in the head by which we see only bare identity in physical things and absolute differences in behavioral processes. But the fact is that whenever we conceive the reality of things in terms of processes, or, as I have called it, activity, there is both functional identity and existential, i.e., qualitative, difference. Probably the most difficult task of man is to see clearly the facts that stare him in the face with a gaze as glaring as that of a cobra.

It is to be noted that just so much of the total existential difference between two or more things is relevant as is necessary for their being particular instances of the functional identity in question. For example two bodies must characterize different spatial volumes in order that there may be instances of the initial identity of bodies. The color, the odor of physical bodies are irrelevant differences. We must recognize only so much qualitative difference as will make possible identical instances. We ignore a great deal and thence fall into the ridiculous fallacy that quantitative science ignores all qualitative differences.

51. The essential character of a given act, then, is its tendency toward a specific terminal result, and this character is independent of any particular organism that may exhibit the act.

52. It therefore follows that if organism X, in making a gesture, by virtue of that gesture stimulated in organism Y a tendency to react, however small this tendency might be (48), which is functionally identical with the response which his gesture would stimulate in another, Y, then X would have a part of his total action the reaction of any other Y (see par. 50) simultaneous with his gesture; and this reaction k would exist in X prior to the actual response of another Y, either by his own organism X or by a different social organism Y. Such a content in the behavior of X would satisfy the conditions necessary for there being an idea. These will be discussed later.

53. It is now necessary to return to the second phase of the problem raised above. The problem was this: Often the appropriate response of Y to X's gesture is not only qualitatively different from the gesture (i.e., the act of which the gesture is the stimulating phase) but also functionally different. For example X's gesture, "I want to buy a suit" is functionally a different kind from Y's response, "I would like to sell you (X) a suit." In such cases, X's gesture is a symbol; that is if X has the meaning or idea of what he is saying, and if the content of his idea is the reaction of the other Y, then X, in making his gesture, must be stimulating in his own organism X a reaction functionally like the response of Y, and this reaction, which X is making simultaneous with his gesture, is functionally different from his gesture. Such is the manner

in which the behavioral content of ideas is conceivable. But its conceivability implies that there is a large measure of structural identity between different organisms. Structural identity of different organisms means that, structurally, any given organism is capable in terms of muscles, bones, and nervous system of performing a great number of functionally different acts, any one or all of which might be expressed in the behavior of another organism. Structural identity means that each of two or more organisms may perform many acts functionally identical with the reaction that another organism may perform. This means any given organism is capable of many behavioral functions and is therefore structurally heterogeneous. But in being able to perform different responses of different numbers of his group, he must have a heterogeneous physiological structure with respect to himself in order to be structurally identical with other organisms.

Functional Identity of Stimulus

1. Let us briefly summarize which seems to be the main drift of the above discussion. First we have tried to show that the result of a gesture of X is the response of another organism Y to that gesture. The gesture of X is related to the reaction of another, Y, back to the oncoming act of X of which the gesture is an early phase. The structure of the gesture is found in the formal social relation of specific behavioral elements of a social act. Second, it was pointed out that what may become the meaning of a gesture of X is the reaction of another form Y to X's gesture. The reaction of Y to some phase of X's action toward Y, defines that phase of X's action toward Y as a gesture. But while the actual response of another organism Y to some phase of X's action defines that action as a gesture, it does not give meaning to X's gesture. X doesn't know the meaning of his gesture simply because another form responds to it. The babe does not know the meaning of his cry simply because another responds to his cry by putting a dry dress on the youngster. The reactions of other organisms to X's action belong to these other organisms. But the meaning or the idea of a given gesture are properties of the organism making the gesture. Hence it is behaviorally impossible that the existential reaction of another organism should be the meaning of X's gesture. Yet the meanings that one has of his gesture are the functionary reactions of any other organism which his gestures tend to stimulate in himself as in another. For what I mean by the gesture "Cut down the tree" is the act of felling the tree. On the basis of such experiments, the generalization is reached that what

may become X's ideas of his gestures are the social responses of others to his gestures which are there in the social acts in which X participates prior to their rise in X's conduct as the meanings of his own gestures.

2. When once the individual has the meaning of his gesture, he may communicate his idea to another at the same time as to himself. He is then endeavoring to signify to another what his gestures signify to himself.

3. Having thus identified the reactions, which are functionally those of another with respect to a given gesture, as that content which might become meanings, i.e., the content of X's ideas, it was apparent that the idea of X was a behavioral content of X functionally identical with the reaction of any other with respect to his gesture. More precisely, if X has the meaning of his gesture, then X in making the gesture is stimulating in his own organism a response k that is functionally identical with the response which that gesture would stimulate in any other organism sensitive to the gesture of X. The *reaction of another* was carefully defined as the reaction of an organism Y to the gesture of a given organism X. Hence, if X stimulated in himself a response to his gesture, the same organism would be performing two acts, the act of gesturing and the act of responding thereto. But in responding to his gesture, his organism would be acting as another organism with respect to the gesture of that organism. The organism would be carrying out (to a small degree, at least) two different kinds of actions. This form of individual social behavior may be symbolized as $P(x, \rightarrow y \rightarrow x)$. It is read: Existential organism P is functioning as organism X with respect to Y, and thereby stimulates himself to function as another organism Y with respect to P functioning as X.

4. The burden of the remaining discussion consists of stating precisely the meaning of functional identity, and when this meaning is applied to social conduct it makes possible the conception of the ideas as embodying a content of identical response between two or more organisms. A behavioral account of meanings, of communicative conduct, thus becomes conceptually possible. But the actuality of such a conception becomes possible only in terms of a statement of the structural mechanism which such a conception implies. What then is the mechanism of communicative behavior?

5. The statement of this mechanism is the great achievement of Mead's life's labor. Its implications for both social philosophy and the philosophy of natural science are profound indeed. They are so great, in fact, that in the twenty-five years of his life after he discovered this mechanism, he never succeeded in catching up with what he saw. To

one who knew him, it is no mystery that he wrote little. He was so busy seeing new ideas that he had neither the time nor the inclination to put any of them into final written form.

6. The first step in the analysis of a communicative act is to note a couple of its general traits.

7. A communicative act is an act of a given existential organism X and not of two or more existential organisms. It is true that such an individual organism would act as two or more organisms. But this is precisely what we do when we act communicatively. The same ideas which we tell another we at the same time announce to ourselves. We play with ourselves, especially in solitaire. And Old Sol usually wins. We talk to ourselves whenever we think. Silent thinking is communication with ourselves. At these times we constitute our own audience. A communicative act is the property of one existent organism whose form of action is that of two or more organisms. Symbolically, this is the form of individual social conduct $P(x \to y \to x \to y - n)$ where n stands for any number of functional organisms.

8. The communicative act, then, is a form of behavior of a given organism X. But, as just intimated, the form of such behavior is identical with the form of a social act involving at least two or more organisms. Let us examine more closely this identity of social form.

9. The minimum essential of a social act is that some phase of the action of one organism shall be a stimulus to the reaction of another organism. When the action of X is a stimulus to the reaction of Y, this total unitary act is a social act, and the relation of the stimulus phases to the response phases of this complex social act is known as the form of a social act.

10. If now a single organism in making a given gesture stimulated in that same organism a response functionally identical with the response that this same gesture would stimulate in any other given organism, then this organism would be exhibiting in its own total behavior a complex act whose form is identical with the form of a social act involving two or more organisms. Its act would consist of stimuli and responses as interdependent parts. The social response to a gesture is a reaction of another. Hence in reacting to his own gesture, X would be reacting as another to his gesture. For example, if I tend to give the guest a chair, and that tendency stimulates in me a tendency to sit as a guest might sit, then my own act involves a social relation of stimulus and response.

11. A communicative act is a social act as exhibited in the behavior of a single organism rather than two or more organisms. What then is the mechanism by which an act formally identical with acts of various

organisms occurs in the behavior of a single form? It is well to remember the precise meaning we have assigned to the term "mechanism."

12. It is well to prepare the answer to this question by contrasting the parts of the social act as exhibited in the conduct of two or more organisms and as exhibited in the conduct of a single organism. First, it is to be observed that the parts of a social act, as they appear in the conduct of a given organism, have the same behavioral stimulus-response properties as do these parts when each appears in a separate organism P in the social act of a group. In the group social act, the gesture is the stimulus for the response of an organism which is another (Y) with respect to X's gesture. So in the social act of the individual, his gesture is the stimulus to the response of another, though his own organism tends to carry out this response. Likewise in the group social act the response of Y to X's gesture becomes in turn a stimulus to the response of X to Y. So in the individual social act the response a' that P functioning as Y makes to his own gesture of P functioning as X becomes a stimulus b from P functioning as X. For example, if an employer reacts to falling profits by a tendency to cut wages, this may stimulate in the employer the attitude of protesting workers. And this reaction in the role of the workers is then in turn a stimulus for some kind of a response to the workers whose role he has taken. The parts of an individual social act retain the stimulus-response relation which they had in the group social act.

13. But in addition to these old functions, the stimulus-response phase of a group social act takes on new properties when they appear in the social act of a single organism P. As pointed out above, the reaction of another which a given organism makes to its own gesture has all the properties that characterize an idea. Secondly, the gesture which stimulates in the organism making the gesture a response functionally identical with the reaction of another organism to that gesture, now takes on a symbolic property. What it symbolizes is the actual reaction of any other existential organism to this gesture.

14. It is to be noted that the logical structure of the symbol is identical with the logical structure of the gesture. We found that the structure of the gesture was a triadic-reflexive relation between the phases of the group social act. The logical structure of the symbol is the same sort of a relation between the parts of an individual social act. The symbol is (1) that part of the individual P's act as X which (2) stimulates P's organism to react as Y back to (3) the later phase of the gestural phase of P's act as X. One difference between the gesture and the symbol is the fact that the structure of the former is found in the behavior

of at least two organisms, whereas with the symbol its complete structure is found in the act of a single organism. The individual has imported into his own behavior, whose form is identical with that of the group social act. The gesture is an adequate stimulus for the group social act, but only a symbol makes possible an individual act whose form is social.

15. What, then, is the mechanism by which symbols and meanings occur in the individual social act? What is the mechanism by means of which an individual act of communication may continue indefinitely?

16. The conditions which such a mechanism must satisfy are clearly exhibited by the definition of the functional identity of response. The functional identity of response means that the individual in making a gesture must be stimulating himself to make a response functionally similar to the response of another who is sensitive to that gesture.

17. The identity of response at once presupposes as its means-condition, an identity of stimulus. The responses of organisms are identical with respect to and by means of an identical stimulus made by some particular organism.

18. That phase of an act of any organism P which occasions an identical response k of organisms Q, R, S–N, is an identical stimulus to all these organisms.

19. To be sure, this conception presupposes an ideal behavioral situation in which (1) a given stimulus is the only factor affecting the behavior of such organisms and (2) that these organisms are alike capable of being affected by that stimulus. These do not correspond to the actual behavioral situations. For organisms differ greatly with respect to the stimulus to which they can react. But in spite of these differences there is experimentally a high degree of capacity to react in similar fashion to identical stimuli. It is just this identity of reference of response of various organisms to the same stimuli that makes possible that system of signs called language. After all, an ideal situation is simply an actual situation where irrelevant matters are disregarded for the purpose at hand. Exact science is full of such ideal situations. For example, the whole science of mechanics is based on the conception of masses on frictionless surfaces.

20. The possibility of there being a stimulus capable of affecting in a similar manner two or more organisms implies first of all that some phase (gesture) of P's (X's) act with respect to another P (Y) is capable of affecting the sense organs of P (X) as they affect those of P (Y).

21. There are some phases of one's response to another which are hardly fitted for this function. Probably there are few phases of P (X)'s gestures to which P (Y) is more sensitive than P (X's) subtle changes of

facial expression, its changes of color, slight twinkle of the eye, lip movement, wrinkling of his forehead. By such slips we often reveal to another what we intend to keep to ourselves. These facial changes are in position to be seen by another but not by ourselves. The actor is probably as sensitive to his facial expressions as is his audience. But he has done it with the assistance of the mirror.

22. The movements of parts of P (X)'s body which subtend light rays to P (X)'s eyes as well as to P (Y)'s eyes, should have the same effect on P (X)'s eyes as on those of P (Y). The movement of the hand and fingers are of very great importance here. For the deaf, the eye, by means of the hand, takes over the function of the voice and the ear. The so-called mimetic language is a language of the hands. In small tribal communities with their various dialects, the great utility of this more universal language of the hand is readily appreciated. In the case of the blind and the deaf the hand alone may take over the functions of the voice, the ear, and the eye. Here the hand is both an organ of sensory response and motor response. It might be possible to train any sense organ to take over the function of the ear, though the same possibility is difficult to imagine in the case of taste and smell.

23. What is essential to communicative action is that the individual shall find some phase of his own response which is capable of affecting his sense organs as it affects those of anothers. The vocal gesture is admirably equipped for this function. It is the loud part of the act. And it is notable that the loud part is the early part. A large part of our conduct never gets beyond its noisy stage. For the vocal mechanism is part of the mechanism of respiration, and the early stages of the act are usually accompanied by changes in circulation and respiration and these may readily involve the larynx. The vocal gesture, then, whose primary function in the social act is to stimulate another, is fitted also to affect the form making it as it affects another, and thus becomes a symbol par excellence.

24. But the vocal gesture has what may be called a rapid temporal and spatial decay which hampers extensive communication. According to the Scriptures, Moses addressed a crowd of 2,000,000 souls, which is probably the largest assembly any orator ever enjoyed. But the voice, however hefty, soon succumbs to space. Then, too, it perishes like the breath of air from which it comes. It is more fleeting than the passing pleasures. The modern radio is extending the space of the voice, but its temporal decay is left unaltered. The prophet of heaven has his vocal day and then he passes to eternal silence. The vocal message can endure only by constant repetition. Such repetition, when extended from

generation to generation, has resulted in charming folk song, powerful stories and sagas of ancestral gods and men. But whatever oral tradition may gain in imaginative beauty it loses in exactitude and accuracy. Thus when it is recalled that social conduct depends on one form stimulating another, it is obvious that the rapid spatial and temporal decay of oral speech implies that social communities must be small in size, especially to the extent that they depend on communication.

25. But this spatiotemporal decay of the spoken word is psychologically easily overcome. As we have said, any given sense-quality may function as a symbol provided it may affect the person making it in the same fashion as it affects another. If we could translate the word into a medium which was relatively permanent in time and transferable in space, and then translate this medium back into the word, there would be no limit, psychologically, to the size—spatial, numerical, or temporal—of the community whose members might stand in significant communicative relations to each other. If such a mechanism could be perfected, one might indeed be "the spectator of all time and existence." The written word is such a medium. It is permanent in time and conveyable in space. It passes from person to person in different times and in different spaces and thus performs the miracle of wiping out these spatiotemporal distances by evoking from all, who read with understanding, some commonality of significant response. By virtue of the written word, then, one may be at once the child of the ages and speak to generations yet unborn.

Index

Absolute idealism: and absolute
space and time, 17; Mead's
revolt against, 3, 4, 13, 21, 22
Abstract relationships: and caste
consciousness, 87; and concrete
relationships, 79-81, 100-102,
105; as detached facts, 101;
and economic process, 96-99;
emergence of, 83-87; over-
coming, 100; and property,
87-88
Abstraction, 78-79; and behaviorism, 132; method of over-
coming, 97; and role-taking,
145; sensa as, 139
Act, 158-59; as anti-entropic,
108-9; beginning of, 113-14;
character of, 112-13; as communicative, 213-14, 215; its
completion by language, 142,
143; completion of as reality,
163; and contact experience,
130; defined, 28; and energy,
110, 114; experience not fully
defined by, 137; and experimental psychology, 109;
functional identity of, 202-3,
213-214; group essential for
its completion, 144, 214; and
idea, 202-3; identified by
result, 208-9; independent of
actual organism, 209; as inten-
tional, 161; later stage controls, 132-33, 159-160, 162,
208; meaning of, 143, 158,
203; and mind-body problem,
121; nature not identified by
quantity, 206; nature in terms
of its tendency, 207-10; as
novelty, emergent, 108; and
percept, 137; phases of, 14;
precondition in imagery, 28;
as process, 203; as purposive,
108; and problem of pleasure,
121; relationship of distant
object, 119; as social, 213-14;
as unit of existence, 8, 14, 27
Alteri: difference with ego, 64-65;
earlier than self, 63; and hostility, 93; and imagery, 104;
as roles taken by self, 75,
92, 94, 98, 103. *See also* Ego
Analysis, 52, 119; and control,
65; in science, 179-80, 181,
183
Angell, James R., 6, 27n, 39n, 59
Aristotle, 164-66, 203; Aristotle-
ian object, 2
Artist, 97; and perception, 137-
38; social function of, 100
Associational psychology, 60,
131, 157-58
Attitude: as beginning of act,
149; as constituting meaning of
thing, 142; as content of
object, 130, 132; as future
present in present, 129, 131,
134-35, 155; as meaning, 16;
of object, as object, 157;
as organization of responses,
137; of other as constituting
self, 152; and perception 16;